I0816219

RUNNIN' DOWN A DREAM

RUNNIN' DOWN A DREAM

HOW TO THRIVE IN A CAREER YOU ACTUALLY LOVE

BILL GURLEY

(WITH MICHAEL J. MOONEY)

CROWN CURRENCY
NEW YORK, NY

CROWN CURRENCY
An imprint of the Crown Publishing Group
A division of Penguin Random House LLC
1745 Broadway
New York, NY 10019
currencybooks.com
penguinrandomhouse.com

Library of Congress Cataloging-in-Publication Data is on file with the publisher.

Hardcover ISBN 978-0-593-79966-6
Ebook ISBN 978-0-593-79967-3

Editor: Paul Whitlatch
Editorial assistant: Coalter Palmer
Production editor: Serena Wang
Text designer: Andrea Lau
Production manager: Christopher Andrus
Copy editor: Elisabeth Magnus
Proofreaders: Kathleen Rizzo, Andrea Peabbles, and Tracy Rothschild Lynch
Publicist: Tara Gilbride
Marketer: Mason Eng

Manufactured in the United States of America

4th Printing

First Edition

The authorized representative in the EU for product safety and compliance is Penguin Random House Ireland, Morrison Chambers, 32 Nassau Street, Dublin D02 YH68, Ireland, https://eu-contact.penguin.ie.

To my wonderful wife, Amy

Did they get you to trade your heroes for ghosts?

—"Wish You Were Here," Roger Waters (Pink Floyd)

CONTENTS

INTRODUCTION: Step Off the Conveyor Belt xiii

THE PRINCIPLES | **PROFILES**

1 *The Never-Ending Quest for the Perfect Restaurant* 1

PRINCIPLE I
Chase Your Curiosity 20

2 *Reading Every Script in Hollywood* 39

PRINCIPLE II
Hone Your Craft 51

3 *The Ballad of Robert Zimmerman* 65

PRINCIPLE III
Develop Mentors in Your Field 75

4 *The Group Text That Changed the Game* 88

PRINCIPLE IV
Embrace Your Peers 99

5 *The Stylist Who Snuck Into Fashion Week* 114

PRINCIPLE V
Go Where the Action Is 124

6 *Learning from the Legends* 136

PRINCIPLE VI
Always Give Back 147

7 *The Music (Festival) Man* 158

IT'S NEVER TOO LATE
Success at Any Age 169

8 *Trusting the Process* 183

CONCLUSION
It Ain't Easy 196

EPILOGUE
The Venture Capitalist (My Story) 204

ACKNOWLEDGMENTS 219
BILL'S BOOK LIST 225
INDEX 239

INTRODUCTION:

STEP OFF THE CONVEYOR BELT

Your time is limited,
so don't waste it living someone else's life.
—Steve Jobs

Have you ever met someone who seemed *born* to play their role in life?

The people I'm talking about aren't just successful or good at their jobs—their enthusiasm for work is infectious. They embody that old saying: *If you love what you do, you never work a day in your life.* These people stand out when you encounter them: the smiling chef at your favorite restaurant who can't stop bragging about a secret recipe; the realtor who relishes the hustle of finding people homes and striking deals; the stylist who loves making clients look their best; the data scientist who delights in the chance to dive deep into raw figures.

When we talk about people who have managed to actually land their dream job, we often use words like *luck* and *destiny*. We attribute their success to inborn genius or special access. You either have it or you don't—and most of us don't. Most of us simply will not catch that big break. We were born without connections, or even if we had them, we would lack some critical, valuable talent.

So what do we do? We make pragmatic calculations. Work is a paycheck, and some days are better than others. True fun and fulfillment happen on our off hours.

If you think this way, I'm here to tell you something: You are buying into a myth.

Consider this: You will likely spend one-third of your life working. That's at least eighty thousand hours. Wouldn't you rather spend those hours doing something you love? Or are you comfortable just passing the time, swallowing a regret or two along the way?

Let's be candid. If living a fulfilling life were easy, more people would do it. There is some luck involved. Monumental pivot points in a career arc—the kind that can launch people into their dream jobs—often feel like good fortune, especially looking back. Natural talent obviously plays a part, too. Many things have to go right.

But focusing on only those parts of a success story—the elements we do *not* have much control over—obscures the larger picture. What we don't talk about nearly enough are the parts we *can* control.

What if I told you that there was a formula, a playbook you could follow that would greatly increase your odds of success?

That's the purpose of this book.

THE CONVEYOR BELT

In the past, most people didn't have much of a choice when it came to work. For most of human history, your work was determined by your blood. During feudal times, the legal code required a father to pass his trade down to his son—and he carried his job for his whole life. It was often in his very name: Archer, Baker, Cook, all the way through the alphabet to Smith, Tanner, and Weaver. Even in America, up until a few generations ago, the son of a steelworker was destined to be a steelworker. The daughter of, well, anyone was going to be a nurse, a teacher, a secretary—or have no job outside the home at all.

Things began to change in the twentieth century. More and more young people found their way to colleges and universities, spurred on by the new idea that each generation should have more opportunities than the last. College became a pathway to high-paying jobs.

In 1978, the great Willie Nelson sang a warning: *Mamas, don't let your babies grow up to be cowboys / Don't let 'em pick guitars and drive them old trucks. / Make 'em be doctors and lawyers and such.* People heeded the advice. In some communities, the pressure to pursue a narrow set of idealized jobs—the doctors and lawyers and such—became intense.

You can see remnants of this primitive thinking still in action today. Plenty of career decisions are still guided by geography or genealogy or gender. But it doesn't need to be that way. A quarter of the way through the twenty-first century, we have more control over our future than at any moment in history. Knowledge has never been more accessible. Mobility has never been easier. There are more ways to work than ever—and more chances for that work to genuinely be something you love.

The goal should be to find a job where hustle doesn't feel like hustle.

The truth is that today's system is broken. Because there are more opportunities, more possible pathways, figuring out how to navigate the transition from education into a career has become more complex than ever.

In the years between kindergarten and high school, you make a relatively small number of decisions—which electives to take or which sports or instrument to play—but you are essentially on a college conveyor belt. Then, all of a sudden, as a high school senior, you are expected to select one out of nearly four thousand colleges and universities, then pick a major, then decide on a whole career. You are expected to make your choices fast, without any training for the decision-making, and with very little guidance, knowledge, or information. Suddenly that conveyor belt becomes a crowded eight-lane freeway, with exits and flyovers every quarter mile.

Add to this chaos the unbelievable pressure applied to young people today. For years, many colleges and universities did not even allow students to declare a major until after they had sampled a variety of courses in different departments. At some schools, you could not pick a major until the end of your sophomore year. Now, more and more, schools are asking students to declare a major before they even apply. That means asking seventeen-year-olds to make decisions that will affect the rest of their lives.

Well-meaning parents, teachers, and guidance counselors (the career conveyor belt industrial complex, you might call them) continue to push kids toward careers they think make more money—doctors, lawyers, engineers—without much regard for how fulfilling that job might be. Where is the time to explore and wonder?

None of this steering is done out of malintent, but the more a young adult is focused on meeting someone else's expectations, the less time they have to figure out what they might truly love.

On top of all of that, so many traditional career ladders have disappeared seemingly overnight. Not so long ago, going to a decent school, earning good grades, and landing an internship was a virtual promise of success, a key that could open almost any door. Now? That just isn't the case. New technologies are sweeping through industries like law and health care—adding new variables to paths that once seemed tried-and-true.

There are so many inputs shaping your career that are out of your control. You do not pick your parents or how much money they have or how encouraging they might be. You cannot help whether you graduate during a recession (although when jobs are scarcer, studies show, job satisfaction is likely to go up). You cannot control the prejudices of any individual you encounter, or whether someone interviewing you at any given moment might just be having a bad day.

But you *can* pursue your career with intention. You can study people who have been successful in different fields. You can learn from those people who are thriving in jobs they love: that great chef, the successful stylist, the rare few who are able to live their dreams. By studying the steps those people took, you can jump off that conveyor belt.

FINDING MY OWN CALLING

I've always been fascinated by the question of how people find the right career and succeed at it. For most of us, it is not a direct route. Some people do not find their way until their forties or fifties. Some people never find it at all.

Like a lot of teenagers in the early 1980s, I was captivated by computers. It started with video games—first Atari's *Pong,* then Mattel's *Intellivision*—and I eventually got a hold of a Commodore VIC-20. This was one of the earliest forms of the personal computer. It had no monitor, but you would attach it to your television like a game console. My unit had no permanent memory, so after you hit the off button, everything was lost. But that did not stop me from mucking around with it for hours and hours.

At the time, computer magazines would publish the actual code for different game programs. I learned programming by typing in these set programs and reverse-engineering the language as I debugged my typing errors.

Coding was magical, and it came easy. So I thought I knew what I wanted to do with my life. I majored in computer science. After graduating from the engineering school at the University of Florida, I landed a job at Compaq Computer Corporation in my hometown of Houston. At that time, Compaq was one of the hottest companies in the industry—and it felt that way. You could sense it in the company culture, and you could feel it in the halls of the building.

Despite all of this, after two years as a computer scientist, I did something that baffled many of the people around me: I quit. I had been making great money at Compaq and certainly did not need to run my bank account in the opposite direction. But as I began work on my third big project, I noticed that it felt quite a bit like the second one, which felt similar to the first. I was starting to go through the motions, and I could sense the future boredom. When I read the industry trade magazines about the products we were launching, I saw a bigger, broader world that I wanted to more fully understand.

As an undergraduate, I did the things that were expected of people that age. But my choices did not feel intentional. I wanted a redo. So I enrolled in the MBA program at the University of Texas in Austin with a purpose. This time around I would be an active learner.

I never read much in high school—or even as an undergrad. I had spent my time programming, playing basketball, hanging out the way college students do. That all changed when I went to graduate school. I was living in a house north of campus and took the bus to school. During my commute, I would read. I started with business books. I distinctly remember Peter Lynch's *One Up on Wall Street,* Carl Sewell's *Customers for Life,* and of course Michael Lewis's *Liar's Poker*. But there were many, many more. As soon as I finished one book, I'd pick up another. I went from never reading to reading all the time—a habit that would stay with me for the next thirty years.

If you start reading books in business school, you inevitably start reading biographies. Lee Iacocca's autobiography was extremely popular at the time, as was Chuck Yeager's. I read them both—and very quickly. Long before he was the figure he is today, I read Donald Trump's *The Art of the Deal*. The book was number one on *The New York Times* bestseller list for thirteen weeks. *The Art of the Deal* and *Liar's Poker* showed me there was a world in New York City that I knew nothing about and it clearly moved very, very fast.

I grew up in Texas because my father moved there from North Carolina when he got the chance to work at NASA, his dream job, so the idea of taking a leap across the country in pursuit of a dream was ingrained early. I had also read some of the great sell-side high-tech analysts at the big Wall Street firms—guys who were quoted in *The Wall Street Journal, Fortune,* and *Forbes*. I wanted to follow them.

So after grad school, I found my way to Wall Street, and then to Silicon Valley—where I found my calling in the world of venture capital. Here, I would combine my love of technology with my love of investing and my love of competition. For me, it's thrilling to make a bet about the future and see it become reality.

A key part of venture capital, and intelligent investing more broadly, is unlocking the components of success. It means figuring out why some entrepreneurs thrive while others flounder, and what makes a great founder, CEO, or executive. I've been fortunate to meet some of the greatest leaders of our time. And because I am addicted to reading, I have met many more in the pages of business books and biographies, some of whom became my heroes.

Over time, I noticed certain patterns.

THE SHOCKING DATA OF CAREER REGRET

How did someone like Bob Dylan start in a town you have never heard of in Minnesota and end up as a generational icon—and a Nobel Prize winner? How did Bobby Knight become one of the greatest college basketball coaches of all time? For years, I thought about how and why certain people seem to land in the perfect jobs.

As time went on, I began to take notice of other successful people, some of whom were a little further from the spotlight of celebrity but nonetheless had forged a remarkable path: the restaurateur who built an empire out of promising a fantastic dining experience; the festival organizer who carved out a career cultivating concert lineups; the Hollywood agent who started as an intern and went on to amass a long list of A-list clients.

In September 2018, I was invited to give a speech at my MBA alma mater, the University of Texas in Austin. The topic: chasing and thriving in your dream job. It was my chance to sum up everything I had been observing about success and passion. It seemed that the students in the room liked what I had to say. But then something remarkable happened. Someone at the school filmed the talk and put it up on YouTube. The camerawork is not the best, and neither is the audio quality. But as the months went on, something unexpected happened. The video racked up thousands of views, then tens of thousands, then hundreds of thousands.

Clearly, I realized, young people had a hunger to figure out the same questions I had been pondering.

Emboldened, I took things a step further. I launched an initial internet poll of one thousand people on SurveyMonkey. I asked, "If you could start your professional career over at the very beginning, would you target a different career?" The results shocked me: Over 70 percent of respondents said they would. Seven out of every ten people were living with what academics call "career regret."

Was this just some sort of statistical anomaly? I repeated the survey a few days later. The results were the same. More than two-thirds of the people who responded to my survey had deep regrets about the thing that they did with most of their waking hours most days of the week.

Flummoxed, I looked through dozens of studies from the small, budding branch of psychology that studies the experience and meaning of work and success. I reached out to some of the top minds in the field, including Daniel Gilbert at Harvard University and Adam Grant and Amy Wrzesniewski at the University of Pennsylvania Wharton School of Business. At Adam and Amy's invitation, in

2023, I teamed up with Wharton to design one of the most thorough studies ever conducted, asking Americans how they felt about their careers.

Our researchers surveyed ten thousand people in various stages of their careers, across a variety of industries and salary ranges. What they found was eye-opening. Nearly six in ten people would do things differently if they could start over. More than 40 percent of those people said they would choose entirely different occupations. About a third of those who would do something different said they wished they had followed their interests more. Nearly 30 percent said they wished they had picked a different major in college. About one in every six people who said they would target a different career said they wished they had gone to a different school entirely. And of course, a ton of people said they wished they made more money.

A few other things stood out to me in the data. Respondents who said they were *hopeful* about work were 66 percent more likely to also say they were working in a "dream job." People who said they had been more thoughtful and reflective when they were initially thinking about a career and people who said they found their work meaningful were both considerably more likely to say they were in or on their way to working in a dream job.

The results of our Wharton research have been echoed in other recent polls. A stunning 2023 Gallup report examining the state of the global workforce found that only 23 percent of employees worldwide said they were "thriving" or "engaged" at work. This survey coincided with a trend on social media that seemed to celebrate notions like "quiet quitting" or "lazy jobs." The survey also found that 59 percent of respondents were "quietly quitting" and that 18 percent were "loudly quitting"—actively disengaged from their full- or part-time jobs.

The report defined *thriving* employees as the people who "find their work meaningful and feel connected to the team and their organization" and also "feel proud of the work they do and take ownership of their performance." The employees who were *quiet quitting,* the study said, "are filling a seat and watching the clock." The final, most desperately bleak group, the employees loudly quitting, "take actions that directly harm the organization."

A similar Gallup report in 2024 found that the numbers were almost identical to the prior year. Yet another Gallup survey released in early 2025 showed a ten-year low in employee engagement and enthusiasm.

So, what's behind all these bleak numbers? Studies going back to the 1960s have examined the relationship between job satisfaction and performance, and the correlation is high. There are also a ton of surveys and studies linking the fulfillment from work to general happiness in life. It is clear that not enough people have managed to navigate into careers they love and that the amount of career regret is at crisis levels.

This is not just about the people looking for jobs. This is about our inability to direct more people toward work they find fulfilling. It is about a massive number of people dissatisfied with what they do with most of their days.

Add to all of this the evolving technology of artificial intelligence, which is primed to change nearly every type of work in one way or another. While AI provides unlimited new possibilities in terms of learning and efficiency, it could also eliminate some jobs entirely within a decade or two. Some of the careers that well-intended parents have been pushing the hardest—law and medicine and computer science, specifically—are among those poised to change the most. Suddenly even the "safe" careers do not seem so safe.

The more I considered it, the more urgent the problem seemed.

But I believe there's hope. Since I gave that talk, and since it was posted on YouTube, I have been moved by the comments I keep receiving month after month about its impact. It not only inspired people, but altered their trajectory so that they moved in a new direction with conviction, determination, and confidence.

LIFE: A USE-IT-OR-LOSE-IT PROPOSITION

It may not feel like it to some people, but there has never been a better time in history to pursue work that you love. Technology and social sensibilities have changed, but the principles of success are timeless. You do not have to be rich to tap into extraordinary resources at your fingertips. Think of all the specialized knowledge available in places like Reddit, ChatGPT, or YouTube, where you can watch an entire lecture series on nearly any subject.

It is also easier than ever to find and communicate with the people who might be able to help you. Today you can email or DM almost anyone. If you ask an interesting enough question, you might just receive a response. And it is easier than ever to find a community of like-minded strangers who share your passions. As artificial intelligence becomes a larger part of our lives, these precious personal relationships—your peer networks and mentors—will become even more important.

Right now, conversations about work focus on "work/life" balance—suggesting that the "life" part is supposed to happen only outside of your job. But I hope this book can demonstrate that personal fulfillment does not have to be crammed into the after-hours but can be a part of work, which is where most of us spend the majority of the day's hours.

I'll be frank: This message is not for everyone. Everyone wants to be successful, but thriving isn't free. It's a grind. Plenty of people will be content putting in their forty hours every week and finding deeper meaning in other parts of their lives. But if you want to have a long, successful career that satisfies you, you'll need to put in the time. If you aren't willing to put in those hours, your chances of success drop precipitously.

Some just don't want to grind. That's fine. But that isn't me. And if you've read this far in the Introduction, it probably isn't you either.

In the pages that follow, you'll discover a carefully structured road map. Chapters will alternate between real-life examples and actionable advice. You will meet remarkable individuals who made the deliberate choice to pursue careers that deeply fascinated them. Each profile features someone starting from humble beginnings—often entry-level roles—and rising to the very top of their fields.

You will also learn what I have come to call the Six Principles for Career Success. These tenets, the result of my decades-long observation of what drives success, are practical strategies that I believe will best position you to succeed in a career you will love. Every profile in the book echoes the wisdom in these six principles, and my hope is that this blend of narrative and tangible guidance will spark parallels and fresh ideas for your own career journey.

I'm writing this book for the young person who has the will to succeed but needs help finding their way. I also hope parents or counselors who want to maximize kids' chances of a happy, fulfilling career will find it useful. And if you are a midcareer worker who knows you need to switch gears the way I did, then this is for you as well.

I'm also writing the book because I find the topic fascinating. Maybe you are just curious, as I am, about what drives success and what distinguishes the people thriving in their dream job. Lastly, I believe a key component of success is giving back—to your industry, to the people who've helped you along the way, to society. My hope is this book is helpful in that way.

Kevin Harvey, my partner at Benchmark, has a phrase that I love. It feels timeless, but when I've searched I haven't found it anywhere else. He says, "Life is a use-it-or-lose-it proposition." If you work forty hours a week from age twenty-five to sixty-five, that's eighty thousand hours spent at work. That's just too long to be doing something you don't love. Most of us only have one career path. If you've got only one shot, then why not do what makes you most happy?

PROFILE ONE

THE NEVER-ENDING QUEST FOR THE PERFECT RESTAURANT

Danny still remembers what he ate for dinner the night he had the most important conversation of his life. He's not great at memorizing phone numbers or dates, but he has a near-perfect memory for meals he's eaten and things he's heard. That night, a Friday in 1983, he was with his aunt Virginia, his uncle Richard, and his grandmother Rosetta Harris at Elio's, an upscale Italian restaurant on Second Avenue in Manhattan. Danny ordered green and white pasta with a cream sauce and Parmesan along with a serving of *pollo al mattone*—Italian for "chicken under a brick," because of the way it's roasted. His family was enjoying delicious Chianti Classico, something Danny, then about twenty-five years old and built like a long-distance runner, usually loved. But that night he wasn't drinking. He knew he needed to wake up at 5 A.M. the next morning to take the LSAT, the law school entry exam, and he was dreading it.

Danny had moved to New York in 1980 to work at Checkpoint Systems, a company that made electronic tags to stop shoplifters. In three years, he'd become the firm's top salesperson. He'd made a lot of money—$125,000 a year, the equivalent of nearly half a million today—and invested most of it in the company's stock, which quintupled in his time there. Impressed by Danny's work ethic, his bosses began sending him all over the country to train other salespeople in Chicago, Los Angeles, and Seattle, and when he traveled he dined in some of the best restaurants in America. His bosses asked Danny if he wanted to open an office in London, so he spent two weeks alone there, trying to obtain a feel for the city. This was before the internet, so he used a Gault & Millau guide to learn everything he could about London's restaurant scene, dining out every single night—including the night he took himself to a Boy George concert.

Danny had a great time on the trip, but at the end of it he did something that shocked his bosses: He gave notice. He liked his job, but he knew that he didn't want to sell electronic tags for the rest of his life.

AS AN UNDERGRAD at Trinity College in Connecticut Danny had majored in political science, though he spent a lot of his free time going down to New York City, planning his trips around where to eat and drink. Still, the obvious path seemed like a career in journalism or politics. He landed a job right out of college as a production assistant at a public television station in Chicago—a few hours from where he grew up, in St. Louis. Then he worked on the short-lived 1980 presidential campaign of John Anderson, who ran as an independent against both Jimmy Carter and Ronald Reagan. When that long-shot campaign flamed out, Danny headed back to New York.

He looked into a few journalism schools, including UC Berkeley and Northwestern University in Evanston—two of the best programs in the country. He ultimately decided on law school, thinking a law degree would provide more options for a career in politics or public service. At the time, it seemed like an eminently reasonable plan. Looking back now, though, Danny realizes he was lost.

He enrolled in an LSAT prep class—and hated every minute. He knew, deep down, that he didn't want to be a lawyer. The legal field thrived on conflict. Danny didn't want to wake up every morning looking for a fight. If anything, he loved bringing people together, making people happy. Now, on the eve of the exam, sitting with his family at Elio's, he observed his tablemates eating great food and drinking great wine while he stewed about the test he would take in a few hours.

His uncle Richard noticed. Uncle Richard was one-of-a-kind: a prolific artist, a father of five, an early writer for *Sesame Street*, and an oral historian who knew how to ask the revealing questions. The ensuing conversation went something like this.

"What the hell is eating you?" Danny remembers his uncle saying.

"I can't believe I'm doing this LSAT thing tomorrow," Danny told him. "I don't even want to be a lawyer."

Danny remembers thinking his uncle looked so mad he might throw his pasta spoon. He didn't. Instead, he asked a series of questions that changed the shape and direction of Danny's life.

"Do you have any idea how long you're going to be dead?" Uncle Richard asked.

"No?"

"I don't know either, but I'll tell you one thing," Uncle Richard said. "You're going to be dead a hell of a lot longer than you're going to be alive. So why in the world would you do something that you have no passion around?"

Danny told him he wasn't sure what else he *could* do. His uncle was incredulous.

"Why don't you just do what you've been thinking about doing your whole life?"

Danny was confused. "What's that?" he asked.

"Since you were a child, all you've ever talked about or thought about is food and restaurants," Richard said. "Why don't you just open a restaurant?"

His uncle was right. Even as a kid, Danny had been fascinated not just by the food in restaurants but by the details: everything from the design of a space to the design of the stemware. As a salesperson at Checkpoint, he had scheduled his sales calls around neighborhood restaurants where he most wanted to stop for lunch. Walking down the streets of Manhattan, he sometimes annoyed his friends by reading nearly every menu he passed on the sidewalk.

Yet the thought of opening his own restaurant had never dawned on him.

"I had never in my mind said, 'Just because you love something, that could be your career,'" Danny told me. "It's not something people were talking about in college. You're either going into insurance or banking or medicine or law. Nobody was talking about the restaurant business. It didn't feel like the kind of thing you want to go tell your parents, 'Here's what you just squandered my whole education on.'"

His uncle's words felt like a wake-up call, almost like an intervention.

"Thank God for my uncle," Danny says. "Thank God someone was there to call me on my shit."

The next morning, that Saturday, Danny woke up early and took the LSAT. "I had already paid for it, for God's sake," he told me. With this new mindset, though, he was totally relaxed. Usually, he hated that kind of fill-in-the-bubble standardized test. But now he wasn't nervous at all. In the back of his mind, he was planning out his next steps.

In the end, Danny did not apply to a single law school. But the following Monday, he went to the New York Restaurant School and enrolled in Restaurant Management 101.

IN HIS TIME as a restaurant-frequenting salesman in New York, Danny had assembled an impressive list of regular dining partners, including a food critic at *The New York Times* and a fraternity brother who was in a bank training program at U.S. Trust. Danny asked his fraternity brother if he wanted to open a restaurant with him.

"You'll be the money guy," Danny told him. "I'll be the food guy."

Banks didn't do a lot of business with restaurants at the time, but his friend agreed. They both paid their $150 and started the eight-week class at the New York Restaurant School. It was an initial, intentional step toward their goal. The class was a mix of people ranging from *vaguely interested in knowing how a restaurant works* to *very serious about starting a business that serves food.* The school rented classroom space on an upper floor in an otherwise dingy Garment District loft building.

That same friend agreed to arrange a job interview for Danny with the only restaurant client the bank had at the time: a San Francisco–style seafood place on East Twenty-Second Street named Pesca. The interview consisted of Pesca's owner sitting halfway down the bar and waving Danny over.

"He looks me up and down," Danny told me. "From my Wallabees to my Brooks Brothers shirt."

Eventually the owner concluded: "You'll do."

So Danny had his first job in the restaurant business. He was the assistant lunch manager. He took reservations, typed up the daily specials, checked in servers, and hosted lunch—which consisted of greeting and seating the mostly regular lunch crowd. Sometimes he would sit in on menu planning meetings or wine tastings.

The 1980s were a fascinating time to be in New York. It was the center of American culture, but it was gritty, too. It was also more affordable back then, which means Manhattan in particular was a mix of clean-cut bankers, mohawked gutter punks, and people from every country you can imagine.

Danny was a preppy, Upper East Side kid, and Pesca's slice of Manhattan seemed like a world away from where he lived. The restaurant was in a changing neighborhood that was only then becoming known as the Flatiron District. A lot of the guests were in glamorous fields like publishing, architecture, photography. Danny got to know them. He remembered their names, their occupations, their dining preferences. One day Danny got to seat tennis legend Arthur Ashe, a thrill he couldn't wait to share with his friends and family. A lot of the people he worked with were also aspiring artists: actors, singers, one especially talented young chef named Michael Romano, who would go on to become one of the biggest celebrity chefs in New York.

Mostly, Danny just soaked up *everything*.

"At Pesca, I was scratching the itch," he told me.

He had gone from making $125,000 a year to a weekly salary of $250, but Danny loved everything about life in the restaurant world. He was exhilarated by the fast-paced intensity. He relished the chance to do the things other people might find mundane or unpleasant, like tossing the seafood pasta or cutting the faces off the soft-shell crabs. He was enchanted by the delicate dance the entire staff performed every day, and how all of those individual efforts—everything from the chef conceiving the specials down to the newcomer stirring the risotto—worked toward ensuring that every single guest had a wonderful experience.

He was learning what made certain restaurants stand out from the city's crowded dining scene. It wasn't just great dishes, a good location, and attentive servers. It was how all of these elements played off each other. For the first time, Danny was starting to understand why some restaurants succeeded and others failed.

In addition to the restaurant management class and the job at Pesca, Danny began taking a wine appreciation course at L'Académie du Vin. Each class focused on varietals from a different part of the world. In all his years in school, Danny had never studied this hard. But he had never loved a subject this much.

Danny also made a point of studying the careers of a new wave of bold young American culinary artists who were making waves across the country. This was years before The Food Network made television stars out of prominent chefs. But people like Wolfgang Puck, Alice Waters, Paul Prudhomme, and Joyce Goldstein were all doing new, fascinating things in their restaurants.

Back then, Danny recalls, restaurants were perceived as shady, cash-oriented businesses, blue-collar endeavors that were somehow beneath clean-cut liberal arts grads like Danny. So seeing these success stories—Joyce Goldstein had an MFA from Yale before launching her cooking career—was liberating for Danny. Observing the success of others gave him permission to think about this path as a legitimate career.

Plus, the more Danny learned about the industry, the more he had to talk about with the chefs at Pesca. As his knowledge base grew, the decision-makers there began to trust him more. After a few weeks, he felt comfortable suggesting lunch specials—and to his delight, some of those suggestions were accepted. Several of the friendships Danny formed at Pesca would last for decades.

He also met someone else there who would change his life. On his first day, while racing down a narrow staircase toward the basement office to answer the reservation line, he passed a magnetic young waitress named Audrey. They both paused for a lingering moment before continuing in opposite directions. Danny really enjoyed the energy of the restaurant, the surging, organized chaos. Knowing he would be working with Audrey, though, made him even more optimistic about this job.

But on his second day, Audrey was gone. She was a commercial and theater actor who was starring in a run of *Guys and Dolls* in Indianapolis. A few months later, when she called the restaurant to say she was back in New York and wanted back on the schedule, Danny answered—and rushed to tell the general manager.

Danny finally got the courage to ask Audrey out about the same time he decided to leave Pesca. Their first date was the night before Danny's last day of work at the restaurant. They started with drinks at the Algonquin Hotel. Then they saw *Noises Off* on Broadway. Then they went down to Tribeca for a late dinner at the Odeon, an after-dinner drink at Le Zinc, another drink at a place in the West Village called Texarkana. They ended up in Audrey's apartment, listening to cassette tapes—demos of her singing.

Danny really liked Audrey—and every other part of working at Pesca. He decided after eight months at the restaurant that the hospitality business was definitely what he wanted to do with his life and that he wanted to take the next step toward his dream of opening his own place. He knew he had a lot more to learn.

Danny called in favors from anyone he could think of: his cooking teacher, family friends, even his father, who owned a tourism business that took people to Europe. Danny's father was one of his best friends and his biggest hero growing up. They played sports together and cooked together. His father would regale Danny with tales of fine French gastronomy, reminding him often that it was far superior to Italian cooking—which he insisted "only uses three ingredients."

Danny arranged a series of *stages* (pronounced *stahjes*)—mostly short, unpaid internships—and set off to spend the last three and a half months of 1984 in Italy and France, learning from some of the best chefs in the world.

Romance would have to wait.

A *STAGIAIRE* IS essentially a brief culinary apprenticeship. For the novice, it's a chance to step into the sacred world of a kitchen to shadow a head chef while performing simple tasks like polishing silverware.

Some stages last a week, some last a little longer. It's a time-honored tradition, a short, intense immersion meant to give the apprentice a glimpse behind the curtain. (One of my favorite episodes of the Hulu show *The Bear* is all about this.)

For Danny, the experience was heavenly—yet another confirmation that he was on the right path. In Rome, Danny studied with a restaurant family at La Taverna di Giovanni, a place he had gotten to know through his father's tourism business. Almost everyone who worked there belonged to Giovanni's family, and at any given time, the same regulars occupied the same tables. It's hard to imagine that the restaurant ever had business or menu meetings. The menu never changed because this was Rome.

Danny spent his mornings at open-air markets, feeling vegetables, smelling fruit, eyeing the dangling cuts of salami and cheese. In the afternoons and evenings he was learning recipes, trying to absorb every detail of the operation. When he wasn't at the restaurant, he was using food and wine guides to eat his way through the city and taking trains to eat his way through other parts of Italy: Florence, Bologna, Sardinia. He took copious notes about what he ate, what he liked, and why. He drew sketches of some of the food and some of the restaurant design concepts. Most importantly, he says, he wrote down how each restaurant made him *feel*.

To save as much as possible, Danny was staying in cheap *pensiones,* low-level Italian B&Bs. He still had a lot of money from his time at Checkpoint Systems, but that money was earmarked to put toward his new restaurant. So he was trying to live frugally. He told himself: *Spend your money on your belly, not your pillow.* Sometimes that meant washing his hair with a bar of soap in a lukewarm bathtub.

But he thought one expenditure would be worth it. After Rome, Danny decided to head to Milan, where he had been set up with a woman he was told was "the Julia Childs of Italy." Danny agreed to pay her $500 a week to teach and mentor him. (If you are keeping track, this means he went from making $2,500 a week to $250 a week to *negative* $500 a week.)

But on the first day they were supposed to meet, the woman was two hours late. She was late the next day, too. She rarely showed up to teach her classes, and Danny was learning more from the woman's diligent assistant. He felt like he'd been conned.

Autumn in Milan was also rainy and dark, and he'd never been alone this long. Back home, America was in the middle of an interesting presidential election. It was 1984: Reagan versus Mondale. Sometimes Danny would listen to debates on a crackly radio station, missing home. More than anything, of course, he missed Audrey. They shared a few expensive long-distance calls—there was no such thing as WhatsApp back then—but that wasn't enough.

This was the lowest point of his journey. But even then—as he felt lonesome, swindled, far from home—he never considered giving up. He never once entertained the idea of quitting on his dream—perhaps just going back to Checkpoint or going to law school after all. Instead, he counted down the days until his overnight train ride from Milan to Bordeaux. His father's friends had arranged for Danny to stage at two restaurants there.

When Danny arrived, one of the restaurants had just lost their second Michelin star (these stars, awarded by anonymous judges, are considered the highest honor in the culinary world). The kitchen was completely dejected. Some of the staff actually quit just as Danny arrived.

"They did not want their résumé to say one star," Danny would later explain. "Michelin stars were everything for the French."

This turned out to be fortuitous for Danny. It meant there were suddenly some openings, and he was doing things like chopping shallots and opening oysters and pulling feathers out of pigeons. Most mornings Danny followed the head chef around the local market as he picked out fresh produce. Danny even got to cook what the restaurant world calls a "family meal"—a dinner prepared for the entire restaurant staff. Danny decided to make his grandmother's version of St. Louis spareribs.

"They didn't even know how to eat these things," Danny would later recall, laughing. "It was just a great, great experience."

On Sundays, both restaurants were closed and the staff took Danny to famous vineyards in the area. He also took a trip to the coast to try blue-flesh oysters and dried sausage. He went hunting for wild pigeon. He was part of the large kitchen crew that catered a grand luncheon in a local palace—and he was there for the enthusiastic round of applause the meal elicited from the guests. He had never seen food have such an effect.

When his stages were over in November 1984, he took a train to Paris to meet Audrey. They spent the week together, taking the Orient Express from Paris to Venice, then renting a car and driving around Italy. Danny introduced her to his restaurant family in Rome. (They encouraged him to propose.)

By the time Danny finally flew back to New York, he had spent the entire eight-and-a-half-hour flight jotting down notes about his trip. He had been keeping a journal each day full of words and illustrations, and now he was tying together all the ideas that had stimulated his imagination.

He also started writing down ideas for his own restaurant.

◢

THE FIRST STEP was to find a location. That meant deciding between Chicago and New York. He convinced Audrey to come with him to Chicago for New Year's Eve 1984. He knew the exact neighborhood where he was considering opening the restaurant and he wanted to show her.

"I don't think she had ever been to Chicago," Danny told me. "I said, 'You're going to love it!' "

Their trip just happened to coincide with three of the coldest days in the history of one of the coldest cities in the country. When the Arctic air moved in, the temperature plummeted to well below freezing and they got more than seven inches of heavy, wet snow.

"It felt like we were being punched in the face by wind," Danny told me.

Audrey told him that with all her family on the East Coast and this frankly miserable experience, Danny was free to open a restaurant in Chicago, but she wouldn't be there to see it. For Danny, that made the question of New York or Chicago pretty easy.

While he toured restaurant spaces in a variety of neighborhoods all over New York, Danny was also wrestling with a different problem. From the beginning, he'd imagined owning and operating this new restaurant *and* being the head chef. In fact, at the time, becoming a chef seemed like his only legitimate entry into the industry. The young, budding culinary innovators he studied were all chefs. They were not *restaurateurs*. Plus Danny loved being in the kitchen. He loved speaking the language of the kitchen.

But his now year-plus of preparation had taught him that as much as he liked cooking, the kitchen was not necessarily where he did his best work. He enjoyed seeing the reservation lists, figuring out who knew who and which guests would spark nearby conversations. He liked solving the puzzles and problems in the front of the house.

"I thought back to my time at Pesca, and as joyful as it always was being in the kitchen, and as much as I loved that time in the kitchen in Bordeaux, I knew the thing that I was best at was being in the dining room," Danny told me. "Being on the front door and making the relationships."

He knew he needed to hire a chef.

He wanted someone like-minded, someone with whom he could

share his vision. He called on his network of restaurant-world friends and eventually narrowed the list of candidates to three. Danny held tryouts, presenting each candidate with a chicken breast, some butter, an onion, some fresh herbs, and a tomato, to see what they could make. He ended up picking a chef who was even younger than himself.

Ali Barker had worked in La Côte Basque, which was known as a training ground for promising young chefs, but he did not have any kitchen-running experience. Ali's chicken breast was succulent and seasoned perfectly, though. And even more impressive to Danny, Ali used the chicken bones and onion to make some delicious stock.

Meanwhile, Danny's search for the perfect location dragged on for months. He looked at more than one hundred places in at least ten New York neighborhoods. After years of sales in every borough of New York, Danny was intimately familiar with the city's real estate and restaurant scene. Every neighborhood offered different pros and cons. He wanted to be somewhere emerging, where he knew a restaurant could bring in both dinner and lunch crowds.

Day after day, he was stepping into restaurant spaces, closing his eyes, walking the streets nearby, trying to imagine his own place. It felt like a hunt—not entirely unlike the wild pigeon hunt he had gone on in France. Even this tedium thrilled him.

He was particularly interested in Union Square. It was only a few blocks from Pesca, but it had an entirely different vibe. It was more artsy—and also a little more dangerous. It had a small farmers' market that reminded Danny of the places he had seen in Italy and France. By day, the neighborhood was home to the men's garment district, which meant the streets were filled with rolling racks of suits and coats—though a real estate executive told him more advertising agencies and publishers would be moving to Union Square soon.

Danny looked at places in Tribeca, in Little Italy, in the West Village, and in the Meatpacking District. But he felt drawn to Union Square. He found a vegetarian restaurant named Brownie's, with a vitamin store attached. It wasn't for sale, but when Danny talked to the owner, Sam Brown, he learned that Sam was planning on retiring and was open to discussing a deal.

One cold, wintry night, Danny went to a tapas bar called El Internacional. He was out scouring the area between Union Square and downtown and he'd had a few drinks to stay warm. As he sat in the tapas bar, he took note of the space: a long bar dividing two square dining rooms—open enough to feel like one big party, but separated enough so that certain spots retained intimacy. He thought back to Brownie's, and how that space could feel like this if he knocked down the wall separating the vitamin store.

Danny immediately started scribbling notes on one of those flimsy white napkins that seems to shred the second it's touched. He sketched out his idea for a layout. He took it to Eugene Fracchia, the owner of Pesca who had given him his start in the industry. Danny trusted and admired Fracchia—and Danny also knew his first boss had an eye for design. When Eugene liked the space, Danny felt validation. He made a deal with Sam Brown and agreed to take over the lease at Brownie's.

It cost $750,000 to take over Brown's lease and another $500,000 for improvements. It was a staggering sum for a twenty-seven-year-old, especially then. Danny put nearly everything he'd saved from the Checkpoint job into renovating and redesigning the restaurant. He asked several family members for loans to cover the rest. As he hired a waitstaff, Audrey—calling on her experiences at Pesca—helped train them.

Danny decided his restaurant would blend elements of his favorite Italian trattorias, the French Michelin-star bistros he loved, and the elevated bar and grill cafés he loved so much in San Francisco. All the restaurant needed now was a name. Some of Danny's early ideas for names included "Gorgonzola" and "Blue Plate Bar and Grill." When he consulted his father, his dad shot down every name idea.

"Why don't you just call it what it is?" Danny remembers his father telling him. "It's Union Square Cafe. Just call it that."

At the time, the Union Square neighborhood of New York was still in relatively rough shape. But Danny's father figured it might be wise to appropriate some of the prestige of the Union Square neighborhood in San Francisco—one of the biggest tourist attractions in Northern California at the time. Danny agreed.

So that's what he called his restaurant: Union Square Cafe.

IN LATE OCTOBER 1985, Union Square Cafe had its opening night party. About seventy-five people attended, mostly Danny's own family and friends. His mother and Aunt Virginia and Uncle Richard were there. So were his grandparents. Friends he grew up with—kids who used to come over for basketball and bacon-wrapped hot dogs or homemade tacos—were there, along with some of Danny's friends from college and his early career in New York. Danny had a little jazz trio playing in the front of the restaurant; his first cousin was the drummer. The woman who used to work as his parents' housekeeper in St. Louis flew out for the event.

Danny was a swirl of emotions. "My entire life was leading up to this moment," he told me. And now he was surrounded by nearly all of the people who were there with him and for him as he developed through the years. (Danny's parents' divorce had become particularly acrimonious by then, and his father did not attend the party.) Danny says that as soon as the doors opened, he burst into tears, filled with a mix of joy, sadness, and relief. But he also did not want to let these people down or disappoint them.

Like the guest list, the menu at Union Square Cafe was an amalgamation of moments from Danny's life up to that point. He had recipes he picked up on his intensive sojourn through Europe. There were pasta dishes from the fake Julia Childs in Milan, and one from his time cooking in Rome. He included both an apple tart and a confit of duck served with garlic cottage fries cooked in duck fat—two dishes he learned to make in Bordeaux.

The menu also included Danny's spin on family recipes and dishes he enjoyed on his travels. Danny's grandmother did not celebrate Jewish holidays, but she did make matzo balls, sauteed in butter and served with roast beef. So he included that but turned the matzo balls into a polenta and served it with a sliced mushroom dish he learned to make in Rome. He also always loved his grandmother's mashed potatoes, made with fried onions on top. Danny included that dish, too, but used mashed turnips and fried shallots. (It would become one of Union Square Cafe's bestselling dishes.) As a kid, Danny had always loved black bean soup, so that was on the menu, too, made with a shot of Australian sherry. He served dessert wine by the glass, something almost nobody in New York was doing at the time—though Danny knew it was common in Europe.

Danny had been studying relentlessly, with that methodical intentionality, for two years by now, but, really, it was clear to the people around him that he had been preparing for this moment all of his life. Everything about the restaurant reflected Danny's personal touch. Every dish, every piece of silverware, every part of the way the space was designed—"as if an architect had never been there" is how he described it—had been filtered through Danny's tastes and preferences. And all of this was aimed at creating an absolutely lovely dining experience for every single customer.

As the party went on, Danny says, he "went into overdrive pleasing people." While his restaurant dreams were driven by his fascination with the nuances of culinary creativity, they were also propelled by his passion for bringing people together and lifting their spirits in a way only food can.

"It all started there," he told me. "That night."

Opening Union Square Cafe was the culmination of one journey and the start of another. Within a few years, Danny brought Michael Romano, the talented young chef he met at Pesca, to Union Square Cafe—where he spent decades as one of the most celebrated chefs in New York, winning virtually every culinary honor possible.

Danny also married Audrey, of course. They went on to have four children, and they're still deeply in love.

It moved locations a few years ago, but Union Square Cafe is still open today. Eleven times, Zagat, once the ultimate guide to New York City dining, proclaimed it the very best restaurant in New York. But as with so many people, Danny's ambition and passion evolved and grew over time. His fascination, it turns out, was not just about opening one restaurant that would survive for decades. His passion was for this particular brand of hospitality that has become emblematic of the white-tablecloth Manhattan dining experience.

Danny Meyer would go on to launch sixteen high-end restaurants in New York City. Four have won Michelin stars. He is the undisputed king of New York City fine dining. But somehow, that's not what he's most famous for.

Most of Danny's restaurants were planted in emerging neighborhoods. He has always looked for places that were on the rise but needed some help, because he believes building a bespoke place to gather helps an entire community—which, in turn, benefits the restaurant too. One area that needed a lot of help was Madison Square Park, not far from Union Square. After he helped launch the Madison Square Park Conservancy that rebuilt the park, he applied to open a restaurant in a kiosk there, a simple burger-and-shake joint that evolved from a hot dog cart. That kiosk, opened in 2004, was the first Shake Shack. You shouldn't be surprised to learn that Danny went on a tour of the nation's best burger joints beforehand.

Shake Shack has gone on to become one of the fastest-growing restaurant chains in the world. There are now more than four hundred locations around the globe, with more than six thousand employees. The company is worth close to $5 billion.

He has come a long way from taking lunch reservations for $250 a week.

I'VE KNOWN DANNY for close to twenty-five years. He's one of the most earnest, warm, wonderful humans I've ever met. He's also a fantastic storyteller and an amazing dining partner. I especially love hearing him tell the story of this transformation in his life: how he went from a successful salesman arcing toward law school and became . . . well, something else entirely.

A lot of people love food. A lot of people are charming and know how to work a room. But Danny possesses one other secret ingredient: intentionality. Once he decided what he wanted to do with his life, he was incredibly methodical in his approach. He sought out knowledge in his chosen field with a relentless tenacity. (He still has that notebook he filled in the autumn he spent in Europe.)

Today, in his late sixties, he takes the same methodical approach to the restaurant business—and he expects the chefs he hires to do the same. Before he opened his barbecue joint in New York, called Blue Smoke, he toured the legendary barbecue restaurants in the Texas Hill Country. He went to the best places in St. Louis. He went to the best places in North Carolina, South Carolina, Illinois, California—you see the point. He studied dozens of iterations of every cut of meat, every sandwich, every side.

As I was talking to him not long ago about his career arc, he was about to leave on a trip with some of his company's chefs to London and Rome, to try dozens of the best restaurants in both cities. "We'll eat eight different kinds of spaghetti *alla carbonara,* eight different kinds of spaghetti *all'Amatriciana,* eight different kinds of artichokes *giudia* style, eight different kinds of eggplant Parmesan," he told me. "The goal is, if you do it with the right people, you debate which is best and now you have a common framework for coming back and trying to make the best version you can of that thing."

He's done countless versions of this through the years, in more places than he could list off the top of his head. And it never gets old. If he wanted to, he could retire tomorrow and live out the rest of his days anywhere he chose. But as he described his plans to eat through two of the best dining scenes in the world, dissecting the tiniest nuances in taste and presentation, he was as enthusiastic as that fresh-faced twenty-five-year-old who ditched his plans for law school, still enthralled with every part of the journey.

"I love this," he told me. "It keeps me happy."

PRINCIPLE I
CHASE YOUR CURIOSITY

I never did a day's work in my life. It was all fun.

—Thomas Edison

Jerry Seinfeld stood at a podium in front of a football stadium filled with thousands of graduating college seniors and their families. Like the graduates, the famous comedian was wearing a deep blue gown, with a cap and tassel to match. It was a beautiful, late spring afternoon in 2024 in Durham, North Carolina. Famous for his '90s TV show "about nothing," Seinfeld was about to give a commencement speech that was as humorous as it was profound.

He started the speech with a self-deprecating quip about his presence—"Let's bring the sophistication and erudition of the Duke experience down a couple notches," Seinfeld joked to the crowd.

Then, addressing the graduating seniors, the comedian turned to a more serious topic, making a point that perhaps, at first blush, surprised many in attendance.

"I can't imagine how sick you are of hearing about following your passion," he said. "I say, the hell with passion."

He suggested letting go of the notion that you absolutely must find "this one great thing" that inspires you to tear open your shirt and heave like Marlon Brando in *A Streetcar Named Desire*. "It's embarrassing," he said. "We don't need the heavy breathing and the outstretched arm from your passion. It makes coworkers uncomfortable in the cubicle next to you."

Instead, Seinfeld suggested a different word.

"Find *fascination*," he told the audience. "Fascination is way better than passion. It's not so sweaty."

I loved Seinfeld's speech—and he's right. "Follow your passion" has become a cliché. While it is an adage meant to direct young people toward fulfillment, it could just as likely push people toward anxiety and dread. *Fascination* might be a better word because it suggests giving real, substantial thought to something, rather than relying on surface-level vibes. And it invokes an equally important word—*curiosity*. If you are fascinated with something, you yearn to understand every bit of detail about it. And that desire to know more will be endless.

So, what are you passionate, fascinated, and curious about? Nothing will make you more successful than loving what you do for a living. If you love what you're doing, you're going to work harder than anybody else. You will study harder than anyone else. If you love what you're doing, it's not going to feel like work. If it's truly your own personal deep curiosity—not your parent's, not your sister's, not simply a social expectation you feel obligated to meet—most of the work is going to feel like fun.

In addition to enjoying your work, a relentless passion also has a fortunate side effect: Other people take notice. As you enter the workforce and begin the process of searching for jobs, you will stand out. People love to hire for passion. You can become a candidate of one.

Most of the top chess players in the world study the game for several hours a day. Magnus Carlsen, often considered the greatest chess player of the modern era, has said that from a young age, his preparation has been more focused on the joy he gets from the game.

"I would still spend a bunch of time reading books, playing—the things I still do, but I do them for fun," Carlsen said on an episode of Joe Rogan's podcast. "That was the difference between me and the other kids. They would go to chess practice. They would maybe even do their homework. But they weren't living and breathing the game in the way that I was."

The greatest athletes of all time echo a similar notion. They don't just love playing the games. They love practice. They love preparation. This may be the ultimate test for whether you are actually pursuing your dream job: *Do you love the work? Do you do it when you do not have to? In your free time?*

THE HARDEST PART OF GRIT

Psychology professor Angela Duckworth has built an illustrious career helping students of all ages discover the inner resolve required for success in the modern world. She has studied West Point cadets, National Spelling Bee finalists, and thriving salespeople in a variety of fields. The thing they all have in common? The shared "secret" to their success? Duckworth calls it *grit*. Early in her teaching career, she noticed that the students who have the best grades are generally the hardest workers—not necessarily the kids with the highest IQs.

Her research on the ways society overvalues concepts like natural aptitude while overlooking stronger indicators of success, like self-control and tenacity, has earned Duckworth a slew of honors, including a MacArthur "genius" grant in 2013. She has been invited to advise the White House, the World Bank, NBA and NFL teams, and Fortune 500 CEOs—and her TED Talk has been viewed more than fifty million times. Her 2016 book *Grit: The Power of Passion and Perseverance* has sold more than a million copies.

But Duckworth says that in the years since her book's publication she has actually changed her mind about one key component of grit, which she breaks into two parts: passion and perseverance. "I used to think that perseverance was the harder part," she told me. "But kids know how to work hard. They can learn to work harder. Some are taught to grind. But passion is the easily overlooked element of grit. Passion is really hard." Working hard, engaging with feedback, practicing tasks we cannot yet do, exhibiting real resilience—all of that, Duckworth says, is easier than knowing what to persevere *toward*.

Plenty of people can run full-speed at a challenge—at least for a while. But it is much rarer for someone to find what Duckworth calls "an obsessive interest," something in life that inspires a fascination strong enough to keep that drive going for the decades it takes to build a successful career.

Finding this "obsessive interest" is what I mean when I say "chase your curiosity." Figuring out what you care about is the most important decision you can make in a career. But it's not a decision in the traditional sense. You can't just *decide* you are passionate about something if you don't actually care about it. You cannot wake up tomorrow and *will* yourself to care more about bass fishing than the people who *actually* care deeply about bass fishing.

A fortunate few realize early in life what field they care deeply about and then never fall out of love. Some people marry their high school sweetheart and never divorce. But those examples are the exceptions, a thin sliver of the population. Research by William Damon, director of the Stanford Center on Adolescence, indicates that only 20 percent of people between the ages of twelve and twenty-six have a strong sense of purpose. Roughly four in five of us struggle to identify where we want to go in life, what we want to accomplish, or why.

If you are in that boat, you are in the majority. It means you must work a little harder to figure out what you want to pursue in life—usually through a long period of trial and error.

SOME SOLUTIONS

So, how do you find fascination? Where should you begin your own journey?

Before we dive in, I want to go deeper on a point I just shared. A study done in 1997 showed that only 52 percent of students who graduated college in 1993 said their job was closely related to their major. And a 2012 survey showed that only 44 percent of students who graduated college in 2008 said they were in jobs closely related to their field. This is just four to five years after graduation. Longer-term studies show that these figures fall to as low as 27 percent of people still in careers that are related to their major.

Why do I expand on this? It is important to realize that *most* people will end up doing something outside their college major. And that is perfectly fine. Said another way, the "major" decision need not be as daunting as it seems. I would think of it as one of the first stops of many on the path to finding your eventual career. If you love it, great. If not, there will be ample opportunity in the future to expand your career horizons. And you will still benefit from the journey.

It is also important to understand that there are different types of job opportunities in every field. Just because you cannot sing does not mean you are blocked from having a job in the music industry. There are many different roles and responsibilities in each field. You are searching for both an industry and the role you will be thrilled to have within that industry.

For this next section I am assuming you have no idea what fascinates you—where you will find your ultimate dream job. I know some of you already know you want to be in STEM or be in theater or study medicine. But I urge you to come along for the ride anyway.

Let's start with a couple of book recommendations. The first is *What Color Is Your Parachute?*, by Richard Nelson Bolles, which is the definitive resource on career choice. It has been in print since 1970. It's a practical, encouraging, hands-on guide for people figuring out what to do with their work life. Bolles was an Episcopal priest, and the book has a pastoral feel—warm and encouraging versus corporate and clinical. This may be too deep a dive if you already have a good feel for your target, but if you still have questions, it is a remarkably well-honed and proven resource.

The second must-read book on this subject is *Designing Your Life,* by Bill Burnett and Dave Evans. This book evolved from an elective class they teach at Stanford under the same name, which is one of the most popular elective courses in the entire university. In the class, Dave and Bill use classic design principles (from product design) but apply them to career and life decisions. It's about prototyping your way forward rather than agonizing over "finding your passion." They are big believers in iteration and experimentation—as opposed to assuming you can figure it all out in your brain and "just start." This is a useful perspective and one I share.

If a whole book is too much for you right now, you may benefit from one of a few exercises that could help point you in the right direction. I would never suggest that any of these is 100 percent proven or guaranteed. They all have quirks, and just because one exercise gives you one answer doesn't mean that is what you must pursue. Later we will talk in depth about how you "really know" if you are in your dream job. Right now is the ideation phase.

1. Myers-Briggs Test with Career Matching

The first is a simple Myers-Briggs test. You can find one easily on the internet. This twenty-minute test will give you a four-character result that attempts to ascertain your psychological type—essentially, *how you perceive the world and make decisions*. Then you can find many tables that map these job types. For example, I am an INTJ. For various reasons I believe many of the top investors are INTJs, and indeed you will find that these tables list "investor" for that type. Now, just because your Myers-Briggs result points you to an occupation, that does not mean you are obsessive about it. We are in the early innings. I just want to help you find a few places to look.

2. "Loves and Strengths" Career Exercise

Tito Beveridge, founder of the highly successful Tito's vodka brand, was forty years old when he stumbled upon this exercise. You take a sheet of paper and fold it in half. On the left side you write the things you love to do, and on the right side you write your skills—things you do well. Once you have been exhaustive on both halves, you try to think about careers that lie in the middle—in the intersection of your "loves and strengths." Believe it or not, this launched Tito in a whole new direction. Simple but informative.

3. Life Design Compass

In *Designing Your Life,* Bill and Dave have two exercises that have proven most popular with students. The first, called the Compass Exercise, is similar to "loves and strengths" but is more focused on alignment with your own values—what you define as happiness and success. They recommend you write two short 250-word essays. The first is titled "What is work for?" and the second is titled "What is a good life?" As above, the goal is then to search for careers that create coherence between the two. This exercise is more about identifying your core values and making sure there is alignment with your actual career direction.

4. Odyssey Plan

This is another exercise recommended in *Designing Your Life,* and it is perhaps my personal favorite. Here you are asked to build three potential five-year plans for your career, all different. For each of these plans you are asked to create a written report that includes a title, a timeline, the key resources needed, and the key questions that arise.

You are also asked to provide an honest assessment of how you feel at the end of working on that particular plan. What is great about this exercise is that it allows you to step outside your current life direction and base plan and to truly think about other alternatives. If you have more ideas than three, I would expand it to four, five, or six. The purpose of the exercise is to allow yourself to truly consider other alternatives and to "dream" a bit about what is possible.

Any of these exercises or programs might help you start moving in the right direction. And they are all quick and simple. There is no reason not to walk through them and see what you learn. It is a small investment to make relative to a lifetime of happiness and fulfillment.

READING TO IMMERSE YOURSELF IN A FIELD

I also recommend that you read as much as possible—not just books of advice but books that immerse you in the world of a given field. In almost every field, someone has written an autobiography—or had a biography written about them—that will reveal more about the actual experience of working in that area than you will be able to glean from any college class or hour-long podcast conversation.

Jerry Seinfeld found his fascination by reading books about Lenny Bruce and other comedians of the 1950s and 1960s. Reading the right books as a teenager or young adult can absolutely change your life. For him, it was *Ladies and Gentlemen—Lenny Bruce!!* by Albert Goldman and *The Last Laugh* by Phil Berger, the first book to explore the world of stand-up comedy.

It wasn't the potential for money or acclaim that drew Seinfeld to comedy. Back then, comedians were not scoring sitcoms or filling arenas or recording lucrative podcasts. Seinfeld has said he was most attracted to the craft of joke telling. Reading about the way comics create their routines gave Seinfeld a kind of *permission* to pursue what he loved. The books were disinhibiting for Seinfeld the same way learning that some of the great chefs in the country had Ivy League degrees was disinhibiting for Danny Meyer.

There are many biographies of the greats in any field. It's an excellent way to test your enthusiasm for the topic. There are also books about entire fields—such as *DisneyWar* on Hollywood, or *Liar's Poker* or *The Buy Side* on Wall Street, or Danny Meyer's own *Setting the Table* on hospitality. Ask ChatGPT (or your favorite AI tool) to give you a list of the top five books on your considered industry and a summary of each. If you aren't eager to pick up these books, I would cross that industry off your list!

I also recommend you read self-help books. Many of the success stories we studied referenced a period in their career where they were inspired and encouraged by these titles. I personally like *How to Win Friends and Influence People* by Dale Carnegie. It's the definitive guide to mastering communication and building strong relationships. Pair that with *The Seven Habits of Highly Effective People* by Stephen Covey for a deeply structured, principle-based system for becoming more intentional and effective in everything you do.

For building lasting behavioral change, *Atomic Habits* by James Clear is unmatched. It's easy to understand, actionable, and rooted in science. Tony Robbins's *Awaken the Giant Within* brings the fire, offering powerful tools for emotional mastery and massive transformation. And *Mindset* by Carol Dweck is essential reading for understanding the psychology of success—the difference between fixed and growth mindsets could change the way you approach every challenge.

Together, these books form a solid self-development foundation.

THE DISCOVERY PROCESS: HOBBIES, SIDE HUSTLES, AND SERENDIPITY

There are other places to look for your abiding interests. Maybe your fascination is a weekend hobby that could actually be a career. Author and journalist Kevin Fedarko had always been enamored with the Grand Canyon. Now he's written two books and countless magazine articles not just about the Grand Canyon but spin-off topics like environmental conservation and the American Southwest. It turns out a lot of people like reading about the history and adventures of this mesmerizing natural wonder.

My fellow Texan Neil Sperry was so obsessed with gardening that he made a career out of it. He's written two books about Texas horticulture, he pens a regular newspaper column about gardening, and he hosts a call-in radio show on the topic that has been on the air for more than two decades. It turns out a lot of people like learning about gardening, too.

Ben Gilbert, cofounder of the *Acquired* podcast, invented his own technique to increase optionality in his career process—he calls it a "side hustle." During each job Ben held, he would search for a side hustle, a different activity outside his employer that would give him exposure to an alternate activity or experience. While he was an undergrad at Ohio State, he created *It's This For That with Eric Kerr*—a parody site of start-up ideas that *TechCrunch* noticed. He and Eric also built a tool that linked *Hacker News* and Twitter. At Microsoft, he side-hustled on events called Startup Weekends. Through these events he made amazing contacts that would shape his career. Microsoft saw it and promoted him to run the Microsoft Garage. Ben told me he did these side hustles to "maximize my surface area for luck to hit."

The connections he made through Startup Weekend eventually led to an offer to join the venture capital firm Madrona in Seattle working on Madrona Labs with Greg Gottesman. There, in 2015, he met David Rosenthal, and the two of them would launch yet another "side hustle," this time a podcast called *Acquired*. Initially the podcast was focused on acquisitions—Pixar was the first episode—but they would broaden into deep company histories and strategic business storytelling (their episodes might help you learn about certain companies and careers!). They would eventually leave Madrona to pursue *Acquired* as a full-time career. Ben had found his dream job.

Today the show explores businesses and strategy in more detail than anyone else in the industry. They did three hours on Costco, seven hours on Nvidia, and nine hours on Berkshire Hathaway. A *Wall Street Journal* story about the show ran with the headline "The Smartest People in the Room Are All Listening to the Same Podcast." Now episodes average more than one million downloads each, and Gilbert and Rosenthal charge sponsors between $1,000,000 and $2,000,000 to advertise. The show's archives generate an additional $75,000 a month, since the podcast's back catalog remains so popular. If you listen, you can hear their passion for learning about the way companies work.

Like Fedarko and Sperry and Seinfeld, the *Acquired* guys figured out what they loved, *then* figured out a way to make money and a career out of it. That order might seem counterintuitive—our society prizes money over passion.

"If your work is unfulfilling," Seinfeld once told fellow comic Neal Brennan on Brennan's podcast, "then the money will be, too."

Little kids are interested in everything. Think of the way a toddler finds wonder in any water tower or dinosaur sticker or Easter egg. Duckworth's research shows the emergence of a deeper level of interest around the end of adolescence. "Unfortunately," she says, "it's given to us in code. We don't get a little memo that says, 'Why don't you become a professor of psychology?'"

Ultimately, Duckworth spent ten years of her adult life figuring out that she wanted to be a psychologist. She compares the process of recognizing an obsessive interest to seeing an old photo of someone you know. "Looking at a kid's photo when they're grown up, you can see the resemblance," she says. "But when you start with a kid's photo, you can't predict what the person's going to look like later."

MOVING TOWARD WARMTH AND NUTRIENTS

The University of Pennsylvania established the Grit Lab, a course based on Angela Duckworth's work, to help students learn the science behind passion and perseverance and to apply it to their own lives. Duckworth tells students (and their parents) to consider the simple, single-celled paramecium. The paramecium survives and thrives using one basic principle: If things are improving, continue in the same direction, and if not, change course.

"Be like a paramecium," she says. "Move in the direction of warmth and nutrients."

Here's how she broke down her metaphor to me: "If you are around people who make you feel better than you used to, hang around them more. If you're at a company that makes you feel better about yourself and about the work you're doing and you feel like you're learning, that seems good. If you can find a better one, then move in that direction."

It's vital, she says, to "wander with a purpose." I really love that phrase. You never know when or where you might hear an idea that sparks something inside of you or disinhibits you the way Seinfeld was freed by reading about great comedians.

Everyone is capable of both deep interest and boredom. Move toward what interests you and away from what bores you. What you should avoid, says Duckworth: prematurely specializing in something "suboptimal," only to end up with burnout.

Interest and boredom are both emotional reactions, but sometimes striving toward achievement, especially at a young age, means learning to push through and discard a lot of emotions, including both boredom and what can seem at the time like a distracting fascination. That self-regulation is vital to modern life. But it also means that we have an easier time understanding what we *do not* like, what we find unpleasant or distasteful. Plenty of adolescents can tell you what they don't like: They don't like being laughed at by their peers. They don't like being rejected. They probably don't like beets.

It is much harder to recognize what we *do* like. It's harder to look inside yourself and figure out what it is about your life that you really enjoy, what inspires and motivates and captivates you. It's harder to pause and contemplate which challenges in life actually feel fulfilling and not just burdensome.

But the sooner you can tap into the emotions on both ends of the spectrum, the better. If you are bored and grinding, especially after multiple years, learn how to change direction. If you are intrigued and engaged—and happy—by all means, keep going.

To be clear, your fascination is not simply something you were good at early in life. It's not just something you did that elicited praise. Everyone likes receiving praise, but the fulfilling feeling of a dream job does not come from the outside world. It's internal, something only you can feel. An obsessive interest also isn't just something you're able to make money doing.

Duckworth told me that the most successful people in society have an "enduring love" of their chosen field. "It's not just like, oh my gosh, I was head-over-heels," she says. "But I'm *still* head-over-heels or I'm *still* committed to this pursuit."

TO WIN, YOU NEED THE WILL TO PREPARE TO WIN

Finding your fascination is the hardest, most mystical of all the six principles in this book. It's difficult because everything that follows is based on solving this.

So how will you know if you've found a deep fascination that's worth pursuing? I think the best test comes from a quote attributed to the legendary college basketball coach Bobby Knight. "The will to win is not nearly as important as the will to prepare to win," Knight said. "Everyone wants to win, but not everyone wants to prepare to win."

When you are thinking about what fascinates you, run through this in your mind. Does the idea of doing whatever your chosen field requires for an indefinite amount of time sound tedious—or does it sound like fun? To be truly successful, your work needs to feel joyful—the way chess feels to Magnus Carlsen. It must be fulfilling all on its own, not just because of the potential outside rewards.

That's the test. Ask yourself: Am I willing to practice this craft indefinitely? Am I willing to put in more time doing this, honing this craft, longer than someone who might be competing with me—without burning out?

When the answer to these questions is "yes," you have found a fascination.

But a "no" is valuable, too. Every time you realize you are not doing something you truly love, you are making headway. These false starts or industry shifts are common in success stories. They happened twice in my own career. So, if you have found the subject matter where you can answer "yes" on the "practice" test—great! If you are not there yet, do not despair.

Jeff Bezos was thirty before he started Amazon. Designer Vera Wang did not enter the fashion industry until her forties. Colonel Sanders did not start KFC until he was sixty-two.

No matter how old you are, there is still time.

LOOK UNDER EVERY ROCK

I am now going to intentionally repeat myself, because it's important: Read as much as you possibly can. And I don't mean social media. Read books, magazines, long online essays—any format that allows someone to thoughtfully investigate and contemplate. Like Seinfeld, plenty of people had their awakenings while reading a book. The more you read, the more you will see how ideas bounce off each other in your mind. You will see which topics interest you most. As a side effect, you will also know more about the world, which is an unquestionably good thing no matter what field you pursue.

Listen to as many thoughtful, ruminative podcasts as you can. Seek out podcasts that involve going surprisingly deep on subjects you might not know much about, that find and interview real experts in those fields. Pay attention to what keeps your attention. Do the same thing with videos on YouTube, Instagram, or TikTok. Right now, you can watch interviews, documentaries, or full-fledged college lectures on nearly any subject you can imagine. It is an incredible resource that previous generations did not have.

Go on a journey with an AI chatbot like ChatGPT. You can ask exhaustive and endless questions. It is immensely patient. It's an amazing tool for going down a "rabbit hole" on any subject. And that's what you are looking for: a rabbit-hole subject. You want to find yourself in a "flow" state where time flies by as you learn as much as you can.

Explore with vigor and enthusiasm because you just don't know which book or article or podcast or video or AI conversation could spark an idea that changes your life. Look in every direction you can, in as many places as possible. Pay particular attention to things that excite you—things about which you love to learn.

In 2009, Todd Burach was meandering through a finance career. He had an undergraduate finance degree from Syracuse, where he had been a walk-on on the basketball team and was working in the

Securities Lending and Prime Brokerage group at Morgan Stanley. He was doing just fine but was not truly inspired by his career. That's when he stumbled upon a 2009 article in *Sports Illustrated* titled "How (and Why) Athletes Go Broke," by Pablo Torre. (The same story was turned into one of the most popular ESPN *30 for 30* documentaries—"Broke.") Millions of people read that story when it came out. It was the most-read article in the history of SI.com. But it resonated differently for Burach. "I was at a point in my career where I was sort of trying to figure it out," he told Torre fifteen years later on Torre's TV show, *Pablo Torre Finds Out*.

Burach felt like he'd stumbled onto a problem in society that he cared deeply about solving. "That was the moment in my career when I focused everything in my power to get onto the track to help athletes and those around them make better financial and life decisions," he said. "I found my passion point. I'm going after that."

Today Todd advises professional athletes and their families on financial matters—the type of job you might see in a TV show. He was able to combine his passion for sports with his knowledge of finance to build a perfect dream job for himself—all because he read that one article.

In addition to reading, ask people directly about their jobs and careers. Take advantage of any chance you have to perform an informational interview. Figure out what people actually *do*, whether they like it, and *why* they like it. This doesn't just apply to the professional world either. Ask friends and family. Ask people at parties. Many young people struggle with conversation starters when they are required to mingle with adults. Here is a simple solution: Just ask them to tell you about their career. Then ask them three things they love about their job and three things that might not be so great. Pay attention to what sounds exciting or intriguing—and what does not.

If an industry or occupation sounds especially interesting, try to schedule a day shadowing someone who works in that field. "Spend half a day shadowing a neurologist and you're going to learn more about whether you want to be a neurologist," Duckworth tells students.

Once you have a potential field targeted, find an entry-level job in that field. Work in the metaphorical mailroom, anything that gets a foot in the door and helps you determine if this is your dream job.

If you're already at a company but feel like you might not be on the right path, think of things you could do that relate to the core business but might also help push a boundary in a way that could be helpful to an organization. This would be your version of a side hustle. Maybe you can leverage something a younger person knows better than someone more established in a field. There might even be a part of the industry where *you* actually know the most, something you care about more than anyone else. See if they will let you work on that.

IT'S THE WHY

There's one more element of passion or fascination—one that doesn't receive as much attention—that we must not overlook. Part of having a lifelong commitment to a career field is believing in what you're doing. It is the purpose—the *why*. A surprising amount of research has been done on the topic, and you are much more likely to find your job fulfilling if it feels like a calling, like you are contributing something important to society. A great comedian believes the audience will benefit from laughing. Great podcasters believe listeners will benefit from listening. A great professor of psychology believes the more society understands about the practices and environments of successful people, the better the world will become. This is one of the key points of Evan's Life Design Compass.

Some of Angela Duckworth's students have parents who push them toward occupations they know can reliably make money, a totally understandable impulse. Parents want their children to be secure in life. "One student said, 'My parents said I should be an accountant because it's a practical job option,'" she recounted to me. "I said, 'If you're not interested in accounting, you will never be a truly great accountant.'"

Persistence is a habit, a practice. But without the other part of grit, whatever we want to call it, your chances of a satisfying career—doing the kind of work you love—drop dramatically. "Persistence without passion," Duckworth says, "is drudgery."

If you haven't found it yet, that's okay. Give yourself some grace, some space, some time. Embrace the journey. Move toward warmth and nutrients. After all, a deep, abiding, meaningful, fulfilling love isn't something you can rush. It starts as some often-imperceptible seed. Then it buds in ways the outside world might not even see. If you're lucky, it eventually blossoms. The trick is watering it at every stage and providing sunlight and paying attention to what grows.

While thinking about the importance of finding fascination, I stumbled upon a poem I found particularly poignant. It's by William Martin, from his collection *The Parent's Tao Te Ching: Ancient Advice for Modern Parents*, and I asked for permission to reprint it here. It's framed as a message to parents, but it is something everyone needs to hear.

Do not ask your children
to strive for extraordinary lives.
Such striving may seem admirable,
but it is the way of foolishness.
Help them instead to find the wonder
and the marvel of an ordinary life.
Show them the joy of tasting
tomatoes, apples and pears.

Show them how to cry
when pets and people die.
Show them the infinite pleasure
in the touch of a hand.
And make the ordinary come alive for them.
The extraordinary will take care of itself.

PROFILE TWO

READING EVERY SCRIPT IN HOLLYWOOD

When the Lyric Theatre opened in Monrovia, California, in October 1925, the marquee teased what was to come. MAGNIFICENT OPENING, the sign on the building read. SURPRISES, MANY PROMINENT STARS. The front page of the *Monrovia Daily News* published stories about the extravagant, celebrity-filled gala planned for opening night, the seven-piece orchestra that would play there, and the four costumed ushers ready to guide audience members to their seats.

The theater, located next to a drugstore that sold root beers for a nickel, was tall and stark white, with ornate flourishes of Spanish and Italian architecture. It quickly became the cornerstone of Monrovia's quaint downtown, nestled near the foothills of the San Gabriel Mountains east of Los Angeles. Programs from the early years advertised films with silent movie–era stars like Buster Keaton and Will Rogers. Later in the 1950s, the Lyric was sold to a California-based chain of theaters and was renamed Crest.

By the early 1970s, the theater was dusty and antiquated. It briefly switched its programming to adult films—before the Monrovia City Council passed an ordinance banning such showings. In the mid-'70s, the Crest started showing Hollywood movies again, and because the theater was more than fifty years old, tickets cost a mere twenty-five cents. It was then and there, in the dark theater in downtown Monrovia, that Lorrie fell in love with cinema.

As a girl, Lorrie would go to the theater every week, excited to see whatever new film was playing. On a good weekend, she'd go back to the movies two or three times. She loved the artistry, the pageantry, the escape of cinema. Whatever stresses or worries she had, once the lights went down in that old theater, nothing outside the room seemed to matter.

When she wasn't at the theater, Lorrie was home watching television—or she had her nose in a book. As far back as she can remember, she was captivated by stories. She was mesmerized by the way entertainment could occupy her mind, the way it could transport her to another time, another place.

Lorrie's father, Bob Bartlett, was the first Black member of the Monrovia city council. When he first ran for office, he advertised on—where else—the marquee of the local theater. When he eventually became the first Black mayor of Monrovia, he overhauled the city's public transportation system and led a redevelopment initiative in town. After a few years, Monrovia started looking more and more like a throwback to a different time. It became a *destination* in the San Gabriel Valley.

Her father was Lorrie's first hero. Inspired by his deft political skills, she decided to major in diplomacy and world affairs in college. She initially wanted to go to school on the East Coast. "I wanted to wear pearls and wear a sweater on my neck," she would say later. But during the winter of her senior year of high school, she toured some of the colleges she liked and decided that cold weather wasn't for her. That is how she ended up at Occidental College, a small, private liberal arts school in L.A.

The diplomacy major was designed to prepare students to enter the Foreign Service. It held natural appeal for Lorrie. She always liked the way her father could make deals for big projects in town, the way he could listen to any problem and figure out what every party involved needed in order to make it happen. Those were skills you could transfer to other settings, to even bigger stages. She imagined working for the State Department, advancing the country's interests, perhaps from an overseas posting.

But at some point in her freshman year, Lorrie realized she didn't want to work for the U.S. government. She was torn, unsure what she wanted to do with her life. As she pondered her options, she thought anew about the world of storytelling and entertainment she had loved so much as a kid.

Though Lorrie grew up roughly twenty-five miles from the studios and sets where so many of her favorite movies and TV shows were made, Monrovia felt like a world away from the glitz and glamor of Tinseltown. She always admired the artistry of great entertainment but had not thought much about the *business* of how all that entertainment was made. She always admired actors, but she knew she didn't want to act. She loved the way great shows and features were written and directed, but she knew she didn't want to do that either. But the business of entertainment? It was a fascinating concept, but where should she start?

With this vague inkling in her mind, Lorrie secured an internship with a movie advertising company called Kaleidoscope Films. The firm created trailers and posters and marketing campaigns for movies. It was an instant fit.

"I thought, *Oh yeah, I like entertainment,*" Lorrie told me.

One day early on, Barbra Streisand came into the office while Lorrie was there. This was in the late 1980s, and Streisand was one of the biggest stars in the world at the time. And here she was, smiling a few feet away. Lorrie felt a little buzz.

She remembers thinking: *This is amazing!*

Then someone at the advertising company told her about an entertainment industry job she didn't even know existed. "I had never heard of an agent," she told me. "But I was given the advice: 'If you are interested in the entertainment business, you should go work at an agency. That will give you a lot of different avenues to explore. You'll meet lots of people, you can get a sense of what you might like to do.' "

Lorrie was enthralled by the idea that it was someone's *job* to help connect the various talents that go into making movies and TV shows. This was the part of diplomacy she always loved—in the service of making the entertainment she always loved. She wasn't sure she would be able to do this type of job, but she knew she wanted to learn as much as she could about what it took to be an agent.

THE ONLY AGENCY that Lorrie knew of at the time was William Morris. She applied for an entry-level assistant job there—and luckily the agency accepted her. She was nervous but excited. She worked for a woman named Joan Hyler, who had started at the agency as a secretary—which was not too different from an assistant at the time—and then ascended the ranks to become one of the most powerful agents in show business. Hyler's clients included certifiable icons of the 1970s and '80s, names like Madonna, Andy Warhol, and Meryl Streep. Karen Allen, who starred in *Raiders of the Lost Ark* and *Animal House,* once said she thought of Hyler as a sister.

"Joan was just incredible in her mentoring," Lorrie told me. "And kind of just pushing you out of the chair saying, 'Go do it.' "

Working under Hyler, Lorrie got to see inside this industry she had admired for so long from afar. She could see how an agent's job was often putting creative people in the same room, and making sure they are on the same page. She saw the way an agent could curate a client's career over time. Sitting quietly in the room during meetings, listening in on phone calls, Lorrie could see that the skills required to be an agent weren't all that different from the diplomacy and political skills she studied in school, the skills she watched her father practice for decades. Everything about being an agent was incredibly interesting—and it didn't take long for Lorrie to realize that this job, this life, was what she wanted.

It also didn't take her long to realize that she didn't want her job to be at William Morris. When she's feeling generous, she'll say things like "It felt very political," or "It felt very male," or "It was not a place where it felt like I could grow." But the truth is, after fifteen months at William Morris, just as she was deciding that this was the career she had been searching for, she says an older executive at the agency told her that despite her doing good work, she would never be promoted there.

"I didn't cry for a week," she says now. "I cried for an hour."

That was when her career path became more intentional. Despite Hyler's stellar mentorship, Lorrie knew she needed to go somewhere else. Lorrie had recently met Bob Gersh. Bob and David Gersh were in the process of taking over the family business from their father, Phil, who started the Gersh Agency in 1949. The Beverly Hills–based boutique agency was one of the last throwbacks to an earlier era in show business, the same era that produced the Bob Hope movies that used to play at the Lyric Theatre in Monrovia. By the early 1990s, the Gersh Agency represented a roster of both big names and up-and-comers, actors like Kathleen Turner, John Turturro, Annette Bening, and John Goodman.

Bob Gersh asked Lorrie to be his assistant—with the promise to reevaluate and possibly give her a chance to be an agent in six months. At the smaller agency, Lorrie had access to the company's top talent. She was invited into meetings and introduced to everyone, and the Gershes regularly asked for her advice.

"They thought I was bright and thought I had good taste," Lorrie told me. "David would always say to me, 'Oh, what have you read that I should be thinking about for Annette Bening?'"

Lorrie then came up with a new idea, a plan to stand out in this world. She would read every script she could. She would make an extra effort to read the scripts and treatments that others were *not* reading. She wanted to know every option that might be available for her clients. She did not just skim through either. She would sit and think about each project, imagining what the final product might look like and who might fit in each role.

For most people, this would be tedious. But Lorrie loved it.

She also got to listen in on Bob Gersh, one of the industry's all-time greats, negotiating his clients' contracts with studio executives. She would watch him calmly insist on what felt like massive sums for a movie role or a part on television. Lorrie noticed that he wouldn't explain how he came to these numbers. He would only say that this was what his client was worth.

"You can say the most outrageous thing," Lorrie told me. "But if you say it in a way that is confident and kind of low-key, it throws people off. It's funny that less is more. He would just say, 'If we're going to make this deal, it's got to be this number.'" She tried to absorb as much as she could, every chance she could. "The way he would negotiate was a great learning experience for me," Lorrie told me. "It's something I continue to use to this day."

Bob Gersh was also true to his word. Within a year, he made Lorrie a full-fledged agent. "This is an empirical job," Lorrie told me. By *empirical,* she meant you have to study it to understand how it works.

"It's not something that you go to school to learn," she said. "That's why assistants listen in on phone calls. So they can understand different scenarios that could happen. It's a great way to learn, but you have to do it. And you hope that the mistakes that you make aren't too big and you learn from them and just keep it pushing."

LORRIE WORKED AT the Gersh Agency for more than a decade, eventually becoming a partner in the firm before moving to ICM, one of the larger agencies in Hollywood, in 2008.

Because she never stopped reading every script and seeing every movie and every short film she could, Lorrie carved out a niche, finding talent in places other agents missed. Sometimes that meant signing an actor she had seen before everyone else. Sometimes it meant recognizing that a veteran actor whose star had faded might be primed for a comeback.

She was also extraordinarily patient. In 1996, she saw a low-budget British movie called *Stella Does Tricks,* about a Scottish woman working as a prostitute in London. It starred the then-unknown Kelly Macdonald in her first big role in a film. "I was freaking out," Lorrie told me. "It was so good!"

But Macdonald already had a British agent, and Bob Gersh insisted his agency wouldn't split commissions. It took ten years, but Lorrie eventually signed Macdonald—right about the time Macdonald starred in the 2007 Coen brothers blockbuster *No Country for Old Men.* The movie was nominated for eight Academy Awards and won four. Macdonald was nominated for a British Academy of Film Award for best supporting actress.

Lorrie loved attending the annual Sundance Film Festival in Utah, where she might sit in a theater watching five or six movies a day for several days in a row. Spending that much time sitting still in a dark theater might sound like torture to some people, but as with so many other parts of her job, Lorrie genuinely loves it. It isn't just about keeping up with the industry's latest or learning about the most impressive new movies earlier than anyone else—though those things are certainly nice benefits. Lorrie is driven by something bigger: Any film could have a future client, a future collaborator, a future friend, the missing piece for a piece of art that doesn't even exist yet.

At one point, around 2013, Lorrie came across the script for a tense action thriller set on the border. It was about a principled FBI agent who joins a government task force trying to find a Mexican cartel leader, written by a relatively unknown television actor. The writer's name: Taylor Sheridan. The script was *Sicario*. This was years before Emily Blunt, Benicio del Toro, and Josh Brolin signed on to star in the movie or Denis Villeneuve agreed to direct, and years before Taylor Sheridan would build a content empire with his blockbuster hit show *Yellowstone* and its various spinoffs and spiritual cousins. At the time, the script had been circulating in Hollywood, and Sheridan's police officer character in *Sons of Anarchy* had just been killed off—not exactly the usual backstory for Hollywood's next hot writer. But Lorrie loved the script so much she wanted to talk to the man who had written it.

She didn't know Sheridan at the time, but she called him up and told him it was one of the best scripts she had read in a decade. Even though Lorrie has never represented Sheridan, she knows hers is a business based on creating relationships. She and Sheridan have remained friendly as he has become the most prolific screenwriter of our time. "People like to be appreciated for their efforts and for their talent," she told me.

Lorrie reads more than scripts. Nearly every day, she reads *Variety, Hollywood Reporter,* and *Deadline,* excited to stay updated on every bit of show business news. As intellectual property became more important in Hollywood—nearly every movie or television show is based on something else—she made it a habit to read narrative journalism in magazines like *The New Yorker, GQ,* and *The Atlantic*. For years, she also read Rona Barrett's syndicated gossip column.

All of this watching and reading became grist for future conversations. A script not many people have seen, a tiny independent foreign film, a magazine story about some surprising heist, a column chronicling the painful details of a high-profile divorce: Any of this could be useful to mention—or not—over a dinner, at a party. Cultivating these morsels of knowledge is an essential part of her craft.

"Information is power" has become an edict Lorrie preaches any chance she gets. "You never know where something interesting is going to come from."

You also never know who you might bump into in Hollywood. One night she was at a party and saw Bob Dylan sitting by himself at a table. *The* Bob Dylan. Unsurprisingly, Lorrie had recently read a movie script that Dylan had optioned. She had taken the time to think about the project, the way she always does. The movie was set in a carnival. Lorrie had a friend, director Penelope Spheeris, who grew up in a carnival owned by her Greek immigrant father. (Her father was also the carnival's "strongman.") Spheeris went on to direct the first *Wayne's World* movie, which grossed nearly $200 million. With her friend in mind, Lorrie decided to approach Dylan.

"I went over and said, 'I've read the script that you optioned. I feel the vision.'" She mentioned that she had a friend who would be a great director for the project. It turns out Spheeris's first movie, a documentary about punk rock in the early '80s called *The Decline of Western Civilization,* was one of Dylan's favorite movies.

Now, everyone knows that Bob Dylan is famously distant and difficult to connect with. Plenty of stars have tried—and failed—to befriend him over the years. Martin Scorsese made a five-hour documentary about Bob Dylan and reportedly did not talk to him once in the process.

But Dylan invited Lorrie to sit down and the two talked for the rest of the evening. They met again a few days later for dinner, and Lorrie brought Penelope Spheeris. The movie was never made; the vast majority of movie projects in Hollywood languish. But Lorrie never forgot her time with Dylan—or the value of reading every script in Hollywood.

THE CREST THEATRE in Monrovia was demolished in 1979. Where it once stood is an upscale assisted living facility. Around the corner is a new, high-tech dine-in movie theater with several amphitheaters featuring laser projection, large screens, state-of-the-art sound, and luxury seating. Customers can order gourmet food from their seats and pay on their phones. From the outside, it bears a surprising resemblance to the old Lyric. The development is part of the legacy of the town's longtime mayor, Bob Bartlett.

Lorrie's dad died in 2015, but a few blocks down from the new theater, at the town's Station Square Transit Village, is a beautiful memorial to Bob Bartlett. It has a mosaic of the former mayor, based on a warm watercolor painting of the man smiling. The memorial also includes several other mosaics: one of Old Town Monrovia, nesting in the foothills of the San Gabriel Mountains; one of a bus with the word "Monrovia" illuminated on the destination indicator, a testament to Mayor Bob Bartlett's dedication to public transit; and another mosaic of a diverse group of residents working together and shaking hands.

The town, and those theaters, have another legacy too: Lorrie Bartlett, a pioneer in the entertainment industry. At ICM, she became the first African American board member of a major talent agency. She also became the first African American head of a talent department. Her clients have, collectively, won virtually every award available in Hollywood—with a few Broadway awards thrown in for good measure.

Lorrie's list of clients includes megastar Regina King, who has won an Oscar, a Golden Globe, and four Emmys. Lorrie also represents Michael Keaton, whose career had a remarkable resurgence after he starred in 2014's *Birdman*. Since she started working with Lorrie, actor Ruth Negga has been nominated for both an Academy Award, for her role in 2016's *Loving*, and a Tony, for her depiction of Lady Macbeth on Broadway.

In 2022, ICM merged with CAA, making it the largest agency in the world—meaning Lorrie had come full circle, back to the type of large agency where she started her career. But Hollywood is different now. Through 2023, Lorrie served as an executive board member of Time's Up, giving her a prominent voice in the creative community's efforts to advocate for gender safety and equality in the workplace. And in 2024, Lorrie was honored with her own award: The Culture Creators Foundation gave her the Icon Award for her "outstanding contributions to the entertainment industry and her steadfast commitment to advancing diversity and inclusion, while spearheading initiatives promoting equity within Hollywood."

Lorrie accepted the award in front of a massive audience of her peers inside the Beverly Hilton International Ballroom. She started by acknowledging the people whose "existence in the representation game" inspired her. She named Bethann Hardison, Dolores Robinson, Darrell Miller, Helen Sugland, Sheila Robinson, Judy Page, Charles King, Nina Shaw, and Donna Chavous, CAA's first black agent.

Then Lorrie broke down her own journey and shared some observations about her industry, though I think this is good advice for just about any industry. Her speech was eloquent and touching—and well worth watching if you pull up the YouTube video.

We'll conclude Lorrie's story with the bits of advice from her talk that impressed me most:

- "Stay ready. You never know when an opportunity will present itself, and in that moment, be excellent. Be consistent. Build your credibility. Let people know who you are, and allow them to understand that they can count on you."

- "Celebrate the wins, no matter if they are big or small. Not only your wins, but all of our wins in our community. We know how hard fought they were."
- "Send a note. That acknowledgment means more than you realize."
- "Analyze the losses. When you don't get the result you expect or someone throws you a curveball, digest it and move on. But there's a lesson to be learned. So often the lesson we learn from our perceived failures can be integral to our success."
- "Find your people. Create that circle of people who will tell you the truth even when it's hard. Those people allow you to show your vulnerability and will never use it against you. Those people motivate you when you need it the most."

Before she left the stage, Lorrie thanked her clients and her family, including her partner Mike, her kids, her cousin Dana, and her mother, father, and grandparents in heaven. Then, as she parted, she reminded the audience of her own passion, what has driven her since she was first curious about what an agent does: "The idea that I have contributed in any way to our beautiful, astonishing, powerful culture," she said, "gives me such great joy."

PRINCIPLE II

HONE YOUR CRAFT

It's what you learn after you know it all that counts.

—John Wooden

The Picasso Museum in Barcelona is spread out over what used to be five adjoining medieval palaces in the oldest part of the city. The collection has grown and evolved over time, but when I visited a few years ago, Pablo Picasso's work—including hundreds of paintings, collages, engravings, and sketches—was arranged chronologically. Moving through the space is like moving through the phases of his prolific career, and the thoughtful exhibition is instructive in ways that go far beyond art. You can see pieces from his blue period, his pink period, his cubist years, his surrealism, and his depictions of the Spanish Civil War and World War II, when his work took on political overtones.

Before all that, though, when you first start your journey through the museum, you see the unbelievably precise portraits he painted as an adolescent, when he was learning his craft. The painting I remember most is called *First Communion.* It's oil on a large canvas, nearly four feet wide and more than five tall, and depicts a girl dressed all in white, kneeling in front of an altar. If you saw this painting out of context, you most certainly wouldn't guess it was a Picasso. It looks like it was done by a great impressionist and employs all the techniques and sensibilities that were popular at the end of the nineteenth century. In fact, *First Communion* won a Spanish art prize when it was first displayed in 1896. Picasso was only fifteen.

Today, Picasso is most famous for his avant-garde work that advanced the limits of what visual art can be. As a teenager, however, he had already mastered the dominant style of the time. Before he could break all the rules of visual art, he had to learn—and master—all the existing rules of visual art. Then, he never stopped learning and experimenting, even after decades of unparalleled success.

You can see this pattern of deep and continuous learning repeated in the titans of almost every industry. Danny Meyer studied every element of the restaurant business—and continues his studies of the field, even after all his success. Lorrie Bartlett, the Hollywood agent, consumed as many stories as she could as a kid and still reads every script she can. Jerry Seinfeld studied the best comics in the world.

Long before Quentin Tarantino became one of the most successful directors in Hollywood, he worked in a video rental store in Manhattan Beach, California, watching and studying as many movies from as many eras of cinema as possible. In 2022, thirty years after he launched his directorial career, Tarantino published a book of essays, *Cinema Speculation*, about some of his favorites, including *Deliverance*, *Dirty Harry*, and *Taxi Driver*.

The author Stephen King has said he has read voraciously for almost all his life, absorbing what makes for a good plot, compelling characters, and natural pacing. In his book *On Writing*, King says he believes that reading widely and continuously is essential for developing a feel for the craft. King also writes two thousand words a day, even when he doesn't feel like it, still practicing his craft daily as he approaches eighty.

Rick Rubin is one of the most important and influential music producers of all time. He has made records with everyone from the Beastie Boys and Run-DMC, to Adele and Lady Gaga, to Metallica and Rage Against the Machine. His albums with Johnny Cash are legendary. He also wrote an excellent book about creativity and has a podcast where he interviews people from all industries. When I asked Rick what drives his desire to learn, he answered with the wisdom of a mystic poet.

"It always starts with curiosity," he told me. "I'm interested in possibilities. I think we know very little, if anything. I'm wildly open-minded. Creativity comes from seeing past the surface."

The reality is: You want learning to be fun. You *need* it to feel like play. We've all been drawn down a rabbit hole of knowledge trying to answer some question or understand something that happened—knowing even in the moment that the entire endeavor might be a waste of time. But sometimes you really want to know something. Studying your field needs to feel like *that*. You would do it even if it weren't your job. The knowledge is its own reward. Your curiosity and drive have to come naturally. You cannot force it.

By now, I hope you are noticing a pattern: In order to be great, you have to do the work. In order to do the work well enough and for long enough to be great, you have to love it. It can't feel like *work* at all. This is an inescapable fact, an immutable truth. If you want to thrive doing something that makes you happy, there is no escaping those two interlocking pieces.

This is also the keystone for the rest of the book. When you find what you love and love what you do, every other step in your career will come so much easier.

KNOW THE HISTORY

There are four different types of learning you need to do throughout your career. First, you should learn the history of your chosen field. Then you need to commit to learning continuously, in a self-propelled way, throughout your career. What's evolving? Who else in your field has big new ideas that you should know about? Third, you need to go deep in some specialized, unique way. In other words, you will develop unique insights and skills in your field that separate you from the rest. And, finally, you need to learn outside your chosen field—following other fascinations—because that type of far-away learning is actually the most likely to spark novel and truly impactful breakthroughs.

The most straightforward of these different types of learning is accumulating foundational knowledge of your field. Study the pioneers. Know the history of the field. Learn the bedrock you want to one day build upon. Learn from the best—the individuals who have done it better or longer or with a higher success rate than anyone else. Be obsessive about understanding everything you possibly can about the field's craft. Consider it an obligation. Hold yourself accountable.

Learning the history of a field is standard in a few industries, including music production and architecture. Some of the best medical schools in America give first-year medical students a class on the history of medicine so they have a general sense of the biggest breakthroughs—and mistakes—physicians have made through time. And just because it might seem optional in other fields doesn't mean you should skip it. Plenty of people can learn the mechanics of the market, but the best investors I've met also know the stories of the greatest investors of all time. They've read books about successful investors who are total strangers to most of the public.

Every industry has a unique language. Learn it as soon as you can. Memorize what abbreviations mean. Learn about the biggest disruptions your industry has experienced and what happened as a result. This is even more important if you're in an emerging field, because that history will be shorter and more recent. Once you start going deep in an industry, reading through the canon of the field, you'll learn quickly how many of your peers are *not* doing the same.

This type of historical learning has three benefits. The first one is obvious. By studying your field intensely, you are going to learn plenty. You're going to absorb knowledge that will be useful at every stage of your career, long after you have forgotten where you actually learned it. You will understand who was successful in your field and why. You will know the key contributions to your chosen craft over time.

The second benefit to studying the history of a field you aspire to join is that it can serve as a good test. Do you find it fascinating or does it bore you? Do you find yourself wanting to go deeper, wanting to read more books and listen to more podcasts? Is learning about the history of your field fun? If not, that's a good indication that this is not your fascination. It is definitely better to understand this early in your journey, so if you become bored learning about a certain field, that's fine. That's great, actually, because now you know that it is not for you. But it's time to go back to that first principle and form a new plan.

The third benefit is social. The more you know about the history of Italian cuisine or open-wheel racing or molecular biology, the more you will be able to converse with established professionals in that field. Veterans of any industry will be more likely to share their knowledge and experience—and opportunities—with someone they believe knows and cares about the canon, the historical texts, and the monumental moments in their field. It proves that the person they're dealing with has passion and respect for the subject and is willing to work hard to learn more. That historical knowledge is a way of bonding with the people who might become your valued peers or mentors.

Knowing someone has read dozens of books about a topic immediately establishes a new level of credibility and differentiation in a conversation. Knowledge opens doors. It gives you an exponential advantage over a peer who hasn't done their homework. In job interviews, this deep understanding of your industry can be *highly* differentiating. It can make you a *candidate of one*.

Witnessing someone demonstrate a high level of passion and

knowledge of their craft is also awe-inspiring. A few years ago, I was super fortunate when a friend of mine brought me along to a dinner with John Lasseter. Lasseter was the longtime chief creative officer at Pixar and personally directed *Toy Story, Toy Story 2, Cars,* and *Cars 2,* and my friend had won a chance to attend the dinner in a charity auction. Lasseter hosted the ten-course meal in his home movie theater and paired each course with a vintage cartoon and a brief, impassioned explanation of its historical significance. He had clips from animation dating back to the 1920s. He told us how much the 1941 *Dumbo* influenced his sense of what animation could do. I did not walk into that room with any particular interest in the history of animation, but seeing a person this engaged with the history of his field was both memorable and energizing. Looking back now, it was one of the most entertaining nights of my life!

LEARNING NEVER STOPS

Mahatma Gandhi is credited as saying, "Live as if you were to die tomorrow. Learn as if you were to live forever." The writer and futurist Alvin Toffler said, "The illiterate of the twenty-first century will not be those who cannot read and write, but those who cannot learn, unlearn, and relearn."

What Gandhi and Toffler are saying is this: Continuous learning is just as important as foundational knowledge.

Warren Buffett famously continues to read investment newsletters. Long after he was already successful, J. D. Rockefeller continued studying every element of the oil business—from the roughnecks pumping it to the pipelines and train systems carrying it—including tedious examinations of his competitors' businesses.

Just like these greats, after you have a broad base of foundational knowledge, you need to keep going. Learn throughout the day, but learn in your off hours, too. I call this *external learning*—learning on your own time, outside the walls of your company. You need to proactively add knowledge about your field. Very few people do this. All too often, people rely on what's being presented to them in their daily activity. It's easy to say, "Well, if the company where I work wants me to know about something, they will put it in front of me."

That type of thinking won't make you great. The most successful people in any field are constantly seeking new information, learning anywhere and everywhere they can.

Seeing what's on the edge of your industry is critical. If you learn about something new that could disrupt your field, and you're the first person to bring that information back into your organization—or if you're the one who has the most knowledge of this particular focus when a company has to adapt—it's going to do wonders for your career.

Pablo Picasso had so many prolific eras of his artistic career—constantly innovating—partly because he never tired of learning. He was a legitimately great artist at age fifteen. He could have spent the rest of his life painting in that same impressionist style. Plenty of great painters went decades without varying styles. But Picasso, like so many greats, continued looking for what to do next.

Think of the way Stephen King keeps reading widely, five decades into his career. Or the way Danny Meyer still loves touring barbecue joints and taking his chefs to Italy to study both new and classic dishes. Albert Einstein once said, "Once you stop learning, you start dying."

A few industries promote this idea of continuous learning. Again, the medical field is generally good about collecting and distributing the latest information available—and encouraging medical professionals to consume it. Other industries are more averse to early adoption of the very newest ideas. NFL coaches are notoriously slow and curmudgeonly when it comes to risky new concepts, for example. But if that's the mentality in your chosen field, continuous learning can give you an even bigger advantage.

When Microsoft was looking for a new CEO in 2013, contenders for the job included the CEO of Ford and the former president of Skype. But Satya Nadella wrote a ten-page memo arguing that Microsoft's return to dominance would have to come from a growth mindset. He later explained that he wanted to change the company culture from "know-it-all" to "learn-it-all."

In his first email to Microsoft employees as the new CEO, Nadella wrote: "Many who know me say I am also defined by my curiosity and thirst for learning. I buy more books than I can finish. I sign up for more online courses than I can complete. I fundamentally believe that if you are not learning new things, you stop doing great and useful things."

Since Nadella became CEO, the company's share price has gone up tenfold.

Continuous learning can have a major impact in any field. In 2009, Kobe Bryant went to Houston in the offseason to ask Hakeem Olajuwon to demonstrate his quick-turn post technique. At this point Bryant had been playing professionally for thirteen years. He had won four championships. He had been the league MVP. Olajuwon had been retired for nearly a decade. But Bryant wanted to improve this very particular part of his game, and he wanted to learn from the best who had ever done it.

KRIV-TV, a Fox affiliate in Houston, got wind of this private lesson and sent a camera crew to the gym. Footage from that day shows a studious Bryant going through Olajuwon's moves over and over, occasionally stopping to ask Olajuwon to guide him.

In an interview afterward, Olajuwon explains that Bryant reached out to him. "He gave me the biggest compliment," Olajuwon says. "He told me, 'You have the best midpost and post move.' And he asked me to show it to him, to show him the footsteps."

Olajuwon says the two men worked on it for two hours. They worked on one move, one set of footsteps, for *two hours*! Olajuwon tells the interviewer that Bryant didn't want to leave the gym until he had the entire thing down "smooth." Even after four rings, Kobe Bryant flew to Houston in his off time to ask a Hall of Famer who played a different position to help him add something to his game, something he didn't have.

It paid off, too. The next season, Kobe Bryant won his fifth championship.

That's the type of continuous learning that ensures greatness isn't random.

FIND YOUR UNIQUE KNOWLEDGE

Once you have established a foundation of historic knowledge and you are routinely adding to that base and keeping up with what's happening in the frontiers of your field, then you'll be better able to spot unique knowledge: areas where you can go deeper than anyone. You can look for the holes in your industry, places your peers are missing. You can find new ways your early awareness of trends could be more useful. Right now, in every industry, there are unexploited pockets of information. Expose yourself to ideas and forums that others in your industry have ignored.

Lorrie Bartlett understood that there were entire communities of talent that were largely overlooked or underappreciated by the rest of Hollywood. Danny Meyer figured out which neighborhoods in 1980s Manhattan were about to blossom. Picasso decided he could paint people from every angle—an entire cubist view—all at the same time.

When he was an up-and-coming young comedian in New York, Dave Chappelle used to walk to Washington Square Park and watch the street performers, including a legendary New York character named Charlie Barnett. Barnett would work public crowds in front of the park fountains. Old footage shows him with audiences of hundreds, and the crowd is laughing uproariously—even at the material that might seem the most offensive. Looking back, this is clearly a lesson Chappelle took to heart.

After the young Chappelle had a bad show at the Apollo Theater, Barnett reportedly gave him time at the park. It's clear watching old clips filmed in the park that flickers of Barnett's delivery style rubbed off on Chappelle, too.

In March of 2024, *Politico* revealed the surprising story of a twenty-year-old economics student at Durham University in England named Kacper Surdy. Over the last few years, posting under the X handle @ringwiss, Surdy has become the most definitive source of knowledge for the many, many arcane parliamentary procedures available to federal legislators in the U.S. But Surdy had never set foot in America's national capitol. He just genuinely loves parliamentary procedure.

Starting in 2020, he started reading massive rule books that even the most powerful individuals on the Hill have never cracked. He described *House Practice*, which is more than one thousand pages, as "a pleasure to read." Now, as more politicians and staffers seek to contort or stretch procedural norms, Surdy's deep knowledge of procedural history is more coveted and valuable than ever.

The account has only a few thousand followers, but they are some of the most connected and powerful followers in the world. *Politico* called the account "a go-to resource for staffers, lobbyists and reporters across Washington," noting that the person operating it "has emerged as a helpful narrator, one whose missives are being read at the very highest levels."

FAR ANALOGIES: CROSS-POLLINATE YOUR MIND

Charles Darwin had a breakthrough in biology by reading about geology. When Darwin boarded the HMS *Beagle* in 1831, he brought with him the first volume of Charles Lyell's *Principles of Geology*—a book that profoundly shaped his thinking about the observable effects of time on the natural world. Darwin later said reading Lyell was like gaining a "grand view of the causes of change."

Reading about geology did not give him the theory of evolution—but it gave him the mental scaffolding to imagine it.

Once you've mastered these various approaches to learning your own industry, you can add a truly pro move to the mix: learning *outside* your industry. This may seem counterintuitive to you. You may be thinking: *Why bother spending my limited time learning other fields if I'm trying to be the best in my field?*

Here's why: Making meaningful, useful connections between seemingly unrelated ideas across a panoply of fields has led to novel discoveries.

This type of outside-your-field learning can push you beyond the best practices of your industry, and in my experience, not everyone can reach this level. But if you can, that will set you apart the most. I think of it as a next-level unlock.

In 2013, I was fortunate to hear UCLA psychology professor Keith Holyoak speak at an event at Stanford. His topic was "far analogies." I had never heard the term before but found it immediately compelling. Holyoak argued that the best and brightest are able to borrow ideas from fields totally unrelated to their own craft. David Epstein's book *Range* also highlights this concept, explaining that many breakthrough innovations happen when someone from a distant field—where they may have deep knowledge—brings new approaches and thinking to a new field of study. Evidence includes the fact that, according to Epstein, "compared to other scientists, Nobel laureates are at least 22 times more likely to partake as an amateur actor, dancer, magician or other type of performer." Epstein also points out, "The most successful experts also belong to the wider world." If you're a chemist and the only thing you ever think about is chemistry, you're not participating in the wider world.

This has also been called "lateral" learning. This type of interdisciplinary research is a founding principle of the Santa Fe Institute, where I'm lucky to spend some time. It's clear that while taking hours away from your own field might seem like ceding ground, it often means building a ramp. You're creating the circumstances for happy accidents. When I asked Holyoak about this recently, he pointed out this fantastic quote from evolutionary biologist Stephen Jay Gould, a recipient of the MacArthur Fellowship: "If genius has any common denominator, I would propose breadth of interest and the ability to construct fruitful analogies between fields."

Think of the way Angela Duckworth could learn about a paramecium and then connect some of those concepts back to her own work in psychology. Steve Jobs studied calligraphy. Magnus Carlsen, the chess player, is also a high-level poker player. When Bobby Knight was a young coach drawing up basketball plays, he also sought out football coaches for their perspective.

When you cross-pollinate your mind like this, you are enhancing the capabilities of your thinking process. You're expanding the well from which you draw ideas.

YOU HAVE NO EXCUSE NOT TO LEARN

At the 2015 Reykjavik Open chess tournament, many of the players gathered one night for a trivia competition—where every question tested participants on historical games, positions, players, and obscure chess terminology. By then, this pub quiz was in its sixth year and becoming a celebrated tradition. It should come as no surprise that the winner of the Reykjavik Open's Pub Quiz was Magnus Carlsen—because of course one of the greatest chess players alive was also one of the best chess *trivia* players in the world—despite the fact that Carlsen was just twenty-four at the time.

Early in the game, Carlsen and his trivia partner, fellow Norwegian Jon Ludvig Hammer, recognized a particular moment from the first game of the Bobby Fischer–Boris Spassky rematch in Yugoslavia 1992—when Carlsen was an infant. They also identified a diagram of an obscure position employed in a tournament that had taken place in 1974, sixteen years before Carlsen was born.

"We already know how strong Carlsen is," a grand master wrote on the U.S. Chess Federation website after the pub quiz victory, "but the breadth of knowledge he showed in the trivia quiz was extraordinary."

Plenty of people are born with talent. Plenty of people have drive. There's nothing you can do about that. You might not be the brightest person in your field. That's fine. You can still become the most knowledgeable.

The great investor Charlie Munger put it this way: "I constantly see people rise in life who are not the smartest, sometimes not even the most diligent, but they are learning machines. They go to bed every night a little wiser than they were when they got up, and boy does that help, particularly when you have a long run ahead of you."

As you strive to know more about your craft or a particular element of your craft, you can also create goals for your knowledge level. You can start with subgroups. Let's say you love esports and you are keen to forge a career path in the world of multiplayer gaming. You decide to pursue an MBA with an esports focus. Within your first six months in a program you should be the most knowledgeable student at your school in your chosen field. That's doable. It probably did not take long for Jerry Seinfeld to know more about the history of stand-up than the other kids at his school, for example.

Then, by the end of your first year, you should be in the top five of all MBA students in the country. Then, hopefully, when you exit your second year, you're the most knowledgeable MBA student out there. This doesn't mean you're the smartest person in the world of esports, but you've separated yourself from everyone else coming out of MBA programs in your class. If you're already working in your field, you can replicate this type of subgrouping.

In fact, with the number of free and inexpensive tools and resources available today, you have no excuse *not* to learn about what you love. If you discovered a new, fascinating topic today, you immediately have Wikipedia, YouTube, and an assortment of podcasts one click away. Chances are, you can also find ongoing discussions of this topic on X or Reddit or some other forum waiting for you on the first few pages of a Google search. When you want to go deeper, you have books, documentaries, research papers—many of which you can access for free.

Now we also have AI. Every week, the artificial intelligence research engines become more capable of delivering concise, digestible information deep dives on almost any subject. For the vast history of humanity, figuring out the answer to almost any question took an enormous amount of time and effort. Now you can learn about near anything in a matter of seconds—and as time goes on, those answers will be more accurate and more nuanced. Unlike human mentors, AI is an inexhaustible companion—always available, infinitely patient, and ready to fuel your continuous learning journey.

It all comes back to this: If you really want to succeed, you really have to learn. And if you really want to learn, there has never been a better time than now.

PROFILE THREE

THE BALLAD OF ROBERT ZIMMERMAN

Robert Zimmerman grew up in a modest blue two-story house on a quiet street in Hibbing, Minnesota, a small mining town about three hours north of Minneapolis. Part of the tight-knit local Jewish community, the family ran an electronics and furniture store. In the 1950s, Hibbing's downtown strip was full of mom-and-pop businesses—drugstores, department stores, small boutiques—but the character of the region, known as the Iron Range, was defined by the blue-collar jobs at the iron mine just outside town. That and the long, merciless winters.

"You couldn't be a rebel," Robert would later say. "It was so cold that you couldn't be bad."

The way he tells it, he was about ten years old when he found two things in this blue house in Hibbing that his father had purchased: a guitar and a big mahogany radio with a turntable. When he opened up the top, he found a country record called *Drifting Too Far from the Shore.* "The sound of the record made me feel like I was somebody else," he'd say later. "That I was maybe not even born to the right parents or something."

Inspired by the music of Hank Williams, young Robert taught himself how to play the guitar and the piano. He'd stay up late at night, when radio signals traveled farther, and listen to stations beaming in through the atmosphere from thousands of miles away. He'd listen to broadcasts from Arkansas and Louisiana, country music and blues tunes that weren't played anywhere in Minnesota. Robert was transfixed by artists like Muddy Waters and Johnnie Ray, who, Robert observed, seemed to be crying as he sang.

As a teenager, Robert formed a band called the Golden Chords. They used to play rock and roll covers, including Elvis Presley and Little Richard songs—though there weren't a lot of opportunities to perform around Hibbing. One year at a talent show, the group played a raucous rendition of "Rock and Roll Is Here to Stay" in the 1,800-seat auditorium at Hibbing High School. The more he heard music from other parts of the country, the more bored Robert got in Hibbing. In his high school yearbook, his photo had the caption "Robert Zimmerman: to join 'Little Richard.'" That didn't happen, but the day after he graduated, he moved to Minneapolis.

"I'd gone as far as I could in my particular environment," he'd say later. He had become what he called "a musical expeditionary."

HE ENROLLED AT the University of Minnesota, but he didn't go to class much. He was hanging out in an area known as Dinkytown, performing at the Ten O'Clock Scholar coffeehouse, honing his skills and building a small following. He'd stay up late, singing and playing his guitar wherever he could. Then he'd sleep all morning. He didn't have any desire to study what the school was teaching, but he'd read books by Beat authors like Jack Kerouac, and they helped him make sense of the world.

"The only people for [Kerouac] that were interesting were the mad people, the mad ones, the ones who were mad to live, mad to talk, mad to be saved, desirous of everything at the same time, the ones who never yawn, all those mad ones," he'd say later. "And I felt like I fit right into that bunch."

Though he grew up playing rock and roll, in Minneapolis Robert became enamored with folk music. He'd heard a bit of this type of music back on the Iron Range—including legends like John Jacob Niles and Odetta—but it was rare.

"Folk music was delivering me something," he'd say. "The way I always felt about life and people and institutions and ideology. It was just uncovering it all."

It was more serious than the vapid rock and roll or country songs he'd heard. Folk songs tended to be about deeper subjects that resonated with the eighteen-year-old: tragic love stories, tales of rebellion, murder ballads, tunes and lyrics that had evolved over decades or even centuries. Captivated, Robert traded in his electric guitar for an acoustic one. He wanted to immerse himself in folk music. He studied every folk album he possibly could. He didn't have a lot of money, but at the time you could walk into a record store and listen in a booth. He would do that for hours and hours and hours, until he knew the songs so well he could play them himself.

He also became friends with other people who liked folk music but did have money. He would go to their houses and borrow their record collections. Over time, though, Robert became one of the most knowledgeable folk fans in Minnesota—perhaps *the* most knowledgeable.

"I had no goal," he'd say later, "except learning all the songs I could."

He was a sponge, picking up accents and mannerisms as he mimicked the songs he'd heard. When he played Odetta songs, he employed her upstroke-downstroke guitar rhythms. When he played Irish songs, he sang with an Irish lilt.

"He was hungry, hungry in a lot of ways," Tony Glover, one of the folk collectors he prolifically borrowed albums from, has said. "Not just for money, not just for fame. He was hungry for experience, for getting out, for doing it, for seeing what was out there, for seeing who he could be."

There was one folk musician Robert liked most of all. Woody Guthrie had toured the country singing about the struggles of working-class Americans. His most famous song became "This Land Is Your Land," but many of his songs were inspired by the trials of hardscrabble people trying to survive. "You could listen to his songs and actually learn how to live," Robert would later say.

Robert even read Guthrie's book *Bound for Glory,* which covers Guthrie's years as a roaming musician and his experiences in the Dust Bowl era. Robert would later explain that he devoured the book "like a hurricane." And the book resonated with the younger musician, opening his mind to a different way of thinking.

The next thing that happened in Robert's story, I think, is one of the most ambitious actions anyone I know has taken to pursue their dream job. Eventually, Robert decided that merely listening to Woody Guthrie albums in Minneapolis would no longer suffice. He wanted to know more about this man. He wanted to meet his folk music idol in person.

So in January 1961, with nothing but a suitcase, a guitar, and ten dollars, he decided to leave Minnesota and hitchhike 1,200 miles to New York City, to Greenwich Village in particular—the center of the folk music world at the time.

WHEN HE REACHED the George Washington Bridge that connects Manhattan to New Jersey, Robert got out of the car and took the subway down to Greenwich Village. The first place he went was Cafe Wha?, a subterranean coffee shop and music venue at the corner of MacDougal Street and Minetta Lane. Five years later, the place would be famous for featuring big-name musicians early in their careers, including Jimi Hendrix and Bruce Springsteen.

The Village was the epicenter of counterculture in America. Poets, musicians, and painters swarmed here from all over the country—and a few came from Europe. The area had been the center of the Beat movement in the 1950s, with poet Allen Ginsberg doing regular live readings. Bars like the San Remo Cafe attracted famous writers and intellectuals like Tennessee Williams, James Baldwin, William S. Burroughs, Jackson Pollock, and Gore Vidal. Jack Kerouac set scenes from his novels there.

By the early 1960s, there were jazz clubs and blues clubs and what seemed like an unlimited number of places to perform. Folk singers Robert had been listening to back in Minnesota—including Dave Van Ronk, Peggy Seeger, and the New Lost City Ramblers—would play short sets at bars and coffee shops all over the neighborhood, earning money by passing a basket around the audience and asking for donations. On Sundays, artists and performers would gather in Washington Square to talk and play.

Years later, the Irish folk singer Liam Clancy would describe the scene like this: "You were suddenly free of all the shackles of family, the baggage of tradition, of bad tradition," he said. "Freedom didn't exist all over America. Freedom only existed really in Greenwich Village."

It didn't take long for Robert to find Woody Guthrie, his hero. But Guthrie wasn't in the Village—he was across the river in New Jersey. Robert took a bus to Morristown, where he found Guthrie in a psychiatric hospital. We know now that the elder folk singer had Huntington's disease, a hereditary neurological illness. But he'd been picked up as a vagrant and misdiagnosed with schizophrenia. Robert was shocked and dismayed to find his hero like this, but he still managed to play a few songs for him and they struck up a friendship.

Robert spent most of his time in New York sitting for hours in venues like Café Wha?, the Gaslight Cafe, and Gerde's Folk City, listening the way he had in the booths at the record stores back home. He studied each performer, each song and style and approach to the stage. Plenty of people have called him a *mimic*. Years later Liam Clancy would say, "He could perform any one of our songs like us, including tonality, tempo, everything."

In a video taken of Robert in his first few months in New York, he looks like a regular teenager, with dirty jeans and a cheery smile. When he played, especially when he first got there, he seemed like a Woody Guthrie impersonator, down to the neck brace he wore to play harmonica. He strummed furiously on his guitar and sang in a nasal twang.

"There's a quality of determination and of will that some people have," fellow folk musician Bruce Langhorne would later say. "When they're doing something, they're really doing it, and you have to pay attention to them."

That was Robert.

When he'd left Minnesota, Robert seemed sort of average. There had been five or six other guys in Minneapolis doing basically the same thing. When he came back for a short visit a few months later, Robert was channeling Woody Guthrie and Dave Van Ronk. He was finger-picking and playing the cross harp. His friends joked that he'd gone to the Crossroads and made a deal with the devil.

ROBERT'S FIRST BIG break came in April 1961, when the owner of Gerde's Folk City gave him a two-week run opening for John Lee Hooker. That led to more regular gigs, opening for touring headliners. A few months later, *The New York Times* music critic Robert Shelton wrote about Robert, with the headline "20-Year-Old Singer Is Bright New Face at Gerde's Club." The article called Robert "one of the most distinctive stylists to play in a Manhattan cabaret in months."

Around that same time, Robert had begun thinking about what went into recording an album. He knew there were talent scouts coming to the bars and coffee shops where he performed, but nobody had ever approached him, so he assumed they'd all passed on him. After all, he didn't sound anything like the smooth crooners on the pop charts.

His first few visits to record labels went poorly. Folkways Records refused to listen to him and threw him out on the street. Executives at Vanguard Records reportedly told him: "We don't record freaks."

But John Hammond at Columbia Records had read *The New York Times* review of Robert's run at Folk City. Hammond was the producer for Aretha Franklin, Billie Holiday, and Count Basie. He was intrigued by Robert. Other executives at the label didn't see it, but they trusted—or indulged—Hammond. So Robert got the chance to record an album.

By then Robert had begun writing some of his own songs, but he didn't want to record most of them. Robert would say later that he didn't want to give too much of himself. Instead, he mostly recorded the first songs that came to mind, including a version of "House of the Rising Sun" that Dave Van Ronk had been performing around town.

He'd given a lot of thought to how folk songs were constructed. He noticed what he'd call the "chilling precision" old-timers used when they came up with songs. The songs were about strange moments someone had experienced or seen, but they were about larger issues, too. Plenty were about real-life events and people. Robert was particularly enamored with a song called "I Dreamed I Saw Joe Hill Last Night," about a Swedish immigrant, labor activist, and folk musician who was convicted of a murder on circumstantial evidence before being executed by a firing squad in Utah. Robert read about Joe Hill's life and musical career, and it seemed like something out of a mystery novel.

Robert thought about how he would have written the song, how he would have immortalized Joe Hill. He imagined writing the song like a man talking from beyond the grave. Robert even had a title for the hypothetical song he never wrote. He would have called it "Scatter My Ashes Any Place but Utah."

In the end, he didn't write a song about Joe Hill. The first folk song Robert wrote that he wanted to share with the world was about another American hero. It was about Woody Guthrie—with lyrics like "I'm a-singin' you this song, but I can't sing enough / 'Cause there's not many men that done the things that you've done." He called it "Song to Woody."

The recording took place over three afternoons in November 1961. Robert had no experience recording, so it was a challenge for producers.

"Bobby popped every *p*, hissed every *s*, and habitually wandered off mic," Hammond would say later. "It occurred to me at the time that I'd never worked with anyone so undisciplined before."

When the album came out in March 1962, it caused a small stir in the Village, but it didn't garner much attention from the outside world. The record reportedly sold fewer than five thousand copies—though Columbia didn't lose much money because it had been so inexpensive to produce.

As soon as he heard it, Robert knew he could do better.

"I was highly disturbed," he'd say later. "I just wanted to cross this record out and make another record immediately. I thought I'd recorded the wrong songs, and I'd already written a few of my own that I thought maybe I should have stuck on there."

IT WAS AROUND this time that Robert Zimmerman officially changed his name to Bob Dylan. He's said over the years that the name change wasn't specifically to honor the Welsh poet Dylan Thomas, but that the name just "felt right" to him. By now the man from Minnesota had fully formed a new persona entirely focused on music.

He went to work immediately on a second record, this time taking an entirely different approach. At this point he was channeling the catalog of folk songs he'd studied so intensely—while processing the turmoil America was experiencing at the time. He wrote songs every chance he got. He wrote on the subway. He wrote in cafés. He'd sometimes stop in the middle of a conversation and start jotting down lyrics.

During this time, he also started dating a political activist named Suze Rotolo. The songs he wrote in this stretch were more political. They sounded both hundreds of years old and at the same time entirely current. Some were bittersweet love songs. Some were explicitly about war.

As he worked on a second album, he was methodical about his song selection, his recording process, even the cover concept—which turned out to be a photo of Dylan and Rotolo walking down a snowy street in New York City. While he had recorded only two original songs on his first album, eleven of the thirteen tracks on his second record were songs he had written.

The Freewheelin' Bob Dylan, released in May 1963, opens with "Blowin' in the Wind," which became an anthem of the 1960s. The lyrics, including the opening—"How many roads must a man walk down before you call him a man"—resonated across socioeconomic lines. The singer Mavis Staples, an icon of the civil rights movement, compared it to gospel music. The album also featured songs like "Girl from the North Country," "Masters of War," "A Hard Rain's a-Gonna Fall," and "Don't Think Twice, It's All Right"—all of which became classics and staples of 1960s folk music.

This time the record was an immediate success, selling more than ten thousand copies a month. It went to number 22 in the U.S. and number 1 in the U.K. From there everything was off and to the races. In '63 he performed with Joan Baez at the March on Washington, where Martin Luther King made his famous speech. A year later he performed for the first time with Johnny Cash, another one of his heroes. Johnny asked Bob for permission to cover his songs.

Bob grew up with a passion. He studied the field meticulously. He found a number of mentors, embraced a group of peers at the epicenter of a budding movement, and ultimately changed the direction of American music. The rest is history, as they say: 125 million albums sold, eleven Grammys, an Oscar, an Emmy. He was inducted into the Rock and Roll Hall of Fame and received a Kennedy Center Award from Bill Clinton. Barack Obama gave him a Medal of Freedom. Then he topped it off with something that had never been done. In 2016, he won the Nobel Prize in Literature—the only musician ever to be given the award.

If you ever find yourself near Tulsa with some time, consider stopping by two interesting museums downtown. The Bob Dylan Center houses and exhibits exclusive cultural treasures created and owned by Bob Dylan over seven decades, and it is a wonderful way to spend a few hours. And why is the largest collection of Bob Dylan history in Tulsa, of all places? Well, because it is just down the street from another museum: the Woody Guthrie Center. Dylan wanted his story to remain connected to Guthrie's.

There is also a quote on the wall of the Bob Dylan Center that sums up his story well. "Life isn't about finding yourself, or finding anything," the quote reads. "Life is about creating yourself and creating things."

PRINCIPLE III
DEVELOP MENTORS IN YOUR FIELD

Find someone who has a life that you want and figure out how they got it. Read books, pick your role models wisely, find out what they did, and do it.

—Lana Del Rey

Before he was one of the most famous investors and one of the wealthiest people in the world, Warren Buffett was a precocious teenager in Nebraska with an affinity for math. He graduated from high school at seventeen, then from college when he was nineteen.

That year, 1949, Buffett had what he's called one of the luckiest days of his life: the day he picked up a copy of Benjamin Graham's book *The Intelligent Investor*, which had just been published. Though Buffett had been interested in the stock market for years, he was blown away by Graham's concept of "value investing" and the idea of a "margin of safety"—meaning, the act of buying shares in a company for less than they are worth. Graham also stressed independent thinking and security analysis—that is, buying shares in a company solely because the fundamental economics are sound, and not speculating at all.

The Intelligent Investor would go on to become one of the most influential investment books of all time. "It not only changed my investment philosophy, it really changed my whole life," Buffett once told the Columbia Business School. "I'd be a different person in a different place if I hadn't seen that book."

Buffett did not stop at devouring the wisdom contained within Graham's pages. Eager to learn directly from the author, Buffett applied to the graduate program at Columbia University, where Graham was an instructor. In his second semester, he took Graham's class. Buffett sat in the front row of the classroom, absorbing everything he could, but he did not stop there. When the course was over, he told Graham that he would work for him for free. Graham did not take him up on the offer, but the two men stayed in touch.

Graham did not forget his plucky student. A few years later, Graham wrote Buffett a letter. By then Buffett had returned to Nebraska, married, and started working at his father's investment firm—while also teaching night courses on investing at the University of Nebraska Omaha. In the letter, Graham told Buffett that if he was ever in New York, he would like to meet. Buffett was in New York twenty-four hours later—not as simple as it sounds in the 1950s—and Graham offered him a job. Luckily for Buffett, Graham did not hold him to the offer to work for free. His starting salary was $12,000 (roughly $125,000 today).

Now Buffett had the chance to soak in his mentor's lessons every day, up close. Buffett observed Graham's systematic, dispassionate analysis, anchored in the idea that the key to investing was figuring out the difference between a company's intrinsic value versus what its shares were going for on the market in a given moment. Graham's investment philosophy boiled down to finding undervalued stocks that were off everyone else's radar.

The two men formed a lasting bond. Over their years of friendship, Graham shared far more than his investment methodology with his eager protégé. Buffett got an up-close view of Graham's generosity, his patience, his integrity in everything from hiring practices to the respectful way he treated employees and competitors. When Buffett's first son was born, in December 1954, he named the boy Howard Graham Buffett, after the two men who had most influenced his life: Howard, for Buffett's father, and Graham, for Benjamin Graham.

In the decades that followed, Buffett applied Graham's lessons as he built his company, Berkshire Hathaway, into a financial empire, amassing one of the world's largest fortunes. The hungry student and the willing mentor remained friends until Graham's death in 1976.

Buffett has said that Graham was so kind, so thoughtful, that it was "impossible to balance the books" with him when it came to gift giving. "He would do things for me or for other members of the family," Buffett has said. "You never could think of anything to do for him."

Buffett hopes to balance the books by preaching the same lessons to new generations of investors. Decades after he first picked up Graham's book, Buffett is a writer himself, publishing an annual report that has millions of investors around the world hanging on his every word. And now, largely thanks to Buffett, Graham's once-radical theories about value investing have become standard practice, transforming an entire industry.

That is the immense power of mentorship.

MENTORSHIP: ROCKET FUEL FOR CAREER GROWTH

Obviously not every mentor-mentee relationship is going to spark a career as illustrious and influential as Warren Buffett's, but a mentor—or a handful of mentors—can make a huge difference in the way your career develops. A whopping 75 percent of executives say mentoring played a key role in their success, according to one recent study. Sometimes that could mean great advice. Sometimes it could be lining you up with a specific job opportunity. There is a reason that nearly every Fortune 100 company has some sort of mentoring program. In late 2024, *The Wall Street Journal* did a nice story about Danny Meyer's forty-year career in the restaurant industry. The focus? His many mentors, and how he *still* reaches out for advice.

I have a phrase I repeat often at Benchmark: *Good judgment comes from experience, which comes from bad judgment.* Why relearn things others already learned the hard way? A good mentor will share hard-earned lessons and industry insights, helping you learn in weeks or months what might otherwise take years. No matter how successful you become, it never hurts to ask for advice from people you trust when you are making hard decisions.

In the early days of Facebook, Mark Zuckerberg would take long walks with Steve Jobs, whose career ups and downs are well known. The two men would discuss management approaches and Zuckerberg's overall company mission. Jobs even reportedly suggested a trip to India when Zuckerberg needed to refocus his goals—advice that proved useful as Facebook suffered through public growing pains. When Jobs died, Zuckerberg posted to Facebook: "Steve, thank you for being a mentor and a friend. Thanks for showing that what you build can change the world."

Mentors also expand your network and your opportunities. They can open doors by either introducing you to key people or recommending you for internships, jobs, or promotions. Imagine a reputable mentor sticks their neck out and recommends you for a job. Once again you become a *candidate of one*, highly differentiated against the field. A great mentor acts as a champion for your growth, and that can become rocket fuel.

Steven Spielberg has seen both sides of that. The future Oscar winner's first big break in show business came at twenty years old, when a short, dialogue-free film he made called *Amblin* somehow landed on the desk of famed Universal executive Sidney Sheinberg. Sheinberg liked it so much, he offered Spielberg a seven-year contract at Universal TV, making him the youngest major studio director in the history of Hollywood at the time and launching Spielberg's storied career.

After experiencing firsthand the way a powerful mentor can shape your career, Spielberg has done his best to pay it forward, championing the careers of directors including Robert Zemeckis (*Back to the Future, Forrest Gump, Cast Away*), Chris Columbus (*Gremlins, The Goonies, Home Alone*), and J. J. Abrams (*Star Wars: The Force Awakens, Star Wars: The Rise of Skywalker*). Together, the films of those three mentees have grossed more than $12 billion at the box office.

At Sheinberg's memorial service in 2019, Spielberg honored the man who launched his career. But when he spoke about the greatest gift Sheinberg had ever given him, it was not that first contract Sheinberg had given him when he was twenty. Instead it was, Spielberg said, "the moral urge to be a mentor."

That's another thing mentors can help with: confidence. Support and encouragement from a mentor can boost your self-confidence and push you to achieve more than you originally thought possible. Knowing that someone powerful and experienced has your back can empower you to stretch your boundaries. Media mogul Oprah Winfrey often credits poet Maya Angelou as a mentor who guided her through crucial years.

"Since the moment I opened *I Know Why the Caged Bird Sings*, I've felt deeply connected to Maya Angelou," Winfrey wrote in the December 2000 issue of *O*, her magazine. Angelou's writing alone seemed to validate her experiences as a young Black girl in the middle of the twentieth century. "Meeting Maya on those pages was like meeting myself in full."

Years later, the two women met in Baltimore and became friends. During Winfrey's twenties, Angelou "brought clarity to my life lessons," Winfrey wrote. The two developed what Winfrey called a "mother-sister-friend relationship." The poet shared in the media mogul's successes and soothed her during some of the hardest times.

Well after she was an international superstar, the undisputed champion of daytime TV, Winfrey would sometimes go to Angelou's home and sit by her feet, by the fireplace, and feel some of the same validation she felt as a girl, reading Angelou's work.

"She was there for me always, guiding me," Winfrey said after Angelou died in 2014. "Mentors are important, and I don't think anybody makes it in the world without some form of mentorship."

TWO TYPES OF MENTORS

There are two different kinds of mentors you can look for as you begin this journey: aspirational mentors you can learn from at a distance, by soaking in their writing or speeches or what's been written about them, and more practical local mentors you can meet with regularly.

1) ASPIRATIONAL MENTORS

James Clear, author of *Atomic Habits,* has said, "The quality of your mentors reflects the quality of your ambition."

Think about the way Danny Meyer identified and started researching all the greatest innovators in the restaurant business. Those were aspirational mentors. Benjamin Graham and Maya Angelou both started off as aspirational mentors for Warren Buffett and Oprah Winfrey, respectively. Then after Buffett enrolled at Columbia and Winfrey met Angelou in person, the relationships evolved.

Start today by studying the greats in your field. Read their books, listen to their interviews, watch their videos on YouTube. If they are on social media, you can follow them and comment on their posts. If they ever follow you back, you can direct-message them—which is an incredibly powerful means to contact someone you idolize directly. If you charm someone, they *might* just respond.

But even if it never gets to that, you can learn what they did to be successful. Understand their achievements, their key areas of interest, how they differentiated themselves. One day you might meet these people, and if that happens, they will undoubtedly appreciate your preparation.

2) LOCAL MENTORS

Identifying local in-person mentors can seem more daunting, but potential mentors are out there in plain sight—often eager to help promising up-and-comers. Finding them can be a significant part of your overall journey. When you begin looking for someone who might be a mentor, start with people you know or almost know. Look around your existing circles first. Is there a senior coworker or a boss you admire? Perhaps a former professor, coach, or family friend in your target field?

If you are early in your career at a company, you might approach a more experienced colleague for advice over coffee. If you are shifting careers, reach out to people in your new industry. Many mentorships start through informal conversations.

Use tools like LinkedIn to identify people in roles or industries where you hope to work. Search for titles and roles that match your interest and see who posts compelling content. Don't be afraid to cold-connect with a brief, polite note expressing admiration for their work and a request for a short chat. The worst that can happen is they ignore the request—not a big loss. Some may respond positively, especially if you have something in common, like an alma mater, mutual connections, or shared interests. My bet: You will be surprised by how willing people are to have a conversation, even if it doesn't evolve into a full-on mentorship relationship.

If you are struggling to identify the right person, double down on your research. Find someone in your target industry who you think is doing great work but who does not have a high profile yet. They might not receive as many asks and might be more likely to say "yes" to a meeting. People are most typically flattered when you show that you paid attention to their work.

Go to in-person events for your industry in your area. Pay attention to the speakers and which ideas resonate with you. The ultimate goal is to create some serendipity.

One place to look for promising events may be a local college or university. Not long ago, a friend of mine wanted to apply to law school at the University of Texas. I suggested attending some of the school's events, and when we looked it up, there were dozens throughout the year. If my friend got to know even four or five faculty members at those events, that could lead to four or five powerful allies on the inside during the application process.

One word of caution, though: Do not aim too high too early. Plenty of people make the mistake of writing to the most aspirational mentors very early in the process and end up sounding less informed than they might have if they had waited until the appropriate time. Try not to make this mistake. Understanding this requires finesse. The right time will come.

Finally, consider having multiple mentors—or what former Facebook COO Sheryl Sandberg has called a "personal board of advisers." *The Wall Street Journal* regularly asks successful people to describe their circle of mentors and advisers. Don't feel like you have to find one person who bumps on every vector, the *perfect* guru. One person might teach you leadership. Someone else might teach you communication. Someone else might teach you specific negotiating techniques. Different people have different areas of expertise.

Having a few go-to advisers gives you breadth in your guidance and you are not overburdening a single individual.

HOW TO APPROACH A POTENTIAL MENTOR (WITHOUT THE AWKWARDNESS)

Be thoughtful about how you go about seeking mentors. Don't ask someone you barely know if they will mentor you, or, if you do, keep your hopes in check. Approaching would-be mentors requires nuance and sophistication. You are trying to build a meaningful relationship that lasts years. Like every relationship, that needs to start with a conversation that interests both parties. So read the room. Take note if someone is in a hurry or if this might not be a good time.

You have to account for how your approach could come across to this other person. As someone who fields a lot of incoming messages from people asking for my time, I know firsthand that many come in hot and sound a little crazy. This kind of communication is hard to perfect. But if you nail it, the rewards are more than worth the time and effort you put into being thoughtful.

When you reach out to people, treat them with unwavering admiration and respect, but don't be sycophantic. Once again, this requires a nuanced balance. You might start by asking if they can have a quick chat over coffee, or maybe you begin with a specific question about how they did something or what they think of an issue. Don't ask something you could find an answer to online, though. Mention what kind of guidance you're seeking, whether it is advice on transitioning into their industry, feedback on your portfolio, or general career insights.

Writing with clarity will help you craft a sincere request that shows this person that you are serious. Being specific also helps them know you aren't mass-emailing with generic introductions and pleas. (To be clear, you definitely should *never* spam or mass email people while looking for a mentor.) Clarity can help them say "yes," since the expectations are specific—and maybe even a little intriguing.

Consider reaching out with a note like this:

"I'm changing careers into marketing after two years in finance. Your posts about storytelling in branding really resonated with me. Could I possibly take thirty minutes of your time to learn how I might pivot into a role like yours? I have a few specific questions prepared."

You should research your targets as much as you possibly can *before* you meet. If they have books or podcasts, read and listen to them. If they speak publicly, attend the speeches. Most people will be impressed by your commitment to learning. Let your prospective mentor know a little about your own journey and how much you care about an industry by asking earnest and interesting questions, but make a point to do much more listening than talking. The last thing you want to do is waste someone's time.

Be genuine when you engage. Be enthusiastic, but don't fake it. If this is your passion and you are committed to learning your craft and industry, your curiosity should be authentic. Your questions should be thoughtful but natural. Most people can sniff out insincerity quickly, and if that happens, you will be worse off than you were before you reached out.

Find ways to stay in touch. Ask them if you can keep them updated on your progress, which gives you a reason to reconnect later. Perhaps you could ask them to review a piece of your own work. For example, if you're an aspiring writer, maybe you can ask to send them your next big story.

Ask if there's anything *you* can do for *them*. Maybe you understand TikTok better than they do. Maybe you see peripheral discussions on Reddit that they would not. Give them a reason to want you around by adding value whenever you can.

Send a thank-you note. If someone takes even a few minutes to talk to you about your career path, tell them how much you appreciate it. The goal should be for the mentorship to develop naturally, without pressure.

RESPECT BOUNDARIES BUT TAKE THE INITIATIVE

Once you have connected with a mentor figure, you need to cultivate a relationship that proves mutually beneficial over time. You want to be a great mentee and make it as easy as possible for your mentor to continue investing in you.

This means that you have to take the initiative. The onus is usually on you as the mentee to drive the relationship. Mentors might be willing to help, but it should be your responsibility to schedule catch-ups and keep the conversation going. Do not wait for your mentor to reach out. Consider setting up a recurring coffee chat once a month, or send them a personalized quarterly update while asking if they have time to discuss some new questions that have come up. Showing initiative demonstrates that you value their time and are committed to your own growth.

At the same time, do not suffocate them. Again, read the room. You do not want to become a burden or an unpleasant obligation. Just as in any relationship, this requires balance and self-awareness. Your mentor is not there to serve you.

Come prepared to every meeting. Treat mentor meetings with a bit of formality—not in tone (you can be casual and friendly), but in preparation. Have an agenda or a few key questions for every meeting. Perhaps you want feedback on a project, help deciding between job offers, or advice on developing a certain skill. Being prepared shows respect and ensures you optimize each interaction. Be ready to show your progress over time, too. A good mentor will love seeing you grow.

If your mentor gives you advice or challenges you to try something, make an effort to act on it and let them know how it goes. This accomplishes two things: It shows that you take their input seriously, and it demonstrates to your mentor that their counsel is making a difference. Keep in mind that *not* doing something your mentor challenges you to do can be detrimental.

Let them know when you have met big milestones. Tell them how their advice specifically helped you and take the chance to thank them again. You want them to root for you. You want them to understand that your victories are also their victories.

Respect your mentor's boundaries. Mentors are not on-call consultants or therapists. Don't send emails or texts like this person is one of your friends from school. Don't expect instant replies to every question. Don't ever be demanding. Ask your mentor early on about their preferred communication style—and frequency. Do they prefer scheduled chats? Is it okay to send quick, short, casual emails? Adjust to their preferences.

By nurturing the relationship, by being thoughtful about it, you can transform a onetime chat into an ongoing mentorship that can profoundly shape your career. If you are lucky, you might build a lifelong friendship like Buffett and Graham's.

DON'T FEAR THE ASK

Here is what I want to stress: Don't be rude, but be fearless. A "no" costs you nothing. A "yes" can dramatically change your life. If someone does not respond to you or outright rejects an invitation for coffee, that "no" might sting, but you are no worse off than you were before asking. Now contrast that to the limitless possibilities a "yes" might deliver. The results are entirely asymmetrical.

Many successful people boost their careers by sending cold emails or striking up conversations with strangers in their industry to ask questions. Do not think of this as networking, though, which can feel forced or transactional. Instead, approach it as a sincere, genuine effort to learn—like you are the new student looking for a friendly face to help you navigate the hallways.

Tim Ferriss, the bestselling author, entrepreneur, and podcaster, has a great quote about mentors. "To learn and grow quickly, identify who inspires you, then reach out. The best mentors respond to ambition." This is a critical insight. Make sure your own ambition is on display during this process. If you are at this point in your journey, where you are searching for mentors, you have nothing to lose and everything to gain. Later in life, many of these people will be your coworkers and peers. But if you are just starting out, put your curiosity, your earnest (and ambitious) desire to learn, on display.

I started this chapter suggesting that aspirational mentors are simply for studying and not actually meeting. I also warned against being too aggressive early on. I stand by that. That said, as you start to grow, gain traction, and climb the ladder of success in your field, opportunities to meet and have a relationship with the greatest in your field will one day arrive, and these will be special moments.

At one point, I recalled that Danny Meyer had made a list of twelve culinary icons at the beginning of his journey. These were the people he studied who gave him both aspiration and permission to pursue the career that he loves in the restaurant business. I texted Danny, "How many of those twelve icons that you studied early on did you end up meeting?" He responded immediately with an emoji: 💯

PROFILE FOUR

THE GROUP TEXT THAT CHANGED THE GAME

Chris grew up in a children's home started by his parents in Taos, New Mexico. This was the early 1970s. His father, who ran the home, was studying to be a priest, and his mother was living with the famous psychologist and psychedelic drug advocate Timothy Leary in Mexico. There were eighty-five kids, mostly wards of the state or abandoned by their own families, living together on a sprawling ranch just outside of town. The children were divided into three houses: ages zero to six in one house, six to thirteen in another house, and thirteen to eighteen in the last house. They shared bunk beds, chores, meals, and stories—some heartbreaking, others hopeful. Early on, Chris learned that teamwork was vital for success in life.

The kids on the ranch were poor and were often treated like outsiders in school. But around the time he turned ten, Chris noticed something: As soon as he or anyone else was competing on a field or a court or a track, it no longer mattered whether you were poor or lived with two parents in a traditional home. Whether it was baseball, basketball, track, or football, Chris gravitated toward anything that helped him fit in. Sports became his lifeline, an avenue to escape the uncertainty of his unusual upbringing, a steadying force amid the turbulence of adolescence.

"I went from not being popular to having a prom date," he told me. "That is the effect of sport."

Chris earned a track and field scholarship to Oregon State University. But just as soon as he arrived, the track program was abruptly canceled. Chris transferred to UC Santa Barbara, where he majored initially in Chicano studies and then sociology. Like so many of us at that age, Chris was not sure what he wanted to do with his life. "My father only had one requirement," Chris says. "You had to do something to serve society."

His senior year in college, Chris got a call from an old family friend named Richard Donati. He had worked at the ranch and had gone on to become a surgeon at Washington State—and he knew Chris was graduating soon. "He says, 'Your dad took care of me way back in the day, so now I want to help you,'" Chris told me.

He asked Chris what he wanted to do in life, what he enjoyed. Chris said he was most passionate about the power that sports have to change someone's life. Dr. Donati offered to arrange a job for Chris doing maintenance for the athletic department at Washington State. Chris decided to write his father an academic-style paper explaining that this—the world of college athletics—was how he wanted to serve humanity. He pointed out how many people receive college scholarships because of sports, and how, as it had been for him, it could be a path toward being socially accepted and building lasting friendships.

His father approved—and Chris was off to Pullman, Washington.

Chris's position in the Washington State athletic department was truly entry level. His early duties included chalking fields, painting fences, managing laundry, and moving furniture. But Chris embraced every task, seeing opportunity in the mundane. He tackled roles no one else wanted, understanding intuitively that building credibility required humility. But volunteering for everything also gave him the chance to familiarize himself with every aspect of athletic operations, from maintenance to logistics to fundraising. Chris was enamored with every part.

Over the next four years, his work ethic caught the attention of coaches, administrators, and peers, establishing relationships that would later become invaluable. In fact, when Chris saw an ad in *The Chronicle of Higher Education* for a job in development at Cal Poly San Luis Obispo, Jim Livengood, the athletic director at Washington State at the time, offered to make a call on his behalf.

The high-level endorsement worked. In 1994, Chris still had almost $60,000 in college debt, but he gladly accepted a job making $18,000 a year. For the first time in his life, he felt like he was working toward a career.

"You can't choose where you came from," Chris told me. "But you can choose your outcome."

Over the next four years, Chris drove up and down California, tirelessly knocking on doors, building relationships, and exceeding expectations. Every dollar from every donor mattered. Within a few years, Chris transformed Cal Poly's modest fundraising operation from $40,000 annually to more than $1 million a year.

Chris also kept learning. That included attending industry conferences where he could learn about the latest trends and issues in college sports. He was at one of those in Las Vegas in 1994 or 1995, when he met a tall, equally energetic fundraiser from Oregon State named Greg. Greg was around the same age, and as they drank the complimentary beer and dined on the free appetizers, they struck up a conversation. The more they talked, the more they realized they had in common. The two men got along so well that they decided to attend a Riddick Bowe boxing match later that evening.

"At the time," Chris told me, "I just thought Greg was a fun guy to have a beer with."

Neither Chris nor Greg could have fully grasped the significance of their meeting that day, but in retrospect, it's clear: the friendship initiated on that trip would profoundly influence both their lives and, ultimately, shape the landscape of American sports.

BORN IN IDAHO and raised in Eugene, Oregon, Greg had a childhood that revolved around the rhythms and rituals of college sports programs. His father, Bill Byrne, served as the athletic director at the University of Oregon from 1983 to 1992, a period when the Ducks were financially strapped but beginning to imagine grander ambitions. As he observed the challenges and complexity of athletic administration that his father was tackling, Greg found himself fascinated, absorbing daily lessons in resilience, ingenuity, and unwavering dedication. Greg initially pursued a business degree at Arizona State, thinking he was bound for corporate life, but an accounting class proved a stumbling block.

"It was a weed-out course," he told me. "And it weeded the hell out of me."

Greg changed course, earning a degree in hotel management—a field that encompassed much of what he loved about business but required much less accounting. After graduating from ASU, he interned at the foundation that organizes the Fiesta Bowl. Then he took a low-level job in the fundraising department at Oregon, where his father had been the athletic director years earlier. From there he went to Oregon State. He was not in that job long when he went to that conference in Las Vegas and met Chris.

Greg noticed that Chris was not just a fan of sports. The two men shared a profound appreciation of the way sports can better society.

"College athletics is one of the few things left that brings everybody together," Greg told me. "You check your differences at the door. We need more of that in our society."

The two men stayed in touch. After Chris's success in San Luis Obispo, he was offered a job in the development office back at Washington State, where just a few years earlier he had been chalking fields and moving couches. Back in Pullman, Chris got the idea to copy one of Greg's fundraising brochures. "I took that brochure," Chris told me. "I reprinted it in my colors and used the exact same verbiage."

Sure, their respective schools met regularly, but the two men knew even then that there was no reason to be competitive. Not many Washington State alumni would be considering donating to Oregon State—and vice versa. Chris and Greg realized they could actually *help* each other. "When someone believes in you, even when you don't believe in yourself," Chris told me, "that's when breakthroughs happen."

When Greg was hired as the associate athletic director at the University of Kentucky in 2002, he met a promising young sports information director named Scott. Greg thought he seemed like-minded, someone who would fit in well with Chris. From there, the group kept growing. Every time Chris and Greg and Scott got together at an industry event, there would be a new face in the group. There was John, who was working at the University of Tennessee at the time. And Ross at Missouri. And Bubba at Notre Dame.

These young men were all working in lower-level positions, mostly in fundraising and development. Over the first few years, the group was just a loose collection of guys around the same age who knew each other and were working all across the country in the same industry. The more they hung out, though, the closer their connections became. Chris thinks it was Greg's idea to start a group text. They called their group chat "Next Gen."

They swapped stories, traded ideas, shared advice, and helped solve each other's dilemmas. They discussed potential opportunities for advancement and made connections in the industry. There were likely a few jokes in there as well.

I asked Chris if they were intentionally networking in an effort to bolster their careers. "No, not at all," he told me. "It was just, 'Hey, that's a good dude,' and realizing, 'Hey, we're all in the same boat.' "

But the idea that they all shared a deep interest in the future of college sports was part of their connection from the earliest stages. Soon they were all moving up in the world of college sports. In 2006, Chris became the athletic director at Rice University—making him one of the youngest ADs in the nation at the time. In 2008, Greg became the athletic director at Mississippi State at the age of thirty-six. A year later, when Greg left Mississippi State for the same job at Arizona, Scott replaced him at Mississippi State. A year after that, Ross became the AD at Western Kentucky and John became the AD at Kansas State and their friend Whit was on his way to becoming the AD at Cincinnati. Around that same time, after three years at Rice, Chris left to become the athletic director at TCU.

Now when the group got together, they were all in powerful positions. Now when they shared their experiences, their approaches to fundraising and hiring coaches and budgeting, it could have a direct effect on the programs they led.

"There's comfort in experiencing life with people who are going through exactly what you're going through," Scott told me. "Just in a different place, different flavor."

THERE WERE SOME obvious advantages to this kind of powerful peer group. First, they could share knowledge and best practices. They could learn from each other, from both the successes and the struggles in the group. The career of a university athletic director is also transient by nature. It involves frequent moves across the country, often to a new town where you might not know many people. But this group of friends provided a level of stability, a real community that transcended geographic differences. There are not many people who know what it is like to run a massive collegiate athletic department, a job that involves managing money, people, and public perception.

Here's how Chris put it: "When you do your press conference, you go back into your office, you sit there—everyone's gone—and you're like, now what? There's no preparation for that."

As an athletic director, you might need to raise tens of millions of dollars or renovate outdated facilities or deal with a coach or a player having legal troubles. Being in Next Gen—they later changed the name of the group text to "Young ADs"—meant having peers who could listen, understand, and help.

Because they all understood the value of working together, they were also able to approach problems together. They could gather as peers—not just competitors—and think carefully and collectively about the future of their industry. They could work together to anticipate and plan for some of the gigantic changes coming to college sports. And boy have there been plenty of *those* over the last fifteen years.

Somewhere around 2010, the group started arranging formal meetings. Often they would see each other at tournaments or conferences and set aside one night for a big dinner. They talked about what was new in the industry in the same way they had been talking for years—though now they each had a decade and a half of experience. At one point, Scott convinced Greg to start a Twitter account. Then Greg convinced Chris to do the same. Chris started using his account to engage fans directly.

Keep in mind that this was a self-directed activity. This was not a directive from any superior. It was an intentional effort to learn and grow beyond the boundaries of their organizations. And there was no playbook.

By 2014, their meetings were scheduled months in advance and programmed with outside speakers and focused discussions. That year they met in Chicago and a trial attorney explained the inevitable lawsuits on the horizon, opening up the possibility of student athletes being paid. The meetings were private, so they could talk openly about what this might mean for college sports and how athletic programs could prepare.

Meanwhile, the jobs in the group were becoming more and more prestigious. In 2016, Scott Stricklin became the AD at Florida, a perennial contender in almost every sport. Ross Bjork became the AD at Ole Miss, then Texas A&M, then Ohio State. In 2017, Greg Byrne took over as AD at Alabama, one of the most esteemed programs in the nation. And later that year, Chris Del Conte, a man who had grown up in a children's home, playing sports in hand-me-down clothes, became the athletic director at the University of Texas, one of the most influential positions in all of sports. (Now he has nearly one hundred thousand followers.)

Around this time, the informal "Young ADs" name shifted to the humorously self-aware "Middle-Aged ADs."

In 2018, Chris hosted the group at a compound just outside Austin. Guest speakers included a Disney executive who talked to the athletic directors about the value of announcing game times months in advance. By then it was also clear that the college football playoffs would be expanding at some point from four teams to as many as twelve or sixteen. For years, even one loss in a season could mean a team missed out on the chance to play for a championship. With two losses it was certain. But with expanded playoffs, even a few three-loss schools would likely have a chance to play their way toward a championship season.

The ADs understood that this meant that strength of schedule would be even more important going forward. Big schools like Texas and Alabama and Florida and Ohio State needed to play each other in the regular season. And oh, by the way, those big matchups would also make incredibly lucrative television programming. These were the discussions that eventually led to the tectonic shifts in college football and conference realignment that college sports fans have witnessed over the last few years.

The group that had started over free beer and hors d'oeuvres at a conference in Las Vegas had become one of the most powerful entities in all of American sports.

CORE MEMBERS OF THE GROUP

Name	Institutions served as AD	Key Connections
Chris Del Conte	Rice → TCU → Texas	Original connection with Byrne (1994)
Greg Byrne	Mississippi State → Arizona → Alabama	Early initiator, key organizer of group
Scott Stricklin	Mississippi State → Florida	Byrne's successor at Mississippi State
Ross Bjork	Western Kentucky → Ole Miss → Texas A&M → Ohio State	Early collaborator, significant SEC moves
John Currie	Kansas State → Tennessee → Wake Forest	Early member, influential in ACC/Big 12
Bubba Cunningham	Ball State → Tulsa → North Carolina	Experienced, steadying voice in group
Whit Babcock	Cincinnati → Virginia Tech	Early participant, long-standing member

In late 2020, Chris found himself at a pivotal crossroads in his tenure as the AD at UT. The storied Longhorns football program was struggling to reclaim its former glory. Despite significant resources, a passionate fan base, and an enviable national brand, on-field results under head coach Tom Herman had consistently fallen short of expectations. Texas fans demand excellence, and Chris knew it was time for a change.

One candidate came to mind immediately: Steve Sarkisian, the dynamic offensive coordinator at Alabama. Sarkisian was known for his brilliant football mind—he was a visionary strategist whose offensive schemes consistently bewildered opponents. But he also had a complicated past. His struggles with alcohol previously derailed his head coaching career at USC. He had been sober for years, but hiring Sarkisian would not be risk-free. It would require a deep understanding of his character, current stability, and potential as a leader. For this, Chris needed insight from someone he could trust. He needed to talk to his old friend Greg.

Chris knew that Greg had spent a lot of time around Sarkisian at Alabama and could give him an honest assessment. At this point, Greg was well aware that Alabama's legendary coach Nick Saban was nearing the twilight of his extraordinary career and that Sarkisian represented a strong internal candidate to eventually succeed Saban at Alabama. Greg also knew that Texas and Alabama would be playing each other twice in the next three seasons. He could have told Chris that Sarkisian wasn't ready for a head coaching job again. He could have avoided the question entirely. But he didn't. Greg helped his friend—and a coach he loved.

"Chris and I were able to talk openly about Sark and why he made sense for Texas," Greg told me. "Sark knew we didn't want to lose him, but if you have an assistant coach who has the chance to go be the head coach of Texas, you have to support them."

On January 2, 2021, Texas announced that Steve Sarkisian would take over the hallowed Longhorns football program. Within three years, the team was back at the top of the national rankings and the Longhorns have consistently made the college football playoffs. (Sarkisian has gone 1-1 against Alabama.) Chris and Greg both understood that a great coach at Texas is good for college football—which is good for Alabama.

Thirty years after the group started, they are all still friends. Most of their wives are friends, too. Chris and Greg also told me they are aware of a new group of young athletic administrators. In fact, they know some of them well. Not long ago, Chris's protégé at TCU, a man named Jeremiah Donati, became the athletic director at South Carolina. Donati is the son of Dr. Richard Donati, the old family friend who helped Chris with his start at the Washington State maintenance department. Greg's son Nick has also gone into the family business. He's the assistant director of development at Florida, where he works with Scott.

When the group—the original Next Gen—gets together now, it's often a family affair. They meet up as often as they can. In 2025, most of them got together at the men's Final Four in San Antonio. They also maintain their group text, though Chris jokes that they need to change the name again.

"It's safe to say we are the old ADs now."

PRINCIPLE IV
EMBRACE YOUR PEERS

Friendship is born at that moment when one person says to another, "What! You too? I thought I was the only one."

—C. S. Lewis

Jimmy was eleven years old when he uploaded his first YouTube video. It was short, about a hack in a niche online video game called *Battle Pirates*, and it contained little more than some screen footage and his own squeaky-voiced commentary. In the small world of *Battle Pirates* players, however, the video struck a chord, immediately racking up twenty thousand views. "That was probably the best thing that could have ever happened to me," Jimmy would say later. "I was hooked from day one . . . I fell in love."

This was back in the early years of YouTube. Most of the popular videos on the site at the time were slickly produced music videos. Few independent content producers were making money, and for kids in middle school or high school, the notion of becoming a professional YouTuber had not yet entered the mainstream. "You were just worried they would try to play your videos in class or make fun of you for it," Jimmy told me.

But Jimmy kept going. While he struggled to focus on school, he had no problem losing himself in YouTube for hours every day. He lived in rural North Carolina, a long way from Silicon Valley, where YouTube was invented. As he turned thirteen, fourteen, fifteen, his videos—still mostly focused on gaming—built a modest following. He taught himself how to edit. He studied pacing, what went viral, everything down to the frame rate and coloring of a video.

His obsession with YouTube created awkward social interactions. He couldn't hold a conversation without steering the discussion back toward the one thing he thought about most. "People would just tell me, 'All you talk about is YouTube.'"

For years, he wasn't making a dime from his YouTube videos. Then when he did start making money, sometime in high school, it was only a few dollars a month. He saved up and bought a better microphone. Then he bought a new computer so he did not have to use his brother's old one. He set a goal for himself: By the time he graduated from high school, he wanted to make enough money from YouTube to make it his full-time job. But when graduation day arrived, he still wasn't there.

His mother gave him an ultimatum: Go to community college or move out. He enrolled in a few classes, but he hated it. Forcing himself to sit there, listening to a teacher read aloud from a book, was so tedious. He did not like doing homework or studying for tests. He loved games and puzzles, and more than anything, he loved trying to "solve" YouTube. He was obsessed with cracking the code for what makes a viral video. The thought of sitting through lectures five days a week for the next four years made him, in his own words, "hate life."

He continued going to the community college campus, but soon, instead of going to class, he stayed in his car and edited videos in the parking lot. His grades were straight zeros, and he knew it was only a matter of time before his mother would learn about his deception. "Now the clock had started," Jimmy told me. He knew that if this didn't work, he'd be in a lot of trouble.

He began working fifteen hours a day on this obsession. YouTube became a game he desperately needed to beat. For weeks, he barely did anything else.

Then something amazing happened: His work began to pay off. A few of his videos started doing big numbers. One month he made $20,000. He showed his mom—when he finally told her that he had been skipping classes. He also announced that he was moving out. “My mom almost had a heart attack,” Jimmy told me. “She didn't understand YouTube back then. She was so disappointed. She cried. I felt so bad.”

Not long after moving out of his mother's house, Jimmy found four other small YouTubers who were obsessed with this burgeoning medium. Two were fellow college dropouts. One was a high school dropout. One had quit a full-time job to dedicate himself to making YouTube content. After seven years of making videos on his own, Jimmy finally had peers with whom he could share this obsession. Looking back now, this is when his YouTube career really got a boost.

They all lived in different places, but they would talk for hours every day, usually in epic Skype calls that would sometimes last from 7:00 A.M. until 10:00 P.M. Then he would go to bed, wake up, and do it all over again. The group dubbed these calls “Daily Masterminds.” Together, they did deep dives on every element of what makes a good video. Once they analyzed a thousand thumbnails to see if there was a correlation between the brightness of the thumbnail and how many views the video got. They studied videos that had more than ten million views to see how often, on average, they cut the camera angles.

In some sense, these fellow YouTubers were Jimmy's direct competitors. But the group did not see it that way. More than anything, they simply enjoyed sharing their love for this particular emerging platform. They loved discussing what might be possible one day. They loved understanding YouTube together. That's why the hours ticked by so quickly every day.

“I had so many years of pent-up desire to communicate these

things," Jimmy told me. "I finally felt like I fit in with other freaks who actually want to make millions of dollars and don't just care to work a nine to five."

But there was something more than that, too. Jimmy told me he also saw this as a fair exchange of value.

"A big part of YouTube is getting people to click on your videos," he told me. "I was horrible at clickbait. But I made really good videos. These guys, back then, were quite literally some of the best clickbait-title and thumbnails makers on the planet. They were so good at it. But their videos were dog shit. So I was just teaching them how to make actual entertaining content. And they're teaching me how to make titles that were good. And so it was like a match made in heaven."

They did this for years. Jimmy estimates they had these calls for one thousand days straight at one point. When they started meeting, each person in the group had ten thousand to twenty thousand subscribers. By the time they stopped the Daily Mastermind calls, everyone in the group had more than one million subs. In fact they all crossed the million-subscriber mark within a month of each other. "It shows that it wasn't luck," Jimmy told me. "We were just all so in tune in helping each other."

Jimmy has also said that if anyone else had been on those Skype calls, they would have been able to crack a million subscribers, too.

Today, Jimmy Donaldson is better known as MrBeast. As of this writing, he has more than four hundred million subscribers to his main YouTube channel, the largest account the platform has ever seen. He is the undisputed king of the medium. Each video makes him millions of dollars. In 2022, he started a chocolate company, Feastables. Within two years, the company reportedly sold $250 million worth of chocolate. He also hosts his own reality show on Amazon Prime, called *Beast Games,* part of a deal with Amazon MGM reportedly worth $100 million. I talked to him about this incredible peer group between his filming sessions a few days after he turned twenty-seven.

If you look at the arc of his career to this point, the big bump did not come from his seven years grinding alone. That was the foundation. He had some moderate success, enough to move out on his own. But when I asked him, Jimmy told me that he grew the most in those years after high school, when he was working with his peers and they were all learning together.

His story is an incredible example of why you should embrace peers in your field.

WHAT WE TALK ABOUT WHEN WE TALK ABOUT PEERS

We often hear about the importance of mentors—the senior figures who provide guidance from experience. But what about peers? Peers, the people walking alongside us in our journey, can be just as powerful in shaping our careers and personal development. Sometimes, as in the case of MrBeast or the group of "Next Gen" college athletic administrators, the peer relationship is the single most important springboard in a developing career.

So, what do I mean by *peer*? A peer is someone on the same professional track as you. They are equally ambitious, striving for success in a way that mirrors your own aspirations. Unlike mentors or senior leaders, peers provide a different kind of support—one rooted in shared experiences rather than hierarchical and experiential guidance. It's a different kind of friendship. These relationships are an extension of your desire to learn more about your craft. The result is more collective knowledge, more people to help you navigate challenges, and friends to help "grease the skids" of career progression.

Despite all this, though, many professionals are hesitant to open up to their peers. They see peers as competitors rather than collaborators and end up trying to navigate their careers alone. This is a problematic mindset. Imagine if MrBeast had viewed those fellow YouTubers only as the competition. He never would have experienced the rapid growth that made him the most popular channel on the platform.

There's also that other element that MrBeast experienced: the shared joy and camaraderie that comes from discussing something you love with someone else who loves the same thing. You immediately have a bond. You have that foundation of a friendship. You can share in the excitement of learning new things from someone else *and* the excitement that comes from sharing something your new friend might not know. And because peers do not have authority over you, you don't have to be your best, most polished self all the time. You can ask the naive questions you might not ask a mentor. This is an incredible way to learn. Have discussions. Have arguments. Share ideas. Hone and innovate concepts the way MrBeast did.

I wish someone had told me this when I was younger. When I arrived at MBA school, everybody said, "Network, network, network," and I thought it was simply a social activity. I thought they were telling me, "Oh, you need to develop your social skills." What I've come to realize is: No, it's not about that. It's about connecting with the people that you have the most overlap with because you will be able to help each other along your journey.

THE UNDERRATED BENEFITS OF ACTIVE PEERS

This may very well be the most important principle in this book. Of all the tools available for growth—coaching, courses, connections with mentors—an engaged peer network might be the most powerful and beneficial. It's one of the most underdiscussed elements in personal and professional development, because embracing the people who might also be in line for a job you want isn't intuitive. And that is why it's a secret weapon.

Here's what having active peers can give you:

1. **Shared Learning:** You are not just growing alone—you're evolving together. Everyone brings unique experiences, interests, articles, podcasts, solutions, and even failures that serve as real-time learning opportunities.

2. **An Extended Network:** You are tapping into not only your peers but their connections, too. That's exponential reach.

3. **Potential Mentors:** Sometimes a peer introduces you to someone just a step ahead—someone who might turn into a future mentor.

4. **Job Opportunities:** Peers hear about openings before they are public. And they are willing to refer people they trust.

5. **Real Talk, Real Advice:** A trustworthy and honest friend will tell you what worked, what flopped, and what they would do differently—without the filter. This is why so many great writers workshop their material before it's published.

6. **Confidence and Validation:** Seeing others wrestle with the same problems affirms that you're not broken. You're just in progress. Seeing your friends succeed is a good indication that you're on the right path. Plus an engaged peer can turn into someone else you can impress, someone else who can provide just an extra pinch of motivation.

In addition to these six benefits, a peer network can also offer another critically important advantage. Not every day is a good day. Sometimes your boss yells at you. Sometimes you make a mistake that haunts you. Some days you are staring down a problem so large it feels like a personal failure. In those moments, it's not *strategy* you need. It's support. You need someone who says, "That sucks. I've been there. You're not alone."

Peers are uniquely qualified to do this because they are not evaluating you. They are not grading you. They are walking beside you. You can be vulnerable. You can share. That vulnerability opens doors to deeper learning, stronger relationships, and real growth. One good conversation with a peer can shift your whole week.

As a side effect, these personal relationships help build useful, real-world skills, like oral communication, self-management, and leadership skills. A good peer network should also expose you to diverse perspectives, which just helps build your understanding of a subject even more.

Besides that, peers give you mirrors. You can see what's possible. Peers can show you how far you've come, even when you can't see it yourself. That builds confidence. They can help shape your professional identity. Peers can also give you a "push." You can have a form of competition that isn't about winning or losing—but raising the bar for each other.

Think of how much and how quickly someone like Bob Dylan improved once he surrounded himself with like-minded performers, fellow students of folk. He left Minnesota with a modest set of skills and a dream. After a year in Greenwich Village, he was *transformed*.

Think of peers as connectors. They are sounding boards. They are future colleagues and future collaborators. They shouldn't be intimidating: They are *career-friends*. And that makes all the difference—because when you are on the same journey, it's easier to be real.

BUILD STRONG PEER RELATIONSHIPS: START SMALL AND GROW FROM THERE

You are looking for like-minded individuals with shared career goals. You want to find people who are a good personal fit for you. These are peers you can trust, people with whom you can be vulnerable. You also want people who share your joy and passion. That rapport is critical. The more comfortable you feel, the better.

You might look for someone in a similar role to yours. If you are still a student, you are probably looking for fellow students or recent graduates. If you are new to the workforce, you are looking for other newcomers who share the same interests and goals. This might even be someone in a slightly different industry. For example, a marketing professional in e-commerce might connect with someone in travel marketing.

Where do you find these peers? If you are still in college, look for people with common curiosities. If you are working, start inside your company. Peers outside of your company are generally going to provide more openness and room for frank discussions, but internal company networking events can also be a good place to find this type of friend. Do you think about the same kinds of big-picture questions in your industry? Do you laugh at the same jokes? If you are comfortable enough, it can work.

Go to industry conferences, public events, and industry symposiums. Happy-hour networking events might seem mind-numbing, but they can be a good place to find someone who shares your interests. The standoffish, quiet types sipping drinks on the margins of the crowd might become the peers that spark your future growth.

Be open to where you encounter your peers. Reddit, LinkedIn, and professional organizations can be great resources for finding and connecting with people. If you see someone posting thought-provoking or inspiring ideas in an online industry forum, consider reaching out and connecting. Connections that begin online can often turn into lasting bonds in the real world.

For me, X, formerly known as Twitter, is the most amazing networking and learning network ever built. For someone pursuing their dream job or chasing a group of mentors or peers, it is remarkable. In any given field, many of the top experts in that field are on X, and they are sharing ideas. You can connect to them and follow them. If you are lucky enough and say something they find interesting, they might follow you. The reason this becomes super-interesting is that it unlocks direct messages. Now all of a sudden you can communicate directly whenever you want with that individual, which is very, very powerful. If you are not using X, you are missing out.

But there are many online communities where these experts might live. For some industries, like enterprise technology, the right platform to look for peers is LinkedIn. For gaming, it is Twitch and Discord. For others, it might be Reddit or even Instagram or TikTok.

You should also feel comfortable leveraging your existing network of peers. Ask your friends for introductions. It should not be awkward. You want to find people you can shoot a text or a quick email asking something simple: "Hey, do you have an email for Peter Barker? I'd love to ask him about that presentation." If your peer hoards contacts or plays power games—that is not the type of peer you need to embrace. And you should not do that either. This lifelong journey should feel like a team sport.

If you don't have active peers right now, start small. Join an online community. Set up a biweekly chat with someone in a similar role. Invite a LinkedIn connection to swap notes on your career paths. Be open-minded and willing to share your own thoughts and goals.

Not every connection will turn into a long-term relationship, and that is okay. Every interaction expands your network. But when you find those people, keep them close. Let them in. Because success never happens alone.

ROOT FOR YOUR PEERS

Meaningful professional bonds, like any important relationship, need cultivation or they will wither. Take intentional steps to maintain these relationships. This can be difficult as you advance in your career and take on more responsibilities. Add growing families to the mix and time becomes a rare commodity. This means it is even more important to set aside some time to make phone calls, send emails, and arrange in-person meetings. Maybe you set up a small group get-together once a quarter. If your peers are local, make it more frequent than that. If you know some of your peers are going to a conference or industry gathering you are attending, plan ahead of time to meet before or after the festivities. Keep in contact online. Maybe you set up a group chat full of like-minded peers. Maybe you have a Discord or a Slack channel.

Think of how beneficial Chris Del Conte's athletic administrator group chat became. Nobody could have known when these guys started grabbing beers together at conferences how powerful their friend group would become.

Try to collaborate with your peers when you can. Sometimes that will be unofficial: volunteering to look at a paper or presentation before it happens and offering notes, or maybe asking for advice on a big project. But collaborate in outward-facing capacities when you can, too. If you are an aspiring journalist with a network of journalist friends, suggest working together on a big story. If you are a YouTuber, invite your peers to collaborate. It pays off.

With that in mind: Always share best practices and don't worry about giving away any proprietary knowledge. It is a good, smart trade. If you worry about what you might be giving away, you're going to fail to advance. The activity of sharing with mentors and peers will lead to so many positive things that any negative costs aren't going to come anywhere close.

Root for your peers. Seriously and vigorously. Encourage them before big meetings or presentations. Champion them whenever you have the chance. Treat them like teammates even if they don't work with you directly. If your friend does not celebrate your accomplishments, that person is not really your friend. And that is a two-way street. If your friend gets a promotion and it makes you grumpy, that is a *you* problem. Celebrate your peers' accomplishments as if they were your own. Cheer them, send them notes, be truly happy for them. That will come back to you in spades.

Do whatever you can to promote shared learning. Pass along interesting news stories or industry white papers. Create an environment where your peers want to share with you, too. Discuss topics of mutual interest. Host miniconferences to debate best practices and solutions. If some of your peers adamantly disagree with a take, that's great! Discuss why and figure out where you agree on the same topics.

One more important point: One of the most valuable aspects of a peer group is helping provide support when one of the members inevitably stumbles. You have a responsibility to support your peers. Lift them up. They will return the favor.

Do all of this throughout your career—not just in the first few years. Like any friendship, a peer relationship will expand and evolve over time. Your peer groups themselves will evolve and grow as your careers advance. But the best peer groups manage to maintain those relationships, and the relationships remain important to everyone involved. You want someone who will keep sending you news articles after fifteen years because they want to keep you informed and they want to hear your take. You want peers who won't bat an eye when you do the same.

The foundation of all these relationships must be the desire to keep learning no matter what you have already accomplished.

ADVANCED PEER NETWORKS

Not all of your peers need to be in your exact field. The college basketball coach Bobby Knight gained valuable knowledge about managing athletes from a swimming coach and a football coach. Some of the CEOs and entrepreneurs I work with find that it's more interesting to go to conferences on topics that are slightly outside their field because they are exposed to more novel ideas that they can bring back to their industry.

This goes back to faraway learning and Professor Keith Holyoak's "far analogies" that we discussed earlier, in Principle Two. Think of faraway peers as an extension of that. If you learn from far away, you may unlock much bigger gains. Your learning will be more nuanced. Your breakthroughs will likely be more creative. Even if they are more rare, these innovations can have huge rewards.

Metcalfe's Law states that the financial value or influence of a telecommunications network is proportional to the square of the number of connected users of the system. This means that when you expand the number and type of people you know and befriend, your reach and the value of that network increase even more. The lesson: Build a tribe.

Bring in people with complementary skills and backgrounds. MrBeast was terrible at thumbnails but good at understanding the arc of a story in a video—so everyone in the group had incentive to both learn and share. If you struggle with one particular element of your job, seek out people who specialize in that and see what you can teach each other. The tribe is more powerful than any individual.

I've personally witnessed several examples of this. I know a group of young, female venture capitalists. They come from different backgrounds, but they gather over Zoom and invite different speakers to meet with their group. This is all intentional, purposeful, because they know that it can spark new ideas, new breakthroughs that might benefit them all. They can also process new thoughts or information as a group, which can be much more effective than a one-on-one meeting.

QUADRUPLE YOUR TEN THOUSAND HOURS

In his 2008 book *Outliers,* my friend Malcolm Gladwell examined what makes some people successful and others fail. There are a lot of variables, which should be evident here, too. But one thing he came back to repeatedly was the "Ten-Thousand-Hour Rule," which asserts that the key to achieving world-class expertise in any skill, is, to a large extent, a matter of practicing the correct way, for a total of around ten thousand hours. The idea comes from a study by the Swedish psychologist Anders Ericsson. The more reps and experience you have with a subject, the closer you come to mastering that subject.

This was actually in MrBeast's mind as he assembled his peer network and spent hours and hours every day learning with his YouTube friends. He easily spent ten thousand hours studying the platform and what goes into making viral videos, but that's not how he sees it. Since each of his peers also spent at least ten thousand hours doing this, and they combined forces, the way he sees it, "We probably put in like forty thousand, fifty thousand hours en masse." This was all they did every day—for years.

This collaborative approach has served Jimmy well. In 2024, he invited fifty of the other most popular YouTubers on the planet to compete in challenges on his channel—for the chance to win $1 million. His video received more than 365 million views. And each of the YouTubers got a boost from the video, too.

"Other creators are collaborators," Jimmy told me, "not competitors."

Think of a strong peer network as a strategic unlock. If everyone is willing to put in their time and do the work, those connections—and everything that comes with them—raise the tide for the group, and each individual can benefit.

More than anything, this is a mindset shift. Once you view your peers as collaborators, as friends and not just competitors, you unlock new doors, new ideas. As your field changes and evolves, you have people you can call. You have friends who might have already experienced the problem you just learned about. You have friends who can toast you when you land the big deal or finally earn the promotion you've been targeting.

The journey to greatness is difficult, but it becomes much easier, richer, and more fulfilling when you are not walking it alone.

PROFILE FIVE

THE STYLIST WHO SNUCK INTO FASHION WEEK

Growing up in a Mormon family in southwestern Utah and Oahu's North Shore, Jen never knew that styling hair could be a job. She knew there was a strip mall salon in her hometown called United Hair-Lines. She knew she liked styling her Barbies. But she did not know any professional hairstylists—and the topic did not come up much in her small, religious community. She also did not see many women styling hair on TV or in the movies. The most popular hair care brands at the time were named after men: Vidal Sassoon and Paul Mitchell.

As a kid in the '80s and '90s, Jen was obsessed with pop culture. While her friends were memorizing scripture, she was buying *Tiger Beat* and *Bop* magazines for the foldout posters of Paula Abdul and New Kids on the Block. She could not watch enough MTV—and she remembers realizing early on how hair and makeup were important parts of self-expression.

She also loved '80s and '90s movies like *Mr. Mom, Troop Beverly Hills,* and *Don't Tell Mom the Babysitter's Dead,* films about women who were empowered and successful but also stylish and beautiful. She particularly enjoyed any makeover scene—the moment in a movie when a character's physical appearance completely transforms, almost always signaling a larger personality shift. Seeing a character change so dramatically so quickly was exhilarating.

"I just really loved the idea of transforming someone into something different and making them feel better," she told me.

Around the age of eight or nine, Jen started to practice doing hair and makeup. Her first client was her younger sister, Marci. Jen was not a great student in school and did not think much about career aspirations. When she graduated high school, most of her friends planned to marry young and stay where they grew up. Her high school boyfriend was away on his missionary trip in Sacramento, California, and his mother was working on the set of the 2003 film, *Where the Red Fern Grows* (later distributed by Walt Disney Home Entertainment), based on the classic children's novel. Her boyfriend's mom asked Jen if she wanted to visit the set—and Jen jumped at the chance.

The movie starred Dave Matthews, from the Dave Matthews Band, in his feature film debut. When Jen got the chance to talk to the musician-turned-actor for a moment, he was actually pretty down-to-earth. It dawned on her that celebrities—even massive stars like Dave Matthews—were still just regular people. They had a completely normal conversation. He asked her what she wanted to do in life. For the first time, Jen admitted out loud that she wanted to work in beauty and move to either New York or L.A.

Matthews, who was at that very moment taking a risk to embark on a new career transition, told Jen she should do it.

It might seem silly looking back, but to the sheltered Mormon girl from Utah, hearing someone who worked around hair and makeup professionals all the time tell her that her dream was, in fact, worth chasing was freeing. She felt like Dave Matthews, of all people, had finally given her permission to leave the safety of home and pursue the life she wanted.

Not long after that, Jen sold her car, packed her bags, and moved to Los Angeles with her best friend. She had no formal training, no connections in the industry, and a total of $300.

AS SOON AS she got to California, Jen started pounding the pavement looking for a job somewhere in the beauty industry. This was the early 2000s—a time before smartphones. All she had were the job ads she found in newspapers and on Craigslist, and to help her find her way, a Thomas Guide, a spiral-bound atlas that featured detailed street maps.

She was at a coffee shop one afternoon, interviewing for a receptionist job—something to pay the bills—when a woman overheard the conversation and asked Jen if she would like to work the front desk at a salon instead. That's how she started working at Estilo, one of the hottest salons in Beverly Hills. Winona Ryder and Jessica Alba were regulars.

Was this chance encounter fate? It certainly felt like that to Jen at the time. But the truth is, this is the type of random optionality that occurs when you are hustling. If Jen had instead been back in Utah or at home watching television or doing anything other than working hard to find a job on the streets of Los Angeles, this lucky encounter never would have happened.

As the receptionist at Estilo, Jen sometimes did tasks like feeding coins into parking meters for stars like Bette Midler or Stevie Nicks. But the job also gave her a front-row view of an entire fascinating world. Jen studied the woman who managed the salon and how she engaged with both the clients and the hairstylists. Jen studied the hairstylists, too—not just how they cut and styled hair but the way they interacted with all the different kinds of clients. Day after day after day, she paid attention to what behaviors and attitudes put people at ease, what was most likely to result in a client leaving the salon feeling transformed and renewed like in the makeover scenes she'd loved as a kid.

She also saw what *not* to do and say. Jen watched some stylists struggle with addiction or overspending—trying to live like the wealthy celebrities they styled. She saw what upset the privileged daughters of Beverly Hills and what reactions failed to calm them when they did not like their hair.

Meanwhile, Jen's move to L.A. did not go over well back in St. George, Utah. Her family worried about her. People from church would approach her mother at the grocery store just to say they were praying for Jen. "I was an outcast for sure," she told me. "But I knew what I wanted to do."

Even sharing a loft with her best friend, Jen could not afford the $21,000 tuition to attend Vidal Sassoon's beauty school at the time, so she enrolled in a free program at the Abram Friedman Occupational Center in downtown Los Angeles to learn as much about cosmetology as she could. For months, she would go to her apprentice program in the morning, go to her receptionist job at the salon in the afternoon, then work as a hostess at a restaurant at night. Eventually, she started assisting some of the stylists at the salon too, seizing every chance she had to work up close with clients.

It was all exhausting, but Jen never complained. She loved the world of the salon, the people she met, the transformations she witnessed. In many ways, it felt like she was already living her dream. She loved L.A., and despite her long days, she still had the chance to go out and enjoy the nightlife. But she was never late to work in the morning.

She read as much as she could—mostly personal development books like *The Secret*. There were no foundational texts about celebrity hairstyling—not yet, at least—but she kept up with celebrity news and pop culture, and she paid close attention anytime a story mentioned a celebrity's stylist.

After two years at Estilo, she had the chance to work with renowned celebrity hairstylist Chris McMillan, known for creating Jennifer Aniston's iconic "Rachel" hairstyle on *Friends*. Suddenly, Jen was working with Lindsay Lohan, Paris Hilton, and Nicole Richie at the height of their popularity. In 2006, she assisted the hairstylist Andy LeCompte on tour with Madonna, styling the dancers before every show. Then she was the personal stylist for British fashion designer John Galliano. But she never stopped assisting other stylists every chance she got. She understood that every time she worked on someone's hair, she improved.

The more Jen worked, the more she built a network of friendly peers and clients. Being in L.A. gave her access to mentors, including Sally Hershberger, one of the few female stylists working at the top levels of the industry. As Jen acquired more experience and her network expanded, so did her roster of celebrity clients. Soon she was the preferred stylist of Sofía Vergara—just as *Modern Family* was becoming one of the most popular shows on television.

Jen did not stop grinding, though. For years, she would pay for her own flights to Paris for the biggest fashion shows of the year. She would sneak backstage, often using that old movie trick of looking at the security guard's clipboard and just saying a name. Then, in the chaos backstage, she would start assisting the hairstylists—sewing wigs, helping models—often from 8 A.M. to 2 A.M. Even after Jen had her own agent, and her own paying contract to do Emma Stone's hair at a massive fashion show, she would sneak away, slip backstage, and start working on models in her spare time.

That all might sound frantic, but, as Jen saw it, if she wanted more reps doing the hair of the most beautiful people in the world, on the biggest, most photographed stages in the world—those opportunities are limited. So she took matters into her own hands.

"It was crazy," she says now. "But I just kept thinking to myself, *When am I ever going to get the chance to do this again?*"

One of the people Jen befriended in her travels was jewelry designer Lorraine Schwartz, whose clients have included a host of famous female celebrities including Beyoncé, Jennifer Lopez, and Angelina Jolie. At one point, Jen was doing hair in Lorraine's suite before the Oscars when she was introduced to Kim Kardashian.

That meeting changed everything.

JEN FIRST DID Kim Kardashian's hair for a *Cosmopolitan* magazine shoot in 2010. Soon she was the personal stylist for Kim and her sisters, Khloé and Kourtney, and Kim's daughter, North. That meant seeing them nearly every day, often in the foggy hours of early morning. With her easygoing demeanor, quick wit, and dependable confidentiality, Jen became a trusted family friend just as the family's reality show was exploding in popularity.

This gave her an insider's view of the way the Kardashian family embraced social media—especially Instagram, which launched in 2010—earlier than most celebrities. Jen could see the fun that comes with building a digital audience of peers, clients, and fans. She also saw the career upside: how sharing some parts of your life with strangers all around the world could make you more famous and in demand than if you merely worked behind the scenes.

Long before hair and makeup tutorials on TikTok were standard content, Jen created an Instagram account to chronicle her adventures in the world of beauty. It started slowly, but her audience grew into the tens of thousands, then the hundreds of thousands, then the millions. (As of this writing she has more than five million Instagram followers.)

As she flew around the world, doing hair for some of the most famous people on the planet, Jen continued reading voraciously. But now she was reading about a secondary interest: business. She never stopped loving hair and connecting with clients, but now she was exploring the other common theme in all of her favorite movies: women in the business world. She read books about self-improvement, about living in the moment, about being ready when opportunity inevitably knocks—as it did for the main characters in those movies. And as it did for Jen one afternoon in late 2012, when she was at her boyfriend's bachelor pad, scrolling through her phone.

That's when Jen received the type of call she had been dreaming of for years. It was Gwen Stefani's manager, frantic, asking if Jen could come to Sony Studios in Culver City immediately. Gwen was shooting a *Vogue* cover with legendary photographer Annie Leibovitz, and Jen was told, "Gwen doesn't love her hair."

"I was like, 'Yes! I'll be there as fast as I can!'" Jen told me. "I remember my whole world just stopped, and I was like, I cannot get dressed fast enough. I cannot get to this place fast enough. I hope they don't change their mind!"

Growing up in the '90s, Jen had a Gwen Stefani poster in her bedroom. By the time she answered this call, in late 2012, Jen had been styling big-name celebrities for a few years, but here she was suddenly doing Gwen's hair for a photo shoot with the most famous fashion and culture photographer of all time—for the biggest, most important fashion magazine in the world. The whole thing felt like a plot twist out of one of the movies she had loved as a kid. She called her agent from the road to tell her what was happening.

"None of us could believe it," Jen told me. "This doesn't happen. It *does not* happen."

She drove so fast that when she arrived, the other hairstylist—the one she was replacing—was still standing outside Gwen's trailer, waiting for his Uber. The world of celebrity hairstyling is small, so of course they knew each other. "That was the most awkward moment of all time," she jokes now.

But Jen went right to work. Inside the trailer, she looked over the mood boards and understood what needed to be done. Gwen wanted a relaxed, casual look for the shoot. Jen was curious what had happened before she arrived—and how she ended up with this opportunity—but she focused instead on the task at hand. "I didn't ask the details," Jen told me. "I just got in there and did what I do."

From there, the day went well. Jen went to the set with Gwen and even managed to grab a selfie with Annie Leibovitz. The cover photo, on the January 2013 issue of *Vogue*, became an iconic moment in Gwen Stefani's career. (The cover tease read: "1 husband, 2 kids, 3 labels, 6-pack abs, and plenty of cool.")

"That moment was life-changing for me," Jen told me. "It put me in a whole other realm."

IN 2014, Jen Atkin expanded her social media presence into a website called Mane Addicts. She hired writers and editors to produce articles on trends, products, and artists in the world of hair care. She lost money on the endeavor for years, but she used her new outlet as a way to pick the minds of some of the most interesting and important people in her industry, some of whom have become mentors. Mane Addicts also brought together the hairstylist community in a new way. "I was planting a seed," she told me, "and I thought, one day it will be something."

Two years later, Jen launched a line of hair care products, Ouai—pronounced "Way." In her decade-plus as a hairstylist, she had seen just about every product line available and she thought the industry could do better. "Everything smelled like an old lady or a little girl," she told an interviewer after the launch.

In a social media launch campaign, Jen and some of her influencer friends told tens of millions of people that Ouai products could save women time and help the health of their hair. Five years after the launch, Proctor & Gamble announced that it was acquiring Ouai and that Jen would remain with the company. The details of the deal were not made public—Jen has always been good about keeping secrets—but *Women's Wear Daily* reported at the time that Ouai was projected to do more than $50 million in net sales for 2021, and more than $80 million for 2022.

In 2023, Jen launched another company, Mane, selling hair care tools and accessories. Her brands are staples at 2,700 Sephora stores around the world.

As her businesses grew, she had less time to work on the incredible roster of clients she had developed. But Jen had cultivated a great stable of assistants through the years. In 2024, she cofounded yet another company, called Highlight Artists, which is an incubator and talent management agency for hairstylists, including many of her former assistants.

Jen never forgot that there were no celebrity hairstylist books when she moved to L.A., so she wrote the book she would have wanted to read back then.

I love Jen's story for a few reasons. I do not know much about the world of the Kardashians or Hollywood hairstylists. But reading her book, *Blowing My Way to the Top*—easily the cheekiest title of any of the dozens of biographies and memoirs I read in my research—I found myself nodding in agreement on nearly every page. Her path reminded me of so many successful people in other fields, from the way she identified her passion to the way she honed her craft and kept learning, to the way she expanded her network and her sense of what was possible. She also moved to her industry's epicenter—even when that was not an easy personal choice, given her upbringing and modest means. And she has been intensely focused on collaboration over competition, that precious and rare mindset that often sets apart the successful people who truly love their jobs.

It is also apparent how dedicated she is to giving back and paying it forward. As of this writing, Jen has 5.2 million Instagram followers, and yet she collaborates with entrepreneurial-minded influencers with much smaller audiences. She does not need to do that, and it probably does not do much for her bottom line, but, she told me, she wants to be the role model that she never had, in the worlds of both beauty and business.

She literally gives back to the places where she learned. In 2018, Jen returned to the occupational center where she had first learned about styling—and brought every student a Dyson hair dryer, valued at $450 each. She also gave the students some of her own products and took the time to share her story with them. The next week, the students won a competition using Jen's products.

Alma Blanco had been an instructor at the school when Jen was a student and was still there when she came back. In a photo from that day, Alma bears an enormous, proud smile. "What stood out the most is her telling all my students not to give up, that it's not easy but if you want it you can achieve it," Alma told me. "She is living proof of it."

When we talked, Jen had just moved from L.A. to Seattle, where life is a little quieter, a little calmer. I asked her what she was planning to do next.

"I have three dogs, two kids, and three brands," she said. "But as long as I have a platform and an audience and I can create, that's what I want to do."

PRINCIPLE V

GO WHERE THE ACTION IS

If you want to start a tech company, go to Silicon Valley. If you want to be in movies, go to L.A. Geography still matters.

—Brian Chesky, cofounder and CEO of Airbnb

By the time Tony Fadell graduated from the University of Michigan, he already had more entrepreneurial experience in his field than virtually all of his peers. As a teenager in the mid-1980s, he created a semiconductor company that sold parts to Apple. He had another company that sold mail-order software for the Apple II, and he also started a third company, with one of his professors, that sold educational software for Mac computers. He skipped his first week of college classes to man a booth at the Applefest in San Francisco.

Tony had spent years reading everything he could about the computer industry, mostly in *Byte Magazine* and *MacWorld*. In story after story, he read about companies based in the Valley. Studying the ads in the magazines, he noted that most of the company addresses were also in Northern California.

He flew out to Silicon Valley a few times a year for meetings, all on his own dime, and he absolutely loved it. On one trip, he rented a car and drove to the original Fry's Electronics in Sunnyvale—"a superstore, like Costco, for everything under the sun in the world of electronics." For a kid who grew up obsessed with computers and building technology—in elementary school he rigged his clock radio to put a headphone jack in it so he could listen to music all night without his parents knowing—this journey felt more like a pilgrimage.

"I was like 'Ho-ly shit!'" he told me. Decades later, you can still hear that original awe in his voice.

Tony knew that when he graduated, he needed to move to Silicon Valley, the epicenter of the industry he loved. At first he thought he wanted an internship at Apple, which was run by John Sculley at the time. The company flew Tony to Cupertino and put him up in a nice hotel with a fruit basket waiting in the room. But when they offered him the internship, Tony declined.

To his surprise, they offered him a full-time job, working at a joint venture Apple was doing with IBM. But again, stunningly, Tony turned them down. He had his eye on a different job. "I said, 'No, I don't want anything to do with that,'" he told me. "I wanted General Magic."

At the time, Tony didn't even know what General Magic was doing, but a few years earlier he read about Silicon Valley computer engineer legends Bill Atkinson and Andy Hertzfeld in a *Rolling Stone* story profiling the Mac team. As Tony was flying to the West Coast, doing these interviews, he read in the back of one of his tech magazines that some of these big names had begun a secretive spinoff from Apple. "I'm like, 'Whatever it is,'" Tony told me, "'that's where I want to be.'"

Despite his remarkable résumé and network of contacts, Tony was told that there weren't any openings at General Magic—but that just made him want it more. So on one of his trips to California, Tony decided to go to the General Magic building, in downtown Mountain View, and present himself unannounced. He found the address in the Yellow Pages and drove over at 8:30 A.M. He wore a jacket and tie and a big, naive midwestern smile. But when he got to the building, it was mostly empty. Security dogs roamed the halls, ready to attack any intruder. When he found the right floor, he walked up with his résumé in his hand. The office door was open. Inside, he found—nothing. "It was just cube wall after cube wall, a desolate cube area," he says.

As he walked through the rows of cubes, he thought he was completely alone. But then he spotted two men in a cube and they looked like they'd been up all night. Undaunted, Tony made sure that this was indeed the General Magic office—they said it was—and offered up his résumé. Without even looking at it, the two men told him the company wasn't hiring. So Tony left and went back home to Michigan.

At this point, leaving the Valley gave him something akin to withdrawal symptoms. Michigan seemed bleak. "I went back to Ann Arbor and it was literally a frozen tundra," he told me. "I kept asking myself what I was doing there."

It is different now, but at the time Michigan did not have a community of technology enthusiasts like those in the Valley. There were no start-ups. It felt like people there barely spoke the same language. So he was even more convinced that he needed to be in California—and more specifically, he needed to be at General Magic.

First, he racked his brain to think of anyone he knew at Apple, anyone who might be able to open a door there for him. He made some calls, pleading his case, and it took a few months, but eventually he got a call back from a woman at General Magic named Dee Gardetti. Tony didn't know it at the time, but Dee was the fourth employee at the company and she was the head of HR. She told him she was impressed with his résumé and she would see what she could do. She told him to be patient.

But Tony is not a particularly patient person. He started mailing letters to the company. He estimates that he sent between fifteen and twenty old-school letters, pleading for a job. As time went by, he graduated from Michigan and moved back in with his parents. He sold his educational software company. He turned down numerous other jobs—much to the chagrin of his parents. He was relentless, but he was also charming. When he called Dee, he was able to make her laugh and win her support. Then, in November 1991, nearly seven months after that original unannounced visit, Tony was invited back for an interview.

He flew back out to the Valley, put on his jacket and tie, and showed up to General Magic's new office in Mountain View. "There were no dogs this time," he jokes.

But now, after all this time and this relentless pursuit, Tony began to feel something all of us have felt at one point or another: imposter syndrome. "I'm like, 'What am I doing here?' I'm totally melting. I'm seeing these people that I've idolized, my heroes, they're interviewing me. I'm just a little kid."

He was told to take off his tie and his jacket. He was told to sit on the floor like everyone else, around an arcade machine in the middle of the office. As he got more comfortable, Tony showed the General Magic team his senior project: a portable touchscreen computer—something most people had never heard of in 1991.

Well, it turned out that General Magic, this top-secret company of superstars, had been working on a portable device with a touchscreen, the earliest iterations of what would become the smartphone. Some of their partners and investors included Sony, Motorola, and AT&T.

Tony thought the interviews went well, but he left without a job offer. He went back to Michigan, where the chill of autumn was morphing into the bitter cold of winter. More than two weeks later, he finally got the call from Dee.

"I want to let you know you're going to be a diagnostic engineer on the hardware team at General Magic," she told him. "And you can start right away."

Tony still remembers running around and screaming when he got the call. His salary was $28,000, below the cost of living in the Valley at the time, but he didn't care. He packed up his car, said goodbye to his parents, left his mother crying in the driveway, and headed to California.

Tony is a good friend of mine, and we'll discuss some of his incredible accomplishments later, but I want to highlight this part of his story for a reason. He made the audacious decision to move, not just to the geographic center of the industry he wanted to work in, but to the one company where so many of his idols had come together.

It's a hard decision and often a hard pursuit, but if you have the chance, put yourself in the center of the action.

GO WHERE THE ACTION IS

As your dream job journey evolves, you may eventually confront a decision with enormous consequences: *Should I physically relocate in order to maximize my chance of overall success?*

Of course, many of us move away for the first time to attend college. And that is not the end of the world. We meet new people, we meet new friends, we are exposed to new cultures and experiences. We learn and grow. Making that decision a second time can and will have a profound impact on your chances of dream job success. It may seem incredibly intimidating, but it may also be the best decision you make in your entire life.

Your journey may not be as dramatic as Bob Dylan hitchhiking from Minnesota to Greenwich Village. I relocated twice in my career—first to New York and then to Silicon Valley—partly because I saw how my dad benefited from moving from Virginia to Houston to work at NASA.

The truth is, different industries are bigger and more prominent in different places—for all sorts of reasons. The tech industry and a disproportionate number of start-ups are in the San Francisco Bay Area. For finance and banking, it's New York City. New York is also the conter of the book publishing world and America's theater scene. But for television and film, the epicenter is Los Angeles. Government and policy? Washington, D.C. Biotech and pharma? That's Boston. Oil and energy? Houston. The automotive industry is still largely based in Detroit. If you want to make it as a singer-songwriter, you'll probably have to spend some time in Nashville, regardless of your genre.

A few industries have multiple hubs, which means you'll have more choices. The fashion industry, for example, is big in Milan, Paris, New York, and L.A. If you want to make it in esports, you can probably pick between Tokyo, Seoul, or Los Angeles—though you'll have a ton of other factors to consider as you decide.

Being in these places puts you in the flow of the industry. You are surrounded by people who speak the language. You are closer to decision-makers, mentors, collaborators. You are able to learn faster, move faster, be seen more quickly. And sometimes, most importantly, you are simply reminded that this is real—that there are people who are doing the thing you want to do, every single day.

Regardless of the geography, there are at least ten ways relocating can help your career.

1. **More jobs**—There are just more opportunities where the industry is dense.

2. **More networking**—You're greatly increasing the chances you'll bump into people in your field.

3. **More mentors and more peers**—The best in the business are often just a coffee shop away.

4. **More events**—Meetups, panels, workshops—they're happening much more often in the industry's epicenter.

5. **Exposure to trends**—You're first to see what's next.

6. **Résumé credibility**—"She's based in L.A." or "He worked in New York" carries weight.

7. **Faster advancement**—Your chances of moving up go up when you're where things are happening.

8. **Higher pay**—It's more competitive and often more expensive, but these places also come with higher compensation.

9. **Serendipity**—The breakthrough meeting, the unexpected connection—it's more likely to happen when you're immersed. You create your own luck.

10. **Fun and energy**—You're surrounded by people who care about the same things. That matters. If you truly love your chosen field, that will excite you.

I saw this in Silicon Valley. I watched people have lunch with billionaires, go to talks by start-up founders who had just IPO'd, meet cofounders over coffee. People in the Valley take time to respond to authentic requests for learning and advice. I felt it on the way up, and I have tried to reciprocate and continue the tradition. It is a vibe you don't necessarily see in other places. I have heard plenty of similar stories about musicians in Nashville. They move there with no guarantees. But they know one thing: *The best people are here. I want to be around that.*

That's the idea. You want to roll around in it. If the idea of being immersed in your industry doesn't appeal to you, you might need to go back to the first principle and reconsider whether this is truly your passion. You should want to be so steeped in your craft that large parts of it become second nature.

Immersion isn't passive—it's transformative. When you're fully submerged in the culture of your field's epicenter, learning accelerates. Opportunities multiply. Your network organically expands. Immersion creates a powerful osmosis effect, exponentially accelerating your growth and visibility.

All of this can seem intimidating, I know. Maybe it sounds *too* competitive. Being nervous about a step like this is totally understandable. My advice: Try your best to remove those thoughts from your mind.

VIRTUAL AND EMERGING EPICENTERS

So what if you just really can't relocate? We live in an era where physical relocation is not the only option. Virtual epicenters can also propel your career. You can engage deeply with Reddit groups and Twitter/X communities. You can consume or even participate in Twitch streams, podcasts, LinkedIn groups, virtual courses on almost any subject.

You can establish yourself with an online presence through content curation, expert interviews, and consistent digital engagement. If you have something interesting and thoughtful to say about a subject on a regular basis, you will build an audience eventually.

To be clear: These are all things you should be considering whether you have already relocated or not. This is part of the learning process, part of building a peer network, and part of seeking out mentors. Physical proximity will likely give you an extra advantage, but in today's world you should be utilizing every tool available.

There are also industry epicenters that seem to bubble up, sometimes in surprising locales. In the 1970s, northern Florida became a hub of Southern Rock, producing a stunning lineup of bands that included Lynyrd Skynyrd, the Allman Brothers Band, and 38 Special—all from Jacksonville. Tom Petty and the Heartbreakers formed around the same time down the road in Gainesville.

A few years ago, comedian Ron White encouraged Joe Rogan to relocate to Austin. For more than two decades, Rogan lived in Los Angeles, one of the two or three big hubs for top-tier stand-up comedy, along with New York and Boston. Rogan was a staple at The Comedy Store on Sunset Strip. For years, he went several nights a week. He honed his act with two or three short sets in a night and spent the rest of his time hanging out with his fellow comedians in the venue's legendary green room.

In March 2023, Rogan opened his own club, Comedy Mothership, on Sixth Street in downtown Austin. He named the bar Mitzi's, after Mitzi Shore, the woman who owned The Comedy Store until her death in 2018. Rogan brought Adam Eget, one of The Comedy Store's bookers, to Austin to help launch the business. Around the same time, other prominent national comedians relocated from both Los Angeles and New York. Within a few years, the Austin comedy scene included Tom Segura and his wife Christina P, Tony Hinchcliffe, and Shane Gillis. They are all regulars at the Mothership, and now nearly every big comic has to stop in Austin a few times a year.

But something else happened, too. Other smaller comedy clubs started popping up all over town. There were more open mics and more paying gigs. As Tony Hinchcliffe's podcast, *Kill Tony*, got more popular, more and more aspiring comics migrated to Austin instead of New York or L.A. Austin has officially become a comedy hub. Though they tour a lot, comedians still need a quality base to sculpt and workshop their material.

Of course, some professions are itinerant by nature. Some industries don't have traditional hubs. Think about sports. If you want to be a college or professional coach, you will probably need to relocate several times. That is true whether you are an assistant or a head coach. It is certainly true for athletic directors. Chances are your next job will not be in the same place as your last one. This is true of journalists, too. As you come up in the industry, you will likely have to move a few times.

But even these itinerant occupations have industry events, reasons to come together in the same place. There are annual conferences, key networking events that function as temporary epicenters. In these industries, it's even more important to seek out and connect with mentors and experts and to stay in touch with peers.

RELOCATING IS HARD

I know this is not easy. Moving is expensive and stressful. Most of us are not nomadic by nature. We crave stability. Relocating is one of the single most disruptive things you can do in life. Maybe your parents live nearby, and you are the one they lean on. Maybe your kids love their school and your weekends are filled with soccer games and birthday parties. Maybe you have built a close-knit community over years, or decades, and the idea of leaving that feels like tearing something sacred.

Moving also means facing more intense competition. You might know more about a subject than anyone else in your graduating class, but once you move to an industry hub, you are suddenly the lowest person on the totem pole. But careers are not zero-sum games. Competition is a tide that raises all boats. Sure, for a while everyone you encounter will know more than you, but that just means you will have the opportunity to learn infinitely faster than you would if you stayed at home.

You might also need a "support job" while you grind. Plenty of struggling actors found other gigs to pay the rent—sometimes for years—before landing a breakthrough role. Some of the best musicians in America spent substantial portions of their lives busking on sidewalks or playing for free in grimy bars. That perseverance can pay off. Sometimes the first job will not be the big career winner. It may just be a critical stepping-stone.

That is what happened with Tony Fadell.

After he finally got that job at General Magic, he worked there for three and a half years. But the company was not a success story. General Magic's failure has become one of the most important legends in the history of Silicon Valley. (It's also the subject of a great documentary that I would *highly* encourage everyone to watch.) However, joining General Magic put Tony squarely in the epicenter of the Valley. And the connections he made there were part of an amazing foundation that would help launch him to greater and greater heights.

After leaving General Magic, Tony continued his pursuit and passion for designing breakthrough portable computing devices. His next stop was building the Philips Mobile Computing group, where he assumed the role of CTO at the age of twenty-five. After four years there and a brief dance with Real Networks, he started his own company in 1999 called Fuse, which aimed to be the "Dell of Consumer Electronics." That timing was not ideal, as the dot-com crash made it difficult for Fuse to raise its second round of financing. Tony kept grinding.

After ten years, Apple hired Tony through an eight-week consulting contract to develop a new MP3 music player. Tony's nine years in Silicon Valley, and the learning he had done through nearly a decade of working on mobile computing products, were finally about to pay off. After a successful consulting gig, Apple hired Tony internally. Within a year, Apple would launch their first MP3 player, the iPod, which would eventually sell over 450 million units. After that, Tony assumed the role of head of engineering for the iPhone. We all know how that turned out. Apple has sold 2.3 billion iPhones, making it the most successful mobile computing device of all time.

Tony wasn't done. He later left Apple to build yet another mass consumer product via Nest Labs. Nest launched a breakthrough product—the Nest Learning Thermostat—which would revolutionize the home automation industry. If you don't have one, you've probably stayed in an Airbnb with a Nest thermostat.

Google eventually acquired Nest for $3.2 billion. Since leaving Google, Tony has become a prolific angel investor and has authored a bestselling book that I would recommend to everyone dedicated to finding their own unique career pathway—*Build: An Unorthodox Guide to Making Things Worth Making.*

Think of your dream as a seed. The epicenter of your industry is the fertile soil that allows that seed to flourish. Embrace the challenge—not as an end in itself, but as the necessary step toward meaningful growth. If the idea of moving ignites something within you, trust that instinct. You already have your answer. Go where the action is.

PROFILE SIX

LEARNING FROM THE LEGENDS

This is a story about a different Robert from the Midwest. Robert Montgomery grew up in the small, blue-collar town of Orrville, Ohio. His father worked for the railroad and his mother was a school teacher who instilled discipline, rigorous study habits, and self-reliance. Robert also spent a lot of time with his grandmother Sarah Montgomery, which taught him a lifelong respect for older people.

Robert made good grades and read voraciously, especially the Chip Hilton young adult sports novels, written by Hall of Fame basketball coach Clair Bee, which were popular in the 1940s and '50s. (Every book followed Chip, an incredible athlete, his buddies, and their smart, tough, reliable coach through a new athletic adventure.) At night, young Robert tuned in to crackling radio broadcasts of Cleveland Indians baseball games and Kentucky Wildcats basketball games. "My lifelong status as a hero worshipper started in those days," he would later write.

He was tall—six foot five when he was done growing—and became a multisport athlete at Orrville High: basketball, football, and baseball.

But basketball was his favorite. Everywhere he went, he had a basketball in his hand. He was a good student, president of the Honor Society, but he had a reputation for making wisecracks in class and occasionally losing his temper. In his junior year he wrote a personal essay he titled "It's Been a Great Life (So Far)" in which he declared his ambitions in life. He knew he was not destined for greatness as a player, so he said he wanted to go to college, join the ROTC, and eventually coach basketball.

College recruiting was different back then. Robert's neighbor, a dentist who earned his degree from Ohio State, called the school to tell them about the young Orrville star. When Ohio State showed interest, the neighbor sent film of Robert playing and arranged for Fred Taylor, the new, thirty-three-year-old head coach of the Ohio State basketball team, to visit Robert at home. (Robert would later say that Coach Taylor was *most* interested in his grandmother's strawberry shortcake.)

Coach Taylor stressed basketball fundamentals, smart team play, and tenacious defense. Taylor also befriended and studied strategies with other coaches, including Pete Newell, who won a national championship with University of California in 1959. Robert wasn't a starter at Ohio State. He came off the bench, and he didn't play a ton of minutes, but this team also had future basketball Hall of Famers John Havlicek and Jerry Lucas. While he was on the bench, though, Robert studied his coach. He took notes on team tactics, player dynamics, and coaching philosophies.

In Robert's sophomore year they won the national championship—defeating Newell's Cal team in the final game. As Robert was out on the court in the final minutes of that game, it occurred to him that one of the reasons his team won was the knowledge Coach Newell passed on to Coach Taylor—and that this fact did not seem to bother the losing coach at all. "That gave Pete Newell a special stature for me," Robert would say later.

Ohio State returned to the national championship game in Robert's junior and senior years, but they lost both times. The losses were painful, but Robert was also gaining invaluable close-up experience in big games.

As some of his Ohio State teammates made their way into the NBA, Robert went into coaching, as he had always hoped. He spent his first year as a JV coach at a high school. Then, in 1963, he enlisted in the Army and finagled his way into an assistant coaching job for the U.S. Military Academy Black Knights in West Point, New York.

The Army's focus on discipline, toughness, and tradition suited Robert. He studied the art and craft of coaching the way he had seen Coach Taylor study back in Ohio. Robert sought out veteran coaches and asked them questions: about their on-court strategies, their recruiting, their motivation techniques.

One trip back to the Midwest was particularly memorable. Robert was in Chicago scouting St. John's, which was on a road trip, when he ended up befriending Joe Lapchick, the St. John's head coach. Lapchick understood why Robert was there—trying to learn enough to have an edge for future competitions—but the older coach still suggested Robert extend his trip, then gave him a train ticket to Chicago, allowed him to stay at the team's hotel, and invited him to a steak dinner at the Diamond Grill. At the St. John's game in Chicago, Robert met Ray Meyer, the Hall of Fame coach at DePaul, who offered to drive Robert to the airport for his flight back to New York. Robert never forgot the graciousness these coaches showed him.

Robert traveled extensively to coaching clinics during off-seasons, seeking out mentors and connecting with established coaches across the country. His notebook from this period was filled with notes from clinics run by legendary coaches like UCLA's John Wooden, whom Robert greatly admired.

When Robert was twenty-four, the head coach at Army retired. Robert begged for the job and the school gave him a chance, making him the youngest Division I college basketball coach in the country at the time.

It would not take long for Robert to prove he was up to the challenge.

AS THE ARMY head coach, Robert drew inspiration from military figures like General George Patton and Colonel Earl "Red" Blaik, the revered Army football coach who won three national championships in the 1940s. Robert read Blaik's book, *You Have to Pay the Price,* for guidance. He adopted the strict discipline of the Academy and blended it with his own ideas, crafting his own hard-nosed, intense coaching style. He demanded excellence and toughness. He took personal pride in developing not just basketball skills but also leadership qualities in his players.

On the court, Robert quickly turned Army into a competitive program. One of his team captains during that era was a point guard named Mike Krzyzewski—better known today as Duke's legendary "Coach K." Robert's mentoring relationship with his point guard would help set Krzyzewski on the path to his own Hall of Fame coaching career. Robert often said that coaching Mike Krzyzewski at Army was like having an additional coach on the floor, and indeed he later hired Krzyzewski as an assistant, kick-starting the career of the winningest coach in Division I history.

What ended up making Robert such a successful coach so early on is not what happened inside the four walls of the West Point gym. It is what he did outside. In the first few years of his coaching career, he sought out living legends in the field, becoming close friends with some of the top basketball minds on the East Coast.

Robert's former Ohio State teammate John Havlicek was now on the Boston Celtics, coached by Red Auerbach. Through this connection, Robert was able to build a mentor relationship with Auerbach, who would lead the Celtics to an unprecedented eight straight NBA championships between 1959 and 1966. The two men would spend hours talking about how basketball teams best fit together and how to instill a sense of pride. Robert was struck by the idea that Auerbach's teams did things "the right way." When Auerbach eventually retired from the Celtics, his first suggestion for his replacement was his old friend Robert.

Robert stayed in touch with Joe Lapchick at St. John's, too. As a rookie head coach looking for guidance, Robert visited Lapchick at his home in Yonkers, New York. The veteran coach surprised Robert by recommending *no rigid team rules*. This might not seem intuitive, especially for someone so focused on discipline and fundamentals. But Lapchick advised him to handle discipline on a case-by-case basis, a policy Robert immediately adopted and maintained the rest of his career.

The young coach also sought out Clair Bee, the Long Island University coach who wrote the Chip Hilton books Robert had loved as a kid. Bee also has the best record of any coach in the Basketball Hall of Fame. Robert met Bee when he was twenty-five. When he was twenty-seven, Robert drove Bee to his induction into the Basketball Hall of Fame—and Robert sat next to him at the ceremony.

Around that same time, Robert noticed that Henry Iba was speaking at a banquet in Ohio. Iba coached thirty-six years at Oklahoma State and was, at the time, one of the most successful basketball coaches ever. Robert, who had already read everything Iba had written about coaching and life, decided to go back to Ohio and attend the banquet so he could hear the coaching legend speak. After the dinner, Robert met Iba and they stayed in touch. A few years later, when Iba coached the 1972 U.S. Olympic team, he invited Robert to be an assistant.

The young Army coach also went to California to meet Pete Newell, the former Cal coach he had seen selflessly mentor Coach Taylor at Ohio State. Pete was the greatest basketball mind on the West Coast at the time. They became fast friends and would remain close for nearly half a century.

Robert didn't limit his peer network to basketball coaches. Bill Parcells, who would become a Hall of Fame NFL coach, served as a part-time assistant on Robert's Army basketball staff in 1966–67, forging a lifelong friendship between the two men. Parcells, then a young football coach at West Point, was curious about Robert's approach, and their exchanges proved mutually beneficial. They bonded over strategy sessions that ranged from X's and O's to motivational tactics. Robert was also friends with Bo Schembechler, who coached the Michigan football team for twenty-one years. Robert would later tell stories about Schembechler calling his locker room, saying something like "It's a hell of a thing when my best friend in this league is a God-damned basketball coach," and then immediately hanging up.

Under Robert, the Army Cadets compiled a 102-50 record across six seasons, with four postseason NIT (National Invitation Tournament) appearances. During Robert's tenure, the Black Knights had only one losing season, his final year, after which he decided it was time to move on.

By 1971, Robert had proven himself as an up-and-coming coach known for discipline, defensive tenacity, and an innovative mind. His success at West Point—combined with his fiery personality—made him an attractive candidate for major-conference programs. In the spring of 1971, Indiana University came calling with an offer to take over the Hoosiers, and at the age of thirty-one, Robert Montgomery Knight—known now simply as Bobby Knight—accepted the job.

He was eager to test himself on a bigger stage.

IN INDIANA, BASKETBALL is not just a sport. It is a deeply ingrained part of the state's culture, history, and identity. Often referred to as "Hoosier Hysteria," basketball is part of Indiana's social fabric. James Naismith, who invented the game in Massachusetts, once said that "basketball really had its origin in Indiana." But when Knight arrived at Indiana University in 1971, the once-proud Hoosiers program was floundering. Indiana needed discipline and a reboot after some tumultuous years, and Knight—with his Army background—was seen as a strict disciplinarian who could instill order. Detractors, however, wondered if his methodical, defense-first style would work in the Big Ten against top-tier competition.

Knight quickly answered those doubts. He immediately applied his rigorous practice standards: He "toughened practices," demanding total attention from his players—which meant banning spectators from practice to eliminate distractions. He emphasized conditioning and defense, requiring boot camp–like running and benching players if they ate too much junk food.

Knight never stopped learning about the game or about coaching. He would later tell a story about a time in the spring of 1972 when he went to Pete Newell's house and sat on the floor with a stack of three-by-five cards he used to diagram plays. He was designing options for a new style of offense, and with Newell by his side, he filled out seventy-four cards. Now, asking a mentor to do something like that with you is audacious—or maybe it is brilliant?—but Knight did it. And Pete agreed.

The impact on the court was dramatic. In Knight's first season (1971–72), Indiana improved, and by his second season (1972–73) the Hoosiers went 22-6 and earned a trip to the NCAA Final Four. That 1973 Final Four appearance signaled to the world that Indiana was back in the elite of the sport. It also validated the lessons he had synthesized from his mentors: Knight's Indiana squad played ferocious man-to-man defense in the tradition of Henry Iba, executed a patient motion offense reminiscent of Pete Newell's teachings, and displayed the mental toughness of a Joe Lapchick team. By the mid-1970s, Knight was widely regarded as one of basketball's brightest minds—intensely competitive, yes, but also a student of the game who was *constantly* refining strategies.

The seasons leading up to 1975–76 brought Indiana closer and closer to greatness. In 1974–75, Knight coached a Hoosiers squad that some people still call the best college basketball team in history. That team went undefeated in the regular season (31-0) before a heartbreaking loss in the Elite Eight of the NCAA tournament after star forward Scott May broke his arm late in the year. Knight channeled that pain into a steely resolve: His team would come back even stronger and this time finish the job. On the first day of the 1976 season, Knight told his team: "Your goal is not winning the Big Ten championship, not winning the national championship, but going through the entire season from first game to NCAA championship game *undefeated*."

He made it clear that an undefeated season was a *reasonable objective*—not an impossible dream.

All of the learning, mentorship, and hard work Bobby Knight had put in up to that point culminated in the historic 1975–76 season. During practices that year, Knight pushed the players to their limits. He ran grueling drills like charge-taking exercises and full-speed scrimmages that left his squad bruised and battered, ensuring that games felt easy by comparison. Knight even occasionally benched his stars, sending the message that no one was above the team.

The Hoosiers had cruised through the regular season the previous year, winning games by an average of nearly 20 points. This year, though, they had several close calls. In a December game against Kentucky, Indiana tied the game with a last-second tip-in from Kent Benson and won the game in overtime. A few weeks later, Michigan had an 8-point lead with only nine minutes to go—forcing Indiana to rally late.

At one point in the game, a guard named Jim Wisman made a few mistakes and Coach Knight grabbed his jersey near the bench. Two photos of the incident—both featuring this young, fresh-faced player looking terrified as his furious coach held a handful of jersey—appeared on the front page of the *Indianapolis Star* the next day, raising new questions about Knight's temper.

Knight did not let any of that distract his team from their mission. The Hoosiers finished the regular season with a 29-point thrashing of Knight's alma mater, Ohio State. This was Indiana's thirty-seventh consecutive Big Ten win and second straight title. The Hoosiers entered the NCAA tournament unbeaten and ranked number one, looking for redemption after the heartbreaking loss the previous year. They beat St. John's and Alabama in the early rounds. In the regional final, Indiana beat second-ranked Marquette to reach the Final Four. Facing UCLA in the semifinal—a clash between storied programs—Indiana's relentless man-to-man defense suffocated the Bruins, earning a convincing 65-51 win.

Then, on March 29, 1976, under the bright lights in Philadelphia, the Hoosiers met Michigan for the national title. After a tense early struggle, Indiana's disciplined motion offense and relentless defense wore Michigan down. Scott May led with 26 points, cementing his legacy as Knight calmly orchestrated from the sideline. As the final buzzer echoed, the scoreboard read Indiana 86, Michigan 68. The Indiana Hoosiers were National Champions, and more importantly, they were perfect, 32-0.

It's been fifty years, and no team has repeated what that Indiana team accomplished. Most years, nobody even comes close.

BOBBY KNIGHT WOULD go on to win three national titles. He won eleven Big 10 titles, and when he retired, he had 902 victories, the most of any coach at the time. He was named NCAA coach of the year four times. Pete Newell inducted Bobby into the Hall of Fame.

He also sparked plenty of controversy throughout his career, and, for some, Knight's infamous temper remains his most memorable trait. I would suggest, however, that the most important aspect of Bobby Knight's legacy is something else. His vast coaching tree continues to reshape the sport decades after he retired. More than two dozen former players and assistant coaches under Knight have gone on to coach basketball. The truth is, Knight never forgot that lesson from Newell, when he sat down with Fred Taylor and ultimately gave him the knowledge that helped Taylor win when the two faced off. Knight never forgot the impact that all of his mentors had, the generosity they displayed when a young coach wanted to learn the craft. Knight actively passed those things on, giving back to the game every time he had the chance.

The most illustrious branch of Knight's coaching tree might be Mike Krzyzewski. After Coach K played under Knight at Army and served as his assistant at Indiana, he embarked on a legendary coaching career at Duke University, amassing over 1,200 wins and five national championships. He also led the U.S. men's national team to multiple Olympic gold medals. He asked Bobby Knight to induct him into the Basketball Hall of Fame.

Steve Alford was a star player under Knight in the '80s and went on to coach in college for more than thirty years, most recently at Nevada. Chris Beard worked under Knight at Texas Tech, where Knight finished his career. Beard later became the head coach at Tech and took the team to the 2019 NCAA Championship game. Other branches of the coaching tree include Mike Woodson, Keith Smart, Isiah Thomas, and Lawrence Frank.

In the 1970s, a college student named Tara VanDerveer transferred to Indiana to be near Knight. She enrolled in Knight's basketball strategy class—a course on X's and O's and coaching philosophy. Knight invited anyone in the class to come observe his Hoosiers' practices, and VanDerveer eagerly took him up on the offer. "I went every day. I think I was usually the only one there," she would recall of those years. She sat high in the stands—she wanted to avoid Knight's eyeline if he got mad and needed to lash out—and became a fixture at IU practices for three seasons, diligently taking notes on everything she saw.

If you know the name Tara VanDerveer now, it's because she was the longtime coach of the Stanford women's team, one of the winningest programs of all time. In December 2020, VanDerveer won her 1,099th game as a head coach, passing the late Pat Summitt for most wins in women's college basketball history. On January 21, 2024, she won her 1,203rd game as a head coach, passing Krzyzewski as the winningest head coach in college basketball history.

Sadly, Bobby Knight didn't live to see this moment, when one of his protégés passed another one of his protégés at the very top of the all-time wins list. Knight died in November 2023 at the age of eighty-three. He's buried in Orrville. He'll be remembered forever, not just as one of the great coaches of all time, who had a ceaseless passion for the game and desire to learn, but as someone who gave himself over to the field he loved.

PRINCIPLE VI

ALWAYS GIVE BACK

The meaning of life is to find your gift.
The purpose of life is to give it away.

—Pablo Picasso

When Shaquille O'Neal was named to the NBA Seventy-Fifth Anniversary Team—a list of the league's seventy-five greatest players of all time—he could have reacted in any number of ways. He could have told the world that he was the best center in NBA history. He could have used the moment to promote any of the dozens of businesses with which he's associated. He could have spoken about the adversity he overcame in his career, or the people who had *not* believed in him along the way, as Michael Jordan did when he was inducted into the Hall of Fame.

But that is not what Shaq did. Instead, in a four-minute speech, made without notes, to the millions of basketball fans tuning into TNT's NBA pregame show, the three-time Finals MVP worked back through his career, thanking as many people as he could. "Magic [Johnson] and Kareem [Abdul-Jabar] and Dr. J [Julius Erving]," he began, showing his reverence to some of the greats who played before him. Then he turned to his own stepfather, Sergeant Philip Arthur Harrison.

"He's the guy that told me one day that I would be here," Shaq explained. "I was a medium level–high level juvenile delinquent. I was always told I would never, ever, ever make it. He convinced me to do well in school." He said his no-nonsense stepfather had taken him to Madison Square Garden once, to watch Dr. J—and that was when Shaq told his stepdad that he wanted to be a pro basketball player when he grew up. His father gave him a list of players Shaq needed to study. "His exact words: 'If you listen to me, I'll make you one of the most dominant big men ever.' And he named Bill Russell. He named Kareem and he named Wilt Chamberlain. I never knew those names."

He thanked his mother, Lucille O'Neal, friends, and family members. He thanked coaches, and fellow players who inspired him, including David Robinson, the Hall of Fame San Antonio Spurs center, and Patrick Ewing, the former Knicks big man. He thanked Lakers guard-turned-team executive Jerry West for settling him down when Shaq first moved to Los Angeles. "All those guys made me persevere," he said. "They helped me get to this point."

He even credited his friendly on-air antagonist Charles Barkley, seated just a few feet away at the time. "Charles taught me how to be ferocious and not give a damn," he said. "Throw them bows, knock some teeth out. When I seen Charles do that, I said, 'Okay, it's okay to be like this.'"

Then Shaq, a traditionally stoic giant, displayed a rare flash of emotion. He held his massive left hand to his chest and spoke with true humility. "It was a very emotional moment for me because all the guys that are greater than me, I can't believe that I'm sitting next to," he said. "When I look at myself play, I was not as good as Hakeem [Olajuwon]. . . . I was not even as good as Bob McAdoo."

Then he reiterated again that he did not do it by himself. "I did it with all these guys, all my teammates." He lamented knowing that he had not thanked everyone and quickly rattled off another half-dozen friends and family members.

After the speech, TNT host Ernie Johnson turned to the big man. "Shaq," he said. "That's one of the greatest things I've ever heard."

Then, of course, Shaq thanked Ernie for saying that.

GIVING BACK AND THE INFINITE GAME

Everyone knows it is good to give back, to pay it forward. The concept is ingrained in us from childhood, reinforced in countless stories, speeches, and lessons from our parents and mentors. It is especially worth thinking about in the context of a career. Stephen Covey advises in *The Seven Habits of Highly Effective People* to "begin with the end in mind." Specifically, he wants you to visualize your own funeral. Imagine what you are wearing or the photo of you that your loved ones have chosen. Imagine who all is there and what they might be saying about you. What accomplishments will they mention? How will they say you treated people on your journey? The suggestion is about setting long-term personal goals and keeping in mind the legacy you leave in your wake.

Too frequently, professionals think of giving back as something reserved for retirement. They envision philanthropy or mentorship as the activities of those who have already "won." But here is my biggest piece of advice on this subject: *Don't wait until the end. Give back throughout your entire journey.*

Embrace humility at every step. I find that all the greats do it. They send letters. They send gifts. When they accomplish something in their careers, they take the time to send messages back to the people that helped them. Like Shaq, they take every chance to give credit to others.

One of my favorite books is *Finite and Infinite Games,* by James P. Carse, first published in 1986. Carse makes the case that most of life can be broken into two types of games: finite and infinite. A finite game, like a marathon race, has a clear beginning and an end. It has a clear winner. An infinite game, on the other hand, continues indefinitely, with no ultimate winner, just ongoing participation and improvement. Careers, contrary to what many believe, are infinite games. There is no single winner. Instead, many participants can—and should—succeed simultaneously.

You might have noticed that this idea has come up a few times, but I think it is worth stressing again. A finite-game mindset is a competitive, zero-sum mentality: "If I win, someone else must lose." This mindset fosters isolation, anxiety, and shortsighted decisions.

By contrast, an infinite-game mindset recognizes abundance. There will always be many, many winners in any field. These winners can coexist, thrive together, and even enhance each other's success. Remember the powerful group of athletic directors or the YouTubers who MrBeast met with every day. Someone who embraces their working community has a better chance of thriving than someone destined to succeed alone—because you can strive forward without pushing someone else back. A career is not a zero-sum game.

Realizing this—and letting go of that competitive attitude—will set you on the right path. If you have that mindset, you need to reorient yourself and start over. Think of the "sharp elbows" people you have encountered—colleagues who believe the path to success involves stepping on others. They are pervasive in athletics, business, and every competitive field. They hoard credit, minimize the contributions of others, and thrive on competition rather than cooperation. Sharp elbows might be useful in the NBA, but ultimately this attitude is self-limiting in the real world. These individuals may achieve isolated victories, but their journeys are often lonely and unfulfilling. Real career success is communal. It's collaborative, not combative.

What you want is people rooting for you. As we have discussed, people naturally root for the colleagues who root for them. Giving back in every direction—whether mentoring a junior colleague, sharing knowledge with peers, or supporting superiors—creates a foundation of goodwill and mutual support.

Some of the benefits are practical for advancing your career. Giving back, being gracious, sharing compliments when you are impressed—all of that can help grease the skids of your career, just like a peer network or good mentors. This attitude smooths interactions, removes friction, and creates opportunities. The nicer you are as a person, the more people will want to help you, and the more likely you are to be recommended or promoted. The people around you will also be more likely to listen to your ideas with an amenable ear.

This is a free value unlock. It is free value creation for your career. Kindness often costs you nothing, but that goodwill is meaningful to the recipient. Goodwill has real value. Genuine goodwill establishes lasting relationships and emotional bonds. You are creating value out of thin air.

More importantly, adopting this generous approach makes your professional journey more purposeful, more meaningful. It aligns with the timeless idea of karma—that the good you put into the world inevitably returns to you. Every act of generosity, kindness, or mentorship enriches your life and career, directly and indirectly. A life full of giving back means more celebrations and more people to celebrate you. It means more joy and more people to share it.

That will always beat celebrating your victories alone.

THE BEST WAYS TO GIVE BACK

In 2013, actor Bryan Cranston received a heartfelt letter from fellow actor Anthony Hopkins. Hopkins, an Oscar-winning icon in Hollywood, starred in *Silence of the Lambs* and was knighted by Queen Elizabeth II. Cranston, a generation younger, starred as Walter White, one of television's greatest antiheroes, in *Breaking Bad*. After bingeing the show, Hopkins was impressed with Cranston's exceptional performance as the high school chemistry teacher-turned-conniving meth cook, and he felt compelled to express his profound admiration. He sent a letter through mutual acquaintances at their agency.

"Your performance as Walter White was the best acting I have seen—ever," Hopkins wrote. "I know there is so much smoke blowing and sickening bullshit in this business, and I've sort of lost belief in anything really. But this work of yours is spectacular—absolutely stunning."

Hopkins let Cranston know he had given the entire season great thought. "From what started as a black comedy, descended into a labyrinth of blood, destruction and hell," Hopkins wrote. "It was like a great Jacobean, Shakespearian or Greek Tragedy."

The letter quickly went viral—not only affirming Cranston's talents but also highlighting Hopkins's graciousness and humility. The letter is striking to me in two ways. First, I have to believe that this letter means as much to Cranston as any physical industry award. It just lands harder—one of the greats calling you one of the greats. Second, I love that when Hopkins was truly impressed, he took the time. It shows an immense level of generosity and respect for the craft that they share.

This is what you need to do in your own career. Look for every opportunity to express thankfulness and appreciation. Anytime you achieve a new milestone—a promotion, an award, some significant recognition worth celebrating—pause and explicitly thank those who contributed to your journey. Always give credit freely and generously. It feels good, and, frankly, it makes you look good.

When super agent Lorrie Bartlett was honored for her contributions to the entertainment industry, she took the opportunity to thank more than thirty people who helped her along the way—in an eight-minute speech. Her name-per-minute rate rivaled Shaq's. Bartlett's acceptance speech at the 2024 Icon Awards overflowed with gratitude, naming colleagues, assistants, mentors, and peers who supported her. Again, this cost her nothing, but it could be priceless to the people she thanked and praised.

Practical actions matter immensely. A simple email or text expressing genuine appreciation can profoundly affect the recipient. What has even more of an impact, however, is a handwritten note. In our digital era, handwritten messages come across as more thoughtful, more meaningful. Consider small gestures or tokens of appreciation, too—a relevant book you picked out for someone or a personal memento. Maybe it is a memento from a sports team or figure you know they favor, another way to show you took the time to know and the care to remember this person's interests. Even a thoughtful meal can leave lasting impressions and make pleasant memories that last a lifetime.

I cannot stress this enough: You can do this for anyone. You do not need a strategy. Just try to be as giving and gracious as possible as a rule. The benefits will come. Sometimes a note earnestly appreciating something is a way of starting a friendship that can last for decades. Sometimes you are impressing exactly the right person at exactly the right time, and you will not know it until later. Consider how future-oriented this mindset is: Every gesture of generosity plants seeds for future goodwill. Your relationships flourish, your community strengthens, and your professional circle expands.

I want to challenge you to send a note of appreciation to someone most people would consider a competitor. Maybe they are at a rival firm. Or maybe they competed for a job you wanted. Make it genuine, earnest. Recognize something that this person has done well. This can be a very powerful exercise.

Another part of giving back is teaching: sharing your experiences, your hard-earned lessons. A lot of people instinctively fear that sharing their "secrets" somehow confers a competitive advantage. But that mindset is profoundly limiting. Just think of the incredibly successful people who have recorded episodes on the website MasterClass. From writers like Aaron Sorkin and Malcolm Gladwell to directors like Martin Scorsese to world-class athletes like Stephen Curry and Bryson DeChambeau—people who are still at the top of their fields openly share their skills through tutorials. Poker is, perhaps, the sneakiest finite game imaginable, but all-time greats Phil Ivey and Phil Hellmuth have both been willing to teach others what they love about the game.

The act of teaching enriches your own understanding deeply—there's a famous adage, "You learn the most when you teach." Sharing knowledge freely not only establishes your generosity but sharpens your mastery.

There are so many ways to teach, too, that have nothing to do with standing at the front of a classroom and assigning grades. Once you've achieved a level of success, you can and should be a mentor. You should share with your peers. But in today's landscape, there are many more ways to give back to your community: podcasts, blogs, workshops, even thoughtful social media posts. Think of Warren Buffett's annual letter: once a year, every year.

This will all be part of the legacy you leave.

I want to share a personal story about why I encourage people to give back as early and often as possible. My favorite professor when I attended the University of Texas was Jim Fredrickson. His corporate strategy class was the highlight of my MBA program—Jim pushed me to think about problems in a way I had never previously considered. Jim passed away in 2018, prematurely. But three or four times along my journey, I took the time to write him a letter, send him a note, send him a gift. I took the time to tell him what an impact he had had on me. So when he passed I didn't have all this anxiety, the worry: *Oh, I never had a chance to tell him something.* I had already thanked him multiple times.

You should do the same thing with the people in your life.

ONE WAY TO JUDGE A SUCCESSFUL CAREER

I like counting the number of people someone thanks when something good happens to them, but there is another way to judge a career that I like even more. How many other careers have you helped? Think of it as the wake of people behind your boat.

Once again consider the career of Bobby Knight, who won 902 games and three national championships throughout his career. But that might not be the most impressive measure of his legacy. His coaching tree—the assistant coaches and former players who went on to become head coaches themselves in either Division I basketball or the NBA—is astonishing.

Mike Leach, head football coach at Texas Tech, Washington State, and Mississippi State, is another example. He did not win nearly as many games as Bobby Knight—he never won a national championship, and he only went 8-9 in bowl games—but he changed the game of football forever. Nicknamed "the Pirate," Leach popularized the modern version of the "air raid offense." His teams prioritized relentless passing, speed, and spreading defenses out across the field. His philosophy didn't just change the tactics of football—it shifted the sport's entire culture at every level, from high school to the NFL.

Leach, who had a law degree from Pepperdine University in Malibu, also left an impressive wake. Several of his quarterbacks, including Kliff Kingsbury and Gardiner Minshew, went on to play in the NFL. At least eleven of Leach's former assistant coaches have gone on to become NCAA Division I head coaches, including Lincoln Riley, who coached three different Heisman Trophy winners, and Sonny Dykes, who led Texas Christian University to a national championship game in 2022.

When Leach died in 2022, he was remembered as an innovator who left an indelible mark on the sport he loved. His impact might not be quantifiable through wins, titles, or accolades—but you can't watch an NFL game now without seeing some traces of Leach's philosophies.

"I certainly believe his legacy will go far beyond his offensive creativity, the wins, the crazy press conferences, all the great stories," Riley said at Leach's memorial. "He truly did invest in other people. It's a great reminder for us all to take a little bit of your time and invest it in other people and get to know them and look to help them."

There are stories like this in every industry. Arnold Sommerfeld, a professor at the University of Munich in the early twentieth century, has an unparalleled academic "tree." He supervised or taught *seven* future Nobel Prize winners in physics. Despite being nominated over eighty times himself, Sommerfeld never won a Nobel Prize, but his influence on his students shaped much of modern physics.

Likewise, Lee Strasberg was never an acting star. But he led the famous Actors Studio, and his list of students includes Steve McQueen, Robert De Niro, Al Pacino, Dustin Hoffman, Sally Field, Faye Dunaway, Jane Fonda, Ellen Burstyn, and Robert Duvall.

Gen. George C. Marshall was the U.S. Army Chief of Staff during World War II—and apparently renowned for identifying and elevating talented officers. He personally groomed future president Dwight D. Eisenhower, rapidly promoting him and entrusting him with commanding Allied forces in Europe. Marshall also oversaw or guided the careers of some of the most famous generals in American history, including George Patton, Omar Bradley, and Douglas MacArthur.

You have probably never heard of improvisational comedy coach Del Close—but you have probably heard of some of the comedians he trained at Second City in Chicago over the years, including Bill Murray,

John Belushi, John Candy, Gilda Radner, Chris Farley, Harold Ramis, Stephen Colbert, and Tina Fey.

When you look back on your career, the true measure of your success will be the lives you've touched and improved, the people you mentored and inspired along the way. The colleagues you've guided, peers you've supported, and successors you've encouraged will extend your legacy far beyond your personal achievements.

PROFILE SEVEN

THE MUSIC (FESTIVAL) MAN

Jay grew up in Essex, Massachusetts, a quiet suburb of Boston in the 1980s. He spent his formative years attending St. George's, a prestigious New England boarding school, where he was the youngest student in his class by a wide margin. What should have been an exciting opportunity turned into a lonely struggle. He felt out of place among the older, more sophisticated students. The experience, he says, left him deeply insecure. He survived those turbulent years largely thanks to an unlikely lifeline: music.

Jay spent countless afternoons alone, absorbed in music. He listened to any and all kinds: punk, jazz, Tuvan throat singing. He discovered the free-spirited jams of the Grateful Dead and the Allman Brothers—and these became his sanctuary. Late at night, headphones on, Jay let music drown out the day's difficulties. He would make mixtapes for friends, family, even strangers who frequented the same diner on weekends. He picked different songs from different albums he felt complemented each other, then listened over and over as the rest of the world faded away.

"If it wasn't for my love of music, I would never have survived," he told me. Immersing himself in those lyrics and melodies gave him solace when little else at school did. After high school, Jay enrolled at the University of Colorado in Boulder—a massive campus worlds away from New England's stuffy prep schools. He initially wanted to major in journalism, but when it came time to apply to the school of communications before his junior year, his grades were not good enough. So he quietly switched his major from journalism to poetry. His professors gave him generally positive feedback on his style, but Jay knew he did not want to be a traditional poet. Unlike most of the other creative writing majors in his classes, Jay's literary idols were not really even authors. Jay wanted to write lyrics. He looked up to Robert Hunter and John Barlow, the famed Grateful Dead lyricists. He dreamed of following in their footsteps—to be the Robert Hunter or John Barlow for some future great band.

He was willing to go to extraordinary lengths to chase that dream. As a student, he even finagled an assignment with an environmental magazine just to score a press pass to a Grateful Dead concert. In 1993, Jay managed to land a brief backstage interview with Dead guitarist Bob Weir. Under the guise of journalism, he boldly asked Weir if he ever visited Barlow's Wyoming ranch—fishing for any hint about meeting his hero. Looking back, Jay says he was "always plotting" ways to be closer to his musical heroes.

After graduation, he took a job as a kayaking guide in Jackson Hole, Wyoming—chosen not just for the career, but for the chance to cross paths with Barlow, who lived nearby. It was a far-fetched plan, but it showed how determined he was to break into music.

Eventually, reality intruded on Jay's songwriting fantasy. His mother, ever practical, made it clear they were done helping him financially unless he got a bartender's license or a master's degree. She suggested a degree in education so he would always be able to provide for himself. So Jay went to grad school and earned a master's in education, figuring it was a sensible fallback while he kept one eye on his musical dreams.

"I think it was my own insecurity that I had never been good at anything in my life except being a rabid music fan," Jay told me. "And if I could just make anybody think I was good at something, maybe it would get rid of this chip on my shoulder—and help me find my place in this world."

Still, one conversation gave him pause. Jay's father confessed that he had once turned down his own dream job—an offer to be an on-air personality at a start-up twenty-four-hour sports network based in Bristol, Connecticut. His father had missed out on the chance to be one of the first employees of ESPN and he had regretted it forever. His father almost never gave Jay advice, but on this occasion he gave his son a stern warning not to ignore his passion in favor of money.

"My father said, 'If you become the single best whittler in the world and you really just love nothing but whittling, eventually people will see your value and start paying you because you're good at it. You have to do something that you can't imagine not doing.'"

Jay took that advice to heart, even as he dutifully completed his degree and entered the working world.

He landed a job teaching English at Princeton Day School in New Jersey—which just so happened to be the alma mater of the band Phish, another jam band that had become something of a spiritual successor to the Grateful Dead. The members of the band would come back to Princeton from time to time, and Jay met Phish lyricist Tom Marshall and eventually Phish frontman Trey Anastasio. In his off hours, Jay witnessed how Marshall and Anastasio collaborated on new songs, giving him an up-close view of the life he wanted so badly.

He watched Marshall's words turn into songs that Phish soon played to thousands of fans. Jay looked on with envy as his friend—who until recently had balanced songwriting with a nine-to-five office job—was now able to quit that job and write music full-time. Phish's popularity was exploding. Soon they were selling out arenas like Madison Square Garden. Jay could not have been closer to his dream career, yet he was still on the outside looking in, grading papers by day while his friend lived the rock and roll life.

After he had spent two years in the classroom, an unexpected phone call finally offered a possible way out. A college friend called to say he was leaving law school to start a music career in Colorado—and he wanted Jay to be his lyricist. It was the chance Jay had been waiting for. He agreed without hesitation, figuring he could write songs on the side until his friend's career took off and Jay could leave the classroom behind.

For the first time in years, Jay felt a sense of hope.

But a few weeks later, tragedy struck. That same friend who had handed Jay his dream opportunity was killed in a car crash. The opportunity vanished in an instant, and Jay was devastated. He mourned his friend and also the cruel twist of fate: An open door that might have led to his dream job was now slammed shut.

Reeling from the loss, Jay found himself at a crossroads. Suddenly all his sensible "backup plan" choices felt hollow. He realized he could not keep waiting for the "right" moment to pursue his passion. So he quit his teaching job, walking away from the stable paycheck and comfortable routine.

Jay packed a bag and bought a one-way ticket to Ecuador, leaving everything familiar behind. He was not moving to be in the epicenter of some industry. He did not know a single person there. Jay was going to South America to escape.

"At that point, I was just done," he told me. "I was done with everything and I wanted to find a real purpose."

JAY ARRIVED IN South America with no clear plan other than to distance himself from the life he had left behind. For nearly half a year, he lived in a cramped, six-by-ten-foot cinder-block room at the South American Explorers Club in Ecuador. During that restless period, Jay chased adventure as if it were oxygen: He scaled Chimborazo—the tallest mountain in the hemisphere—kayaked the headwaters of the Amazon, and explored the isolated wonder of the Galápagos. Despite the thrilling escapades, Jay was still haunted by his lost dreams.

Like a true poet, he decided to turn some of that pain into art. Sequestered in his tiny room, Jay poured his broken heart into two raw screenplays. One script laid bare his grief and guilt over the lost friend who'd dared chase their shared dream—while Jay played it safe. Writing became therapeutic, but his savings dwindled, and a few coups—and a few arrests—in Ecuador had Jay pondering a return home.

Then he got a fax telling him that one of his scripts had earned honorable mention at the Nantucket Film Festival. With excitement and trepidation, he found his way back stateside. He landed in Miami, hitchhiked up to Washington, D.C., took a train to New York, and then got a ride up to Boston. On his way to Nantucket he struck up a conversation with a stranger. Jay told the man that he had spent the last few months in Ecuador writing after the death of a friend—and that he was finally returning home.

That stranger turned out to be Peter Farrelly, the filmmaker behind comedy hits like *Something About Mary* and *Dumb and Dumber*. Farrelly took a liking to Jay's easy charm and genuine passion for music. He told Jay to email him if he needed work. Weeks later, Jay had a job on Farrelly's film *Outside Providence*, a movie starring Alec Baldwin. He was the art department coordinator. In his off time, he made mixtapes for Farrelly and the two men bonded over their tastes in music.

Farrelly invited Jay back for his next movie, *Me, Myself & Irene*, which starred Jim Carrey. As they talked around the set, Carrey recognized Jay's passion for music, gently nudging him toward music supervision. After giving him one of his special mixtapes, Jay remembers Carrey's advice vividly: "You're doing the wrong thing," Carrey said. "I hear how you talk about music—everybody does."

Farrelly told Jay he would pay him to find the perfect song for a scene in *Stuck on You,* a movie in which Matt Damon and Greg Kinnear play conjoined twins. It was an "ah-ha" moment, he told me—a gift to feel like his talents were finally being put to the right use.

Jay proved himself a natural for this type of work, and soon he found himself handling music suggestions for a range of projects and directors, who were impressed with his instinctive choices. Jay left his comfortable role with the Farrellys, taking a risk as he became a music supervisor for hire. Early projects included small commercials, but gradually, bigger opportunities arose. Soon, he was working with legends like Pete Townshend, Radiohead, and the Grateful Dead—merging his creative instincts with business acumen.

Around this time, in the early 2000s, Jay started writing again, too—about music, of course. He wrote vividly candid articles for early issues of *Paste* magazine, immersing himself alongside bands like the Flaming Lips, the Roots, and My Morning Jacket. He was not a pretentious music snob. He was an earnest and passionate walking musical encyclopedia who loved to talk (and talk and talk) about music. Long before Spotify or Apple Music, if Jay learned you liked a certain band, he could offer five or ten recommendations of other bands you might like, too.

"After my ten thousand hours I had fully mastered the art of the mixtape, by far my greatest skill set," he jokes.

His writing style—part Hunter S. Thompson gonzo, part Cameron Crowe sincerity—attracted a devoted readership. The time he had put into his musical enthusiasm was now paying off in multiple ways.

As Jay's reputation as a music insider blossomed, he was offered a new role: festival consultant. A company named Festival Network, aiming to acquire and consolidate live music festivals, hired him to travel the globe evaluating festival viability. He became what he calls a "professional festival connoisseur," reporting back about everything from band selection to venue to overall vibe. It seemed like the ultimate music nerd dream job.

Eventually, he was sent to evaluate the legendary Newport Folk Festival, a once-iconic event that had grown stale. This was the setting of the famous moment when Bob Dylan broke out his electric guitar. Newport had once been a beacon for the likes of Joan Baez, Pete Seeger, and Johnny Cash. But now it felt dead.

"It was just lost. It felt jaded and faded," Jay says.

Rather than a cursory report, Jay delivered an exhaustive, passionate eighteen-page, single-spaced document detailing precisely how to revive the festival's dormant soul. This was the music festival that had started them all, Jay explained. While nearly every other festival had been taken over by corporate overlords, Newport was the original and it had never sold out. And that meant something.

His investors were convinced, ready to revive the classic festival. They even started the process of acquiring it—but the 2008 financial crisis struck before Festival Network could realize its ambitions. The company crumbled, leaving at least a dozen festivals in limbo and Jay adrift. Around this time, George Wein, the festival's original founder, was able to take back control of the Newport festival due to a savvy contractual clause. Reading Jay's impassioned report, Wein called him, skeptical, yet intrigued by Jay's audacity and passion.

Wein was toying with the idea of having Jay run the festival, but he wanted another opinion. So the octogenarian music impresario invited Jay for what would become the most crucial interview of his life—not with Wein himself, but with the legendary Pete Seeger and Ramblin' Jack Elliott around the time of Seeger's ninetieth birthday celebration at Madison Square Garden. Jay faced intense scrutiny from the folk icons, who peppered him with detailed queries on his musical values.

Seeger probed deeply, testing Jay's authenticity with pointed questions about his favorite Dylan tracks and his understanding of folk's cultural legacy.

"I said 'Buckets of Rain,'" Jay says. "But I told them I could quote anything from *Blood on the Tracks*."

By the end of their conversation, Seeger was convinced. He placed a decisive call to Wein, advocating firmly: "I like him because he's music-first. He'll learn all the other shit, but he's pure at heart when it comes to music."

That endorsement altered Jay's trajectory. It validated his meandering path from prep school isolation, through uncertain years of teaching, to Ecuadorian adventures, Hollywood flirtations, and journalistic explorations. For the first time, Jay saw his disparate experiences aligning into something coherent—something real. He had spent years running from doubt, but now he was running toward a purpose.

IN THE EARLY days after taking over the Newport Folk and Jazz festivals, Jay found himself up against a harsh reality. The festivals had been reclaimed by George Wein from the collapsing Festival Network, and now Jay was working with a shoestring budget—a stark contrast to the lavish resources previously available. Gone were the comfortable days of six-figure salaries and financial security. Instead, he faced the stark truth: His paycheck in 2009 amounted to just $16,000. He was forty years old. With a family, mortgage, and dwindling savings, Jay realized this was more than a career move—his family was now depending on his ability to make this festival a success.

Jay committed himself to building a community and reviving the festival. The early years were difficult. Newport's infrastructure had been neglected, its reputation had been tarnished, and its legacy had faded. But Jay embraced the challenge, driven partly by pride and partly by an enduring passion for music. He poured himself into reviving the festivals with a gritty determination, intent on proving himself—and honoring the trust placed in him by legends like his legendary predecessors.

One inflection point came when Jay, committed to honoring Newport's historical roots while breathing new life into its performances, faced resistance over inviting Beck. Critics dismissed Beck, who was sometimes categorized as an alt-rock musician, as incompatible with the festival's traditional image. Undeterred, Jay appealed directly to Seeger, sending him a mixtape that included Beck's emotionally charged album *Sea Change*. Seeger responded warmly, acknowledging Beck as a "troubled soul but lyrically brilliant." With Seeger's endorsement, Jay won the confidence he needed to push forward boldly.

Slowly, Newport began to regain its prestige. Jay's thoughtful curation resonated deeply with both artists and audiences. His authenticity and genuine love for music created an environment of trust and respect rarely seen in the commercialized festival industry. Artists returned year after year—not for extravagant paychecks, but out of loyalty and affection for Jay and the unique spirit he nurtured at Newport. People like Hozier, Dolly Parton, and Jack White performed for a fraction of their usual fees, understanding that their involvement meant directly supporting a greater cause.

This commitment was exemplified vividly one afternoon in the summer of 2023 when headliner Noah Kahan canceled his performance with less than three hours' notice. Jay, ever resourceful and connected, quickly sent a text message to James Taylor, who lived across the bay: "Hey, any chance you're around? We're short a set."

Taylor immediately replied, took his boat across the water, guitar in hand, and delivered an impromptu performance that left both the audience and fellow artists in awe. "James just said, 'Well, if you need me, I'll be there,'" Jay says. "That is the kind of community we've built and what a kind soul Sweet Baby James is at his core." Maggie Rogers, whose set had overlapped a bit, rushed from her own stage to witness the unexpected moment, openly weeping with joy.

This was Newport at its finest—where music was personal, community reigned supreme, and artists were family. Taylor later slipped away quietly. He never asked for payment, satisfied merely with having contributed to something meaningful.

There have been a few other incredible moments since Jay took over. In 2019, the supergroup the Highwomen, featuring Brandi Carlile, Natalie Hemby, Maren Morris, and Amanda Shires, made their debut at Newport, performing songs that celebrated women in music before surprising everyone by bringing out Dolly Parton. In 2022, Paul Simon and Joni Mitchell both came out of retirement and made a surprise appearance on stage with Nathaniel Rateliff, Lukas Nelson, Brandi Carlile, Wynonna Judd, and Marcus Mumford.

As the festival has become more and more popular, Jay has continued giving back to the musical community. Under his guidance, the nonprofit Newport Festivals Foundation established various music education initiatives, including free music lessons and new instruments for young musicians. Jay recalls the emotional moment when he handed a brand-new saxophone to a twelve-year-old girl who had previously had just twenty-five minutes a week to practice on a borrowed instrument. Her joyous tears, her immediate, soulful playing, reminded Jay exactly why he was doing this. It wasn't about fame or headlines—it was about creating "moments of hope," he says.

Before Jay's arrival, in the early 2000s, the festival struggled to sell tickets. These days, it sells out in under a minute, months before the lineup is even announced. The community trusts Jay implicitly. And if you manage to purchase a ticket and see Jay in his element, you will see nearly every musician hug him and thank him for inviting them. Several profess their appreciation for Jay over the mic on stage. Most of the audience—thousands of people—greet him by name when they see him walking through the crowd.

His route was circuitous, but Jay never let go of his passion for music. He was forty before he found the job his professional life had been building toward. And when he got it, he took every advantage to give back to the world of music.

Today, Jay Sweet remains humble, deeply aware of his responsibility as the guardian of Newport's legacy. He treasures each moment that reinforces the festival's purpose. Whether it's supporting artists in crisis, funding music education programs, or simply creating unforgettable musical experiences, Jay continues to lead with an authenticity that is both rare and inspiring.

In a rapidly commercializing industry, Newport stands apart, a reflection of Jay's own journey from uncertainty to fulfillment. He has embraced his role, not as a gatekeeper or curator, but as a community builder and hope creator. He literally went from listening to music alone in his bedroom for personal solace to building a community that gives solace to thousands.

And Newport is no longer defined by its past struggles but by the endless possibilities it offers for connection, growth, and joy. Under Jay's stewardship, the festival has become a musical sanctuary, a place where dreams are nurtured, friendships are forged, and hope reverberates in every song.

IT'S NEVER TOO LATE

SUCCESS AT ANY AGE

It is never too late to be what you might have been.

—George Eliot

There's a particular type of regret that keeps people awake long into quiet nights—the kind that's born not from the mistakes they've made but from the risks they never took. Daniel Pink, in his book *The Power of Regret*, calls these "boldness regrets." They haunt us not because we tried and failed but because we never found the courage to try at all. Pink describes boldness regrets as those moments when we chose safety over adventure, stability over passion, comfort over possibility.

When it comes to careers, boldness regrets often intensify as we age. They start as quiet whispers—maybe the desire to write novels, start a business, or become a teacher—but grow louder each passing year, eventually drowning out even the most reasonable excuses. However, regret, as Pink argues, is not entirely a bad thing. Regret can swallow people up, but it can also be life's greatest motivator.

It is never too late to silence those quiet whispers of regret by taking action. The fear of failing at something new pales in comparison to the lifelong ache of never having tried.

There are loads of people who summoned the courage later in life to chase their dream jobs—and their stories make a compelling case that regret, even decades old, can still be redeemed with renewed motivation. Boldness regrets are painful, but they are also instructive. The best time to start pursuing the work we love might've been twenty years ago—but the second-best time is always right now.

History is filled with people whose greatest successes came later in life. Consider Toni Morrison, who published her first novel at thirty-nine—and went on to win both a Pulitzer Prize and the Nobel Prize in Literature. Ray Kroc was selling milkshake machines until he bought his first McDonald's franchise at fifty-two, revolutionizing fast food forever. Samuel L. Jackson was working minor roles for decades until breaking through at age forty-three with *Jungle Fever*. Stan Lee, the creative force behind Marvel's iconic superheroes, didn't achieve comic book success until he was nearly forty. Vera Wang shifted from figure skating and journalism to design her first wedding dress at age forty, becoming a global fashion icon in the process.

Rodney Dangerfield famously returned to comedy at forty after years spent selling aluminum siding, going on to influence generations of comedians. Arianna Huffington began building the Huffington Post media empire at age fifty-five, redefining online journalism. Morgan Freeman spent years in theater and TV before landing his breakout film role in *Street Smart* at fifty. Laura Ingalls Wilder didn't begin publishing her beloved Little House books until she was sixty-five years old. Alan Rickman was forty-two when he appeared in his first movie, embarking on a film career that would leave a powerful legacy. And Bram Stoker, whose novel *Dracula* reshaped the horror genre, was fifty years old at the time of publication.

Just because you did not start when you were twenty or twenty-five or thirty-five or forty-five does not mean you can't start today. Here are a few of my favorite stories of people who found their calling a little later in life.

THE COSMETICS QUEEN WHO TURNED A HOBBY INTO AN EMPIRE

Estée grew up in Corona, Queens, New York, in the first decades of the twentieth century, with immigrant parents of Hungarian-Jewish heritage. Her first memory, she would later say, was the scent of her mother's perfume. As a child, Estée was obsessed with what she called "touching faces"—applying makeup products.

When Estée was sixteen, her uncle John, a chemist from Hungary, arrived with formulas for creams and lotions and set up a small lab in Brooklyn. Estée learned to mix creams and experimented endlessly—and she began selling her uncle's concoctions to anyone who would listen: family, friends, even strangers. By her own account, she was "mesmerized by pretty things and pretty people" and spent her youth practicing makeovers on anyone within reach.

In her early twenties she dreamed of a glamorous life (even imagining herself an actress), but instead Estée followed a more traditional route—at first. She met Joseph Lauter (also spelled Lauder) and they were married in 1930, when she was twenty-one. During the 1930s, Estée continued to promote and sell her uncle's skin care products, repackaging the creams and giving live demonstrations in beauty salons. In her free time, she went to the library to study the history of the beauty industry going back to ancient Rome and Egypt and the beauty routine of Cleopatra.

Estée started mixing her own creams, conducting small experiments using her own face to see which products worked best together. She invited friends she met at the salons she visited over to her home for lessons on makeup application. For years, this was a hobby. She would give her creams away for free, because initially she did not think of this as a business.

Then one day a salon owner asked Estée what she did to keep her skin looking "so fresh and lovely." Estée excitedly showed her some of the products she'd been experimenting with, and the salon owner asked if she might be interested in running a small concession in her salon. Estée would pay rent, but she could keep anything she made from selling her products.

This was a breakthrough. It was the moment her hobby became her career.

She was already in her early thirties, but her journey as an entrepreneur—what Estée really wanted to do—was ready to launch. At her stand in the salon, if a customer bought one product, Estée slipped extra samples or even a small freebie into their bag. If a customer didn't buy, Estée still sent them off with a free sample to try at home. This strategy won women's loyalty and spread goodwill, compensating for the fact that the fledgling company could not afford big advertisements.

By 1944, thirty-six-year-old Estée was selling her own homemade creams in several New York beauty parlors, mixing batches in her kitchen. Customers loved the products and told their friends. It was still a small-scale operation, but Estée decided it was time to throw everything she had at it. In 1946, when she was thirty-eight—an age when many would be afraid to start anew—she and Joseph committed all their savings and energy to the venture. They decided to name it after her: the Estée Lauder Company.

One of the company's first big breaks came the next year. In 1947—when Estée was almost forty years old—the upscale department store Saks Fifth Avenue ordered a modest $800 worth of creams and lotions (about $10,000 today). Estée had relentlessly courted Saks' beauty buyer for months despite repeated rejections. Her lucky break actually came from a clever stunt: Estée had handed out free samples of her lipstick at a charity event in New York's Waldorf-Astoria Hotel, causing society women to flood Saks asking for the product. Saks sold out Estée's initial shipment in just two days.

With that success, the Lauders closed their small salon concessions and focused on supplying department stores. Estée Lauder—the brand and the woman—was officially on its way. In the first year, the company did $50,000 in business—an impressive start for a brand-new business in the 1940s.

One of Estée Lauder's landmark achievements was the creation in 1953 of Youth-Dew, a product that would revolutionize the cosmetics industry and turbocharge her young company. Noticing that in the 1950s women wore expensive French perfume only on special occasions, Estée sought to create an affordable fragrance women could use every day. The result was Youth-Dew, a bath oil that doubled as a perfume. Priced at $8.50 a bottle, Youth-Dew was marketed for daily use—a clever way to encourage women to buy it for *themselves* rather than wait for a gift of perfume. By the late 1950s, Estée Lauder was grossing about $800,000 annually.

Her business grew exponentially from there. By the mid-1980s, she was selling millions of bottles of perfume—and many other products—all over the world. She was the only woman on *Time* magazine's 1998 list of the twenty most influential business geniuses of the twentieth century.

Today, of course, Estée Lauder is one of the biggest cosmetic companies in the world. In the fiscal year 2024, the company reported more than $15 billion in sales. When Estée Lauder died in 2004, at the age of ninety-five, she was lauded as one of the most influential self-made businesswomen of the twentieth century.

THE MIDLIFE CELEBRITY CHEF

Julia's life initially followed a conventional path. Born in Pasadena, California, in 1912, she grew up in comfort and privilege, attending private schools and Smith College, where she graduated in 1934. After college, she bounced between various jobs in advertising and publishing in

New York. When World War II broke out, Julia joined the Office of Strategic Services (OSS), the precursor to the CIA, initially working clerical jobs before taking on more significant roles overseas in Ceylon (now Sri Lanka) and China. There she met Paul Child, a diplomat and artist who shared her adventurous spirit. They married in 1946, and two years later, Paul's assignment took them to France—a country Julia had never visited.

On a gray November afternoon in 1948, Julia sat down to lunch at a restaurant in Rouen, France, and unknowingly stepped onto a new path in life. The thirty-six-year-old barely knew a word of French and, by her own admission, did not even know how to boil an egg properly. But then the waiter brought out a dish of *sole meunière*—a whole Dover sole expertly browned in butter—and Julia took a bite. "It was the most exciting meal of my life," she later recalled. The tender fish, the nutty *beurre noisette* sauce, the squeeze of fresh lemon—it was a revelation. It was the instant that Julia discovered an insatiable curiosity for food.

Before that moment in France, Julia had never been particularly interested in cooking and had been happy to let others handle the cooking. But France changed everything. The sensory jolt of Normandy butter and briny oysters sparked an intense curiosity. How could food be this good? What secrets of sauce and seasoning did the French know that Americans didn't? Those questions lit a fire in Julia. Within weeks of that Rouen lunch, this tall, outspoken Californian boldly enrolled in cooking school in Paris, determined to master the mysteries of French cuisine.

She was nearly a foot taller than some of her instructors, and one of the few women in a professional training program filled mostly with young American GIs taking advantage of their veteran benefits. Undaunted, Julia plunged into the hard work of learning to cook *à la française*. The classes—taught entirely in rapid-fire French—covered everything from knife technique to elaborate sauces. At first, Julia struggled to keep up with the language and the younger men in class. But she attacked her new tasks with zeal. She practiced obsessively, chopping mountains of onions and perfecting classic dishes like *boeuf bourguignon* in her tiny Paris apartment at night. Her determination paid off: She graduated and earned her Le Cordon Bleu *diplôme* in 1951. Julia was now officially a trained cook.

Around that same time, at a cocktail party in Paris, Julia met Simone "Simca" Beck, a forty-four-year-old Frenchwoman from Normandy who adored cooking just as much as she did. "It was an immediate take," Julia later wrote of her first encounter with Simca. Despite coming from different worlds, the two women bonded over a shared love of cuisine and a desire to do something with it. Along with a younger French friend, Louisette Bertholle, they began cooking together, experimenting with recipes and hosting informal classes for American acquaintances.

As Julia and Simca's friendship deepened, so did their ambitions. Simone Beck had been laboring on a French cookbook geared toward Americans, and in Julia she found the perfect partner to bring it to life. In 1952, the three women officially set out to coauthor a comprehensive guide to French cuisine for beginners. Julia found Simone's draft recipes charming but imprecise—measurements were vague, steps skipped. So Julia painstakingly retested every dish, translating French techniques into precise English instructions. She insisted on explaining why each step mattered, determined to give readers the know-how and confidence to cook like trained chefs. What began as a modest recipe collection ballooned into an encyclopedic manuscript. By 1957, their draft ran to nearly nine hundred pages, jam-packed with classical recipes from *boeuf bourguignon* to chocolate soufflé.

It took nine relentless years of work, testing and tweaking hundreds of recipes, before the manuscript was ready for a publisher. When *Mastering the Art of French Cooking* hit American bookstores in October 1961, Julia Child was forty-nine years old. Renowned *New*

York Times food editor Craig Claiborne pronounced the book an instant classic, marveling that its hundreds of recipes were "written as if each were a masterpiece, and most of them are." Thus, as she entered her sixth decade of living, Julia's career was just now coming to a boil.

Promoting a cookbook was not commonplace in the early 1960s, but Julia and Simca were determined to spread the word. The two middle-aged coauthors gamely embarked on a book tour across the United States, giving cooking demonstrations in department stores and on local radio. In January 1962, they even appeared on NBC's *Today* show—an extraordinary sight at the time: two unglamorous, apron-clad women cooking an omelet on live TV. But the jovial, six-foot-two Julia came across as warm and approachable, effortlessly translating French cooking to a mass audience. That morning, millions of Americans heard Julia Child's distinct voice for the first time. It was the beginning of something neither she nor Simca had planned for: Julia's second act as a public figure.

Back home in Cambridge, Massachusetts, Julia was soon invited to host a new educational cooking show on public television, leveraging the buzz from her book tour. In 1963, at the age of fifty-one, Julia Child made her debut as "the French Chef" on national TV. Her on-screen persona was a hit: viewers were charmed by this witty, unpretentious woman who cheerfully showed them how to truss a chicken or whisk a hollandaise, all in a warbling patrician voice. America's *first* celebrity chef, Julia Child continued to appear regularly on television for the next three decades—well into her eighties.

In 2000, she was presented with a Knight of France's Legion of Honor, the highest and most prestigious order of merit the French government awards. She was awarded the U.S. Presidential Medal of Freedom in 2003. She also received honorary doctorates from Harvard University, Smith College (her alma mater), Brown University (2000), and several other universities. When she died, in 2004, she was mourned around the world.

Not bad for someone who did not even recognize her passion until she was nearly forty.

THE PRESIDENT OF THE MATH CLUB WHO WENT ALL IN

In high school, as the president of the math club, Sal tutored his fellow students, running after-school sessions for classmates struggling with algebra. Later, as an undergraduate at MIT in the 1990s, Sal gravitated toward physics. He wanted to explore "the grandest way of understanding the universe," as he told me. But soon Sal found himself drawn to the budding world of software and the internet. It seemed like both an exciting and a practical path.

After graduating, Sal launched into the late-'90s tech boom. His first job was as a product manager at Oracle, but it lasted just over a year. He then dabbled in a dot-com start-up and a tech consulting firm during the frothy internet bubble. Looking for a fresh start, Sal decided to go to business school. He earned his MBA from Harvard Business School in 2003, where he discovered a new interest in finance, especially the analytic challenge of capital markets.

Armed with his MBA, Sal landed at a small hedge fund in Boston. The fund had just two people managing money, and Sal thrived on the job's intellectual breadth. One day he might be analyzing a biotech company, the next day he might be looking at a tech firm or a logistics business.

"It satisfied that curiosity of how the world works," he says.

By his late twenties, Sal was successful, well paid, and enjoying the work. He settled into married life and started paying off student loans. Yet deep down, he felt a pull to do something more meaningful. He had never forgotten his experience as a math tutor in high school, where he saw how "if kids just got a little bit of personalized help, they could learn a lot." Even as he climbed the ladder in tech and finance, Sal had harbored a quiet ambition to refocus his energy on education.

He began telling his wife that if all went well, in ten or fifteen years he might follow through on that dream of starting a school.

In 2004, opportunity arrived unexpectedly. Sal's twelve-year-old cousin Nadia, who lived across the country, was struggling with math—unit conversions—and asked for his help. Sal agreed to tutor her remotely, working through problems over the phone and using an online notepad. Nadia's math grades quickly improved, and soon word spread in the family. More relatives began approaching Sal for math help.

To manage this growing tutoring circle, Sal started writing small software scripts to generate practice problems and track progress. He also began recording short video lessons—informal doodles and explanations—and posting them on a then new, fledgling site called YouTube.

What began as a family favor was steadily morphing into a passion project. Sal's YouTube videos were simple and low-tech—just a voice narrating hand-drawn math explanations—but they struck a chord beyond his relatives. Strangers started finding the videos online and left grateful comments about how these free lessons helped them finally grasp algebra or pass a class. Sal was both surprised and motivated by the feedback.

"I was finding *intrinsic joy* from doing this," he says.

Evenings spent creating math tutorials felt rewarding in a way that analyzing stock portfolios did not. Sal had not set out with any business plan—in fact, he resisted suggestions to monetize his budding YouTube channel. By 2008, though, the channel had grown to hundreds of videos and tens of thousands of views. That year, Sal Khan incorporated the "Khan Academy" as a 501(c)(3) nonprofit organization, his first deliberate step to turn his hobby into a broader mission. His mission: "to provide a free, world-class education for anyone, anywhere."

He continued working at the hedge fund by day and recording

lessons by night. By 2009, Sal was in his early thirties and had spent six years in finance. He had a comfortable salary and a new baby at home—and yet, he was seriously considering quitting his job to focus on Khan Academy full-time. It was a leap that defied the typical career script, and most people around him thought he was crazy to even contemplate it.

By the summer of 2009, Khan made the pivotal decision. With his boss's encouragement, he left the hedge fund and dedicated himself to Khan Academy. Sal and his wife set a one-year timeline for the experiment, budgeting their savings to go through a full year without salary. It was a bold risk.

The first months working from home were daunting. Sal describes 2009–10 as "a very hard year." He was essentially a solo entrepreneur of a nonprofit start-up, with no steady funding and a newborn in his arms. He spent his days producing more videos, improving the software platform, and courting philanthropists in hopes of donations—all while watching his bank account shrink. Doubts crept in. But then, precisely as the savings deadline neared, Khan Academy's fortunes began to turn.

In the summer of 2010, Microsoft founder Bill Gates praised Sal's videos in an interview, revealing that his own kids were using Khan Academy at home. Gates even quipped that Sal Khan might be "his favorite teacher." Soon after, Google selected Khan Academy for a major grant aimed at supporting innovative charities. Prominent Silicon Valley donors like Ann Doerr (wife of venture capitalist John Doerr) also reached out to help—which was a critical turning point.

By 2011, Khan Academy had skyrocketed in visibility. Sal Khan took the stage at TED 2011, where he told the story of quitting his job to teach the world. He showcased Khan Academy's approach to self-paced, online learning. The TED Talk went viral, spreading his mission to millions more. The nonprofit grew from just Sal himself to a small team of engineers and educators. They expanded content beyond math into science, history, and more. Usage exploded—students, teachers, and adult learners around the globe were watching Sal's YouTube lessons and practicing on the site in increasing numbers. One early observation stunned Khan: Even back in 2009, with just a camcorder and some math videos, Khan Academy reached more students via the internet in a single month than Khan's alma mater Harvard could teach on campus in its entire 350-year history. And the numbers only kept climbing.

Today, Khan Academy is a global educational force. The platform has over 180 million registered users in 190 countries. Its library of ten-thousand-plus free videos has been translated into dozens of languages. Amid the 2020 pandemic, usage spiked as students everywhere turned to online learning. And Sal Khan has continued to innovate—recently introducing an AI-powered virtual tutor. Sal has some powerful supporters, too. According to analysis of its IRS tax returns, from 2008 through 2021, Khan Academy received approximately $365 million in donations.

Looking back, Sal Khan is grateful he made his bold leap. "I consider myself one of the luckiest people on the planet to be able to work on something that I care about, something that I feel might be able to make a dent in the world," he says.

THE MORTGAGE BROKER WHO CREATED AMERICA'S FAVORITE SPIRIT

Raised in San Antonio, Texas, Tito studied geology and geophysics in college and entered the oil business in the 1980s, dreaming of striking it rich. But by the time he graduated, the Texas oil boom had gone bust, and steady jobs were hard to come by. Over the next decade, Tito chased opportunity wherever he could find it: working as a roughneck and geologist in Texas, running seismic exploration crews in South America, even founding a small drilling company. When oil prices collapsed again in the early '90s, he switched fields—first to environmental consulting, then to selling mortgages. By his midthirties, Tito was a mortgage broker in Austin, making a decent living but feeling restless and unfulfilled. He knew he hadn't yet found his calling.

As a fun side project, Tito had begun infusing cheap vodka with fresh ingredients—habanero peppers, black cherries, oranges—and bottling these homemade flavored vodkas as gifts for friends. In 1992, at a party, a stranger tasted one of his concoctions and exclaimed, "Hey, you're the vodka guy!" The nickname made Tito chuckle (after all, he still thought of himself as "the mortgage guy"), but it also planted a seed of an idea.

Around that time, he saw the late-night public broadcast show about a technique for discovering your true calling. Tito divided a piece of paper down the middle and made a list of what he loved to do on one side and what he was good at on the other. In the end, he decided that distilling vodka was worth pursuing full-time.

Tito threw himself into the project with all the determination and grit he had honed in the oil fields. First, he faced a legal hurdle: No one had ever licensed a distillery in Texas before. In 1995, after two years of pushing, he secured the state's first permit to legally distill spirits. He bought twelve acres of scrubland on Austin's rural outskirts and built a small shack that would serve as his one-man distillery. Using spare parts and even photocopies of old moonshiners' still diagrams as his guide, Tito engineered a makeshift pot still and taught himself how to distill vodka by trial and error.

When investors refused to fund his unlikely start-up, Tito financed it the only way he could—by maxing out nineteen different credit cards. He quit his day job and did every task himself, from cooking the corn mash to hand-bottling each batch of vodka. His initial product looked humble, packaged in a plain glass bottle with a simple brown-paper label, but inside was a spirit he believed could rival any top-shelf brand.

The next few years were a grueling test of perseverance. Tito sold just a few thousand cases in the late 1990s—barely enough to stay afloat—and he faced constant financial strain. His big breakthrough moment came in 2001, when he entered his vodka into the prestigious San Francisco World Spirits Competition—and won the top prize, a Double Gold medal, beating all the established vodka brands. The little Texas vodka that no one had believed in—Tito's Homemade Vodka—was suddenly on the industry's radar. Orders picked up, and by the late 2000s Tito's had expanded well beyond Austin.

By 2013, the brand was selling millions of cases, and by 2019 Tito's had even overtaken Smirnoff to become the top-selling spirit in the United States—a mind-boggling achievement for a venture that started in a dusty backyard shack by someone who had spent the first twenty years of his professional life pursuing other careers.

Today, Tito Beveridge—now in his early sixties—remains at the helm of his company, and he still embraces the passion that launched his second career. He has no plans to retire; in fact, he often says he feels like his best years are still ahead. Looking back, Tito has no regrets about his long, indirect career path.

"You're not a failure," Tito told me, "until you quit trying."

PROFILE EIGHT

TRUSTING THE PROCESS

Sam was born in the Netherlands, where his father was working at the time, but he grew up mostly in Marlow, Oklahoma, a town with a population just under five thousand. Sam's dad worked for Halliburton, the oil and gas company, which was founded in Duncan, Oklahoma, ten miles down the road. Sam went to Marlow High School, where he played defensive back for the football team and point guard for the basketball team. Unfortunately, Sam was five foot nine and 140 pounds, so he did not keep playing in college.

But Sam was also gifted with intelligence and was his high school's valedictorian. From an early age he loved numbers. He loved math. He was fascinated by the power of exponential growth. At the University of Oklahoma, he majored in finance. He still loved sports—he briefly considered becoming a coach—but if you had asked him at the time, Sam probably would have told you he wanted to become the CEO of an industrials company or something similar. After his freshman year, he applied for an internship at Conoco. He was invited in for an interview—and it was going well until the interviewer asked Sam where he imagined he would be in five years.

Sam was honest. He said he figured he would go to business school.

"The interviewer was like, 'What? You don't want to work at Conoco in five years?'" Sam remembers. "I was like, 'No, definitely not. I'm not interested in that.' So that clearly changed the tone of the conversation."

Sam went to the career services office at his school to ask for advice. He was told he should consider looking into some of the big consulting companies. At most of those firms, it is not unusual for someone to work a few years, then take off for an MBA program. He interned in the accounting group of Ernst & Young, in Dallas, which happened to be the world leader in providing third-party opinions on the purchase of professional sports teams—giving Sam some early exposure to the world of sports business.

After he graduated, Sam was offered a job at the Dallas office of Bain Capital, as the first University of Oklahoma student hired by Bain. His class of incoming associate consultants was the largest ever at the time, and soon Sam understood why. This was in the spring of 2000, the height of the dot-com boom. "Everyone with a pulse was leaving corporate America to work in start-ups," he told me.

Meanwhile, Sam enjoyed the work at Bain. It was long hours of rigorous analytical work with a strong team atmosphere. He liked being able to consult with Bain's clients, to bring large amounts of data to important decisions. He had a variety of clients, usually one at a time for three to nine months. He was tasked with helping the companies that hired Bain in a number of ways: from improving profits and growing revenue to forming strategies and occasionally purchasing other companies. And being an Oklahoma kid, he even used his rare off time to go fishing in the cement pond behind his apartment complex.

About eighteen months into his time at Bain, Sam was at lunch with some other young analysts and two men he considered mentors. The two older men went around the room, asking the young analysts: If you could do anything, any job in the world, what would you do? Most of the answers were something along the lines of "private equity" or "CEO."

When they got to Sam, he said, "Sports GM." It was the first time he verbalized this idea, but it had been forming in his mind for a while. A general manager of a professional sports team is responsible for assembling the team of players and signing each of them to contracts within a budget—plus hiring and managing the coaches and staff in an effort to win games.

"This was not well thought of at all," Sam told me. "I remember they laughed at me. It made me so mad."

It is different now, but at the time, almost nobody was bringing the tools of data analytics into the world of professional sports. Sam was admonished. He was told that he was not being trained to be the general manager of a sports franchise.

For the next year or so, he continued pursuing his career path as he thought he was supposed to, but he didn't forget about his dream. In his third year at Bain, the company relocated Sam and his wife to Sydney, Australia. He worked on the forty-fourth floor, in a building that looked out over the iconic Sydney Opera House.

By now, the world of sports was beginning to change. The San Francisco 49ers and New England Patriots had both hired former Bain analysts. Then in 2002, the Boston Red Sox hired Theo Epstein, an espoused fan of advanced data analytics, as the team's general manager—making the twenty-eight-year-old Epstein the youngest GM in baseball history. (During his time as an undergrad at Yale, Epstein famously wrote letters to several different teams, expressing interest in working for them, and eventually began his baseball career interning for the Baltimore Orioles.)

Sam also recognized that the landscape of sports was on the brink of a dramatic shift. For decades, most of the sports franchises in America were owned by wildcatters or families with old money. They tended to hire guys who did things the old way. But that was changing. Mark Cuban, who bought the Dallas Mavericks in 2000, made his money in tech. John Henry, the man who purchased the Red Sox in 2002 and hired Epstein, made his money as a hedge fund manager. Sam knew the future of franchise ownership would come from the world of private equity and investment banking and tech founders.

"What would surely happen was these guys would buy sports teams," Sam told me. "And what would almost certainly happen on a two-year delay is they would bring in the talented young people they had always worked with."

As Sam was thinking about all of this, the author Michael Lewis published the book *Moneyball,* a look inside the innovative approach of Oakland Athletics general manager Billy Beane to assemble a competitive baseball team on a small budget. Beane used an analytic tool called sabermetrics that deploys more advanced metrics that better reflect a player's true contribution to the team's success. The book explained that several of the statistics traditionally used to evaluate players—including stolen bases and runs batted in—were antiquated relics of another time and that newer statistics like on-base percentage were a much better measure of a player's value.

Sam read *Moneyball* in two days. He loved everything about it. He could not stop thinking about it. Like Jerry Seinfeld reading about Lenny Bruce or Danny Meyer talking to his uncle, Sam decided then and there that he was going to quit his lucrative job at Bain, move back to the U.S., and start working toward his dream of becoming a general manager.

When he told his parents, they confessed that they thought he was "crazy"—but, he says, they were supportive. Ever the quantitative analyst, Sam tried to assuage their fears by telling them: "I think it'll take me ten years. Right now the odds are zero. I think I can push them all the way to 10 percent."

Then he added: "If I'm wrong and I come up snake eyes, I think it's going to be fun anyway."

SAM STARTED APPLYING to business schools. He was accepted at Harvard and Stanford. As he was deciding where to go, he traveled to both schools, starting with Harvard. While he was on the East Coast, he set up meetings with members of the school's administration, but he also met up with friends from Bain who had gone to Harvard Business School. In every meeting, he gave his one-minute spiel about wanting to disrupt professional sports by using data to make better decisions.

"You could just see their eyes roll," he told me. "You could see them thinking: *Our brochure says 99 percent of our people are employed six months after graduation, and our average salary is X, and this guy's going to screw up both those numbers.*"

His trip to Palo Alto went differently. He noted the entrepreneurial spirit there, the openness to new ideas.

"Stanford was much warmer, both physically and metaphorically," he says. When Sam told someone from the career services office his plan to be a GM, they were enthusiastically supportive: "That sounds awesome. We've had five people go to professional sports. You come to my office, we'll flip through my Rolodex."

At Stanford Graduate School of Business, Sam was able to take a sports management class for the first time. He also reached out to Paraag Marathe, the former Bain analyst who was already working with the 49ers. Sam had never met Paraag but told him in an email that he had heard of him, that he thought his path was interesting, and that he had been thinking a lot about this and would love to ask him some questions. Paraag agreed to meet. "We went and ate burritos across the street from Stanford," Sam told me. "And I didn't ask him twenty questions. I asked him two hundred."

While attending Stanford, Sam also met with Billy Beane, the A's general manager at the center of *Moneyball.* He spent time with Michael Lewis, the former Wall Street trader-turned-bestselling author who wrote the book that so dramatically shifted Sam's career path. Lewis lives in the Bay Area. At the time, the author was working on a follow-up to *Moneyball* about the undervalued positions in football. That book was called *The Blind Side,* and it became the Oscar-winning movie starring Sandra Bullock.

His first year at Stanford, Sam also took a move from Theo Epstein's playbook. Sam sent both emails *and* physical letters to NFL franchises all over the country, offering to work as an unpaid intern in the front office. He suggested that he could bring a new way of thinking about value in the salary cap era. His pitch was simple: *I can help you. You have a limited pile of chips and you need to turn it into as many wins as you can. I can help you reduce risk or boost return or both. I'll be in your town. We should talk.*

When spring break came around, most of his fellow students went to places like Aruba or Cancun. But Sam was focused on his goal. Instead of a trip to the beach, he went on what he calls a "roadshow on Southwest Airlines." He visited five or six different football teams that week, mostly to introduce himself.

"I was just trying to get a foot in the door," Sam told me.

One of those teams was the Houston Texans, a franchise that was only a few years old at the time—and losing badly. Sam was invited to intern at the team's front office. The initial internship lasted eight weeks, but the team asked Sam to stick around during his second year of business school, too, which meant that sometimes Sam had to fly back and forth from Palo Alto to Houston several times a week. But Sam was willing to take every chance to be in the building, to learn the language and culture of the world he was hoping to disrupt. He asked questions as often as he could without burdening anyone. In most meetings, he didn't say anything at all.

He spent most of his time building a software tool for the draft that could help the team evaluate each player's relative value in an effort to maximize return on draft day. Sam had observed there was still a lot of old thinking in football. For example, teams often rewarded running backs with big contracts after big breakout years—despite ample data showing that was exactly when a running back would most likely revert to the mean. Sam could explain why a mid-second-round draft pick is often half as valuable as a first-round pick, but at 10 percent of the cost—but position coaches and coordinators and scouts were all set in their ways and resisted any new approach to personnel, especially from a baby-faced twenty-six-year-old from Stanford.

Sam realized that succeeding in this career would involve not just analysis but also "earning the right" to influence these stakeholders in the team. "Earning the right to get them to listen, to make good arguments, to realize the facts are on this side and that it's in your best interest to do this for the particular goal."

FOLLOWING HIS GRADUATION from Stanford in 2005, Sam had a two-hour conversation with Les Alexander, who owned the Houston Rockets NBA franchise at the time, about how data could be used to make better basketball decisions. Les was a bond trader in the '80s, so when Sam talked about "reducing risk" and "boosting return," Les understood immediately.

At just twenty-seven years old, he was hired as a special assistant to the general manager—about three weeks before that year's NBA draft. So Sam and his wife moved to Houston and slept on an inflatable mattress while Sam worked from 6:00 A.M. until midnight or later every day. While they waited on their belongings to ship from California, the couple had only one car, which meant Sam's wife drove him both ways.

Within a year, Les Alexander hired Daryl Morey as the team's assistant GM. Daryl had begun his career at STATS, Inc., a pioneer sports data firm where Bill James, the legendary statistician who created sabermetrics, also worked. Daryl shared Sam's analytical philosophy. A year later, Daryl was promoted to general manager, making the Rockets the first NBA franchise to hire a GM dedicated to integrating advanced statistical analysis. In 2007, Sam was promoted to vice president, making him the youngest VP in the league.

Together, Daryl and Sam built the best basketball sports analytics department in the country. At the time, the Rockets had superstars Tracy McGrady and Yao Ming—which meant the team had to deal with injury challenges often. Eventually, Houston acquired James Harden in a trade widely praised as a strategic masterpiece, propelled by data-driven insights on Harden's undervalued potential.

Sam also spearheaded numerous analytical initiatives aimed at player evaluation, contract negotiation, and resource allocation. His role involved extensive use of predictive models, valuation frameworks, and statistical assessments—concepts traditionally foreign to NBA management. Together, Daryl and Sam pushed forward the NBA's adoption of advanced metrics, introducing terms like *true shooting percentage, efficiency,* and *wins above replacement* into mainstream basketball discourse.

Most importantly, the Rockets won a lot of games with Sam and Daryl in the front office. They made the playoffs every year Daryl was GM, and Daryl would go on to win "Executive of the Year" in 2018. They proved their model. It was only a matter of time before other teams wanted to try the same approach.

In 2012, Sam was invited to interview for the general manager job at the Philadelphia 76ers. The conversations did not go well. "We could not get on the same page in a bunch of ways," Sam told me. "And I was aggressive about it in a bunch of ways that surprised them. And so I told them I wouldn't come, and I didn't."

Sam decided to stay in Houston for another year, but he made a few predictions for what would happen that year in Philadelphia—most of which came true. Impressed, the owners of the 76ers came knocking again. So in 2013, at age thirty-five, almost exactly ten years from the moment he told his parents he wanted to be a GM, Sam Hinkie was hired as the general manager of the Philadelphia 76ers.

NOW, IF YOU are a basketball fan and you remember Sam's tenure in Philadelphia, you know it was . . . *complicated*. Sam's time in his dream job was covered pretty extensively both in Philadelphia and in the national press. Sam told me he did not have anything to add to what he has already said on the subject—which I totally understand.

I also want to explain this in a way that even non–sports fans can understand. See, Sam and Daryl had spent a lot of time studying the ways you could turn a program around. (I've had long discussions with Daryl about it, too. The way they analyze things is fascinating.) If your team is in a particularly tough spot, the only way to turn around an NBA franchise is to shed your current talent, improve your salary cap room, let your young players have tons of playing time, and use your draft picks wisely. This means sacrificing the chances of winning in the short term for the chance to win big down the road.

That was Sam's plan. And like any good entrepreneur or businessperson, he told all his constituents—the fans, the media, team sponsors and partners: "It's about the long term, not the short term. You've got to stay with me on this." He wrote open letters to the fan base explaining his plan. The rebuilding effort was dubbed "The Process," as in "trust the process," which became a popular meme at the time.

Sam's strategy led to three of the worst seasons in the history of the NBA.

But it also led to drafting Joel Embiid, who has become one of the best players in the league. Embiid has been an All Star seven times. Twice, he's led the NBA in scoring. In 2023, he was the league MVP. But Sam was not in Philadelphia for any of that.

After nearly three seasons of losing, the ownership cut ties with Sam. Sam's resignation letter, which quickly made its way to the internet, was truly epic. Clocking in at seven thousand words, the letter is a manifesto, combining introspection, philosophical reflection, and strategic advice—highlighting Sam's analytical approach to team building, leadership, and life. He openly discussed mistakes, viewing them as opportunities for growth rather than as setbacks. He argued passionately for a forward-looking perspective: "The longest view in the room always wins." He championed intellectual humility: "I hope to continue learning forever." He used a quote often attributed to Abraham Lincoln: "If you give me six hours to cut down a tree, I'll spend the first four sharpening my axe."

Then something interesting happened. Just about the time Sam was pushed out, the team started improving. Joel Embiid was finally healthy—and dominating. The 76ers started winning. A few of Sam's draft picks were suddenly looking like superstars. The next year, Philly vaulted into the top three teams in the Eastern Conference, at one point winning sixteen consecutive games—a moment that felt like it came straight out of the pages of *Moneyball*. They continued to compete at the top of the league for almost ten years. Three down years for seven to ten good years? Most fans would take that trade.

There were some fans who supported him the whole way, holding up signs like: "Now we're stinky, but I trust Hinkie." As the team started winning, more and more fans insisted on giving Sam credit. A few made memes depicting Sam as a martyr. No one was a bigger fan of Sam's than Joel Embiid, the 76ers star player who has become a close personal friend of Sam's. Embiid would often post some variation of "Trust the Process" on social media. He once retweeted Sam with the note: "Trust the process. He died for our sins."

For years, fans begged the 76ers franchise to rehire Sam—despite Sam's insistence during rare public interviews that the chances of his returning to the NBA were "zero." In 2020, though, the 76ers hired Sam's close friend Daryl Morey as president of basketball operations, a clear effort to continue what Sam started.

Personally, I hope Sam never goes back to basketball. It's more legendary that way.

◢

SO WHAT DO you do if you finally have your dream job, then lose it? That was the thesis of a *Sports Illustrated* story about Sam a few months after he left the 76ers. Sam didn't seem angry or bitter, exactly. He knew when he started his journey that a job as the general manager of a sports franchise could be tenuous. He knew there was some personal risk involved with his rebuilding plan. And now he knew he needed to take some time to think about what he wanted to do next.

He moved his family back to the Bay Area and started teaching a few courses at Stanford, including a class about negotiations. He tells his students: "You have two ears and one mouth. Use them in that proportion." Initially, he thought teaching was just something he would do while waiting out his noncompete clause with the 76ers. But Sam found that he really enjoyed it. He loves sharing teaching duties with his old friend Paraag Marathe right across the street from where they had shared burritos twenty years ago.

Sam also used this time to start his pathway toward a *second* dream job. He wanted to be even more intentional about this journey than he was the first time. He ran a series of what he calls "experiments" to see what else he wanted to do next. Sam talked to a few other teams in other sports about how they were doing things. He asked if he could sit in on meetings at private equity firms, to see how that felt. He was invited to sit in on a few partner meetings at venture capital firms, where he could listen to pitches and then listen to the partners debate and talk about them. These meetings were inspiring.

In 2020, Sam raised more than $50 million and launched his own VC firm, called 87 Capital. The name comes from a key moment in Robert Caro's *Means of Ascent,* which recounts Lyndon Johnson's 1948 Senate election victory, which he won by a margin of only eighty-seven votes. (Of course, Johnson went on to become one of the most powerful senators in the country, then vice president, then president.) In true Sam fashion, the firm calls itself "a den for data-driven dreamers." They invest in technology and internet businesses.

I've had the pleasure of knowing Sam for almost a decade now. He is one of the smartest people I know. Sam has been thoughtful and methodical at every stage, even when he was pursuing a career at Bain. He has been lucky enough to find multiple dream jobs, but each has played into his deep fascination with large numbers. He was earnest and direct in reaching out to peers and mentors. He gives back; he teaches, he mentors, he wants to help fellow dreamers.

He has also been willing to work really, really hard every chance he gets. And he has never stopped learning. He wants to know about any new way of thinking, any new statistic that might give new insights. He is a voracious reader, and not just in business or sports. As evidenced by the name of his firm, he reads Robert Caro, too. Sam has a long wall in his home entirely dedicated to books, with thousands of volumes.

These days, Sam sports a sharp salt-and-pepper beard that makes him slightly less recognizable to the people who know him only from his time in Philadelphia. When he talks about his long and winding career journey, he seems happy, content. He stressed to me how much he loves working with the people he works with now. He talks about his firm the way so many people talk about their dream jobs.

"I'm investing money on behalf of other people," he told me. "I like them. I like them a lot. And that is meaningful in ways that I wouldn't have guessed. If one of them calls me, I'm excited to talk. They're not calling me to browbeat me about something. They're not calling me with a dumb idea. They're not calling me with some deadline or something. I know our conversation will be fun and generative. And I didn't always have that with the people I worked for before."

Mostly, he says, he loves being in a world of infinite wins. In the world of sports, you have one winner every year and twenty-nine losers. In the Valley, that is not the prevailing mindset.

"I am surrounded by colleagues and people now that are really abundance-minded and really bright and really curious, and I'm curious about them."

CONCLUSION
IT AIN'T EASY

Nothing in the world is worth having or worth doing unless it means effort, pain, difficulty.

—Theodore Roosevelt

I wrote this book to give readers the permission and courage to pursue a career that will be exciting and meaningful to them. I want fewer people to spend their lives with deep career regrets. But not everyone thinks this way. For a variety of reasons, most of them well-intentioned, many people—parents, guidance counselors, and other authority figures—will try to talk you out of this pursuit. The number one reason they will cite is money. They want you to do well financially, and if you choose to pursue a hard, less traditional path, they will be anxious that you might need to move back home. For people who have chosen the well-trodden path in their own lives, dreaming can appear quixotic, especially when the dreamer is young.

I stand on the other side of these arguments. If you have a deep ambition, passion, and curiosity about a potential career—I want you to go for it. I want this book to be the catalyst that propels you on a journey that will give you lifelong satisfaction and happiness. Life, after all, is a use-it-or-lose-it proposition. Why waste it?

But when I give people advice about their career path, I always include a two-part warning. First, you really need to make sure the passion is truly deep and not just a passing interest. Second, every successful pursuit requires a tremendous amount of hard work. I would not want to leave you with the belief that these principles are an alternative to hard work. Rather, it is the combination of the principles alongside hard work that will lead to success.

It all starts with identifying your key curiosity. James Clear has a simple rule for life that rarely fails: *Optimize for enthusiasm. Make as many choices as you can that leave you feeling energetic and interested. Pay attention to when you have the urge to pursue or participate in something and do more of it.*

After passion comes learning. I want you to become the most voracious learner of anyone in your field, and I want that enthusiasm for learning new things to continue for your entire career. Does that sound exhausting? It will be if you are not truly excited about the field. External learning (learning outside the four walls of your organization) requires true and deep curiosity. Passion and learning are deeply, symbiotically intertwined.

If pursuing this kind of high-metabolism learning feels like work, you will eventually burn out. You need to be so damn curious and driven to learn about a field you aspire to join that spending most of your spare time on it will feel like fun, not work. It is not a coincidence that many of the people I profile in this book turned a hobby into a career.

All of this learning and the inner drive that sustains it will give you an unfair advantage. And that is a good thing. I suspect you have seen this trait in others—people who simply cannot stop talking about a particular subject. They know more about it than anyone else in your friend group. They "bleed" the subject matter. For people like this, the practice of learning feels effortless. This comes with true passion.

If that does not sound like you, keep searching. If you cannot imagine that ever sounding like you, then the path I am describing—the path of relentless dreamers—is probably not for you.

Being successful may also require that you start at the very bottom of an organization. Lorrie Bartlett started as an executive assistant and Jen Atkin started as a receptionist. Their first goal was just to be inside the front door. Danny Meyer left a high-paid sales job and a potential career as a lawyer to take a very low-paying entry-level position in a restaurant. In Hollywood, executives such as David Geffen, Barry Diller, Mike Ovitz, and many others all got their start in the "mail room." David Rensin wrote a book about it—*The Mailroom: Hollywood History from the Bottom Up.* Ironically, this meme has outlived the *actual* mail room. If you want to break in, you have to be willing to take "any job you can get" and do the work.

Achieving your dream job may require taking what feels like excessive risks. It would be hard to outdo Bob Dylan hitchhiking to New York City with just ten dollars in his pocket. This action redefines determination. Jen Atkin moved to Los Angeles with just $300. It would be hard for any parent or adviser to imagine themselves saying, "Yeah Jen, that's a good idea." Sal Khan left a high-paying job in a successful hedge fund to focus on making an impact in learning. He even assumed it would be a nonprofit and told his wife he would "give it a year." Bert "Tito" Beveridge maxed out as many credit cards as he possibly could and may have even cut some corners on the applications. I doubt I would ever encourage someone to load up on credit card debt, but the point is that all these people put everything on the line in pursuit of success.

You will need to be able to endure tough feedback and not let it bring you down or dampen your enthusiasm for the pursuit. When Dylan first received some press about one of his performances, one of the leading folk artists of the time told the writer, "He can't sing, and he can barely play, and he doesn't know much about music at all. I think you've gone off the deep end!" At that same time, Dylan's first record sold only five thousand copies. But he kept going.

Lorrie Bartlett has spoken openly about a horrific event early in her career, when a boss at a talent agency she worked for told her she would not be promoted because she was, in his words, "too fat." Fortunately, her father told her how to use that moment to push even harder. "You're always going to have adversity. You're always going to have people who tell you that you can't do something, right? Your job is to show them that what they think doesn't matter," Bartlett said. "You're going to show them by how you behave, what you do, your work ethic, who you are. You're gonna show them that they're wrong."

When Tito decided to enter the vodka business, he was met with skepticism at every turn. There were no craft distilleries in Texas, and state law required three-tier distribution. He knew none of this when he started, and he refused to let these roadblocks affect him. Like Lorrie's father, he now recommends entrepreneurs to use the negative energy from naysayers as encouragement.

Bartlett's and Tito's stories remind us that if you are determined to succeed and want to rise to the top of your field, you are bound to run into negative feedback and unwelcome comments. It is part of being out on the field competing, and frankly you have to find a way to not let it affect you. One time when I was called out by a competitor, my partner told me, "You know, the opposite of love is indifference." His point was that there were thousands of other people this individual did not take a shot at—clearly they viewed me as a threat or someone of importance. The bottom line is you have to put this stuff in the rearview mirror as fast as possible. If you can turn it into positive energy, great. If not, let it slide off you like water off a duck's back. Do not let other people's words become mental anxiety for you.

In order to succeed, you may need to hustle at a level beyond what you have ever imagined. To my eyes, Tony Fadell's pursuit of a position at General Magic is unprecedented. I have heard no story of anyone trying that hard to pursue a single company. Equally, Bobby Knight's insistence on having a learning discussion with literally the top minds in basketball coaching is nothing short of legendary. Why not start at the top? And he would come to those meetings with a long agenda. What audacity.

But perhaps the story that takes the "hustle" top-prize award for me is Jen Atkin's assault on the famous Paris fashion shows. Jen would fly herself on her own nickel to Paris, would literally sneak in through the back door, and would essentially volunteer to style hair (of course, the talent thought she was hired)—all to have more practice, increase her exposure, and make connections. It's hard for me to imagine the moxie it took to do that.

A final reminder: You will almost assuredly need to endure failure. Jay Sweet's lifelong dream was to be a lyricist—he loved music. After he had dreamed about this for years and years, his good friend who had finally committed to developing music with him shockingly passed away at an early age. Later, after he had invested ample time into developing a thesis on the festival industry, the firm he worked for decided to back away from investing further. This second huge "failure" is what led Jay to proactively pursue the opportunity at Newport, where he is now a living legend.

Perhaps no one likes to talk more about failure than "Tito" Beveridge. Tito shares a document with aspiring entrepreneurs he meets titled "Failure and Success." In it he argues the two are inseparable. Tito believes the best way to put yourself on the path to success is to become comfortable with "failing gracefully." He also believes that you never have more raw energy than immediately after failure. The key is to empower yourself to channel it in a positive way—versus giving up. He also reflects on his own success as the compounding of previous failures:

> Was it easy? Hell no. Did I have failures and setbacks? Hell yes. Did I ever give up or give in? No way. How did I do it? I did it with the wealth of knowledge I had learned studying geology and geophysics along with the can-do oilfield spirit I had developed as a roughneck and running seismic crews. I learned from my failed businesses about cash flow management and employee expenses. I learned how to deal with bureaucratic red tape and regulators in the environmental business, and I learned from the mortgage business about finance and credit. Had I not have had all those failures under my belt I would not be successful today. Period.

It reminds me again of our favorite saying at Benchmark Capital: "Good judgment comes from experience, which comes from bad judgment."

THE PERFECT ANSWER TO THE MOST COMMON PUSHBACK

In March of 2022, I was invited to speak at SXSW on the topic of "Helping Artists Navigate the Modern Internet." I shared the stage with my good friend Tom Gimbel, who most notably managed the lineup for the famous *Austin City Limits* TV series for over thirteen years. We did our best to help young artists sort out the many new trends around representation, digital distribution, social media, and how technology would help lower the cost of music production. It was curiosity in this latter topic that led me to drop in on a different SXSW panel later that day titled "The Bedroom Music Producer Takeover."

Increasingly powerful music production software has enabled very high-quality music to be produced literally anywhere, and metaphorically "in a bedroom." Billie Eilish's brother Finneas produced *When We All Fall Asleep, Where Do We Go?* in his home on Logic Pro. This new reality means that artists no longer need expensive time in an expensive studio to produce world-class music. Quite a shift. One of the panelists that day was Gregg Lehrman, a music industry veteran who, in addition to composing and producing, founded a company called Output that helps these bedroom producers thrive, including even Finneas, who is a customer.

I was surprised to see that the room for the Bedroom Producer panel was packed—standing room only—which was humbling, as it was better attended than my speech earlier that day. As the panel finished, a long line formed behind a single Q&A microphone that sat ready in the aisle between the attendees. Somewhere in that line, a young woman asked a question I have heard hundreds of times, especially as it relates to industries like music. I do not remember her exact words and am therefore paraphrasing, but the very prototypical question was something like this: "I really want to have a career in the music industry. It's the favorite thing in my life. I am very passionate about it. *But*—everyone I talk to, including my parents, says it's just too hard to make money, to hold a *real* career in the music industry. They say I should get a real job and just have music as a hobby."

Gregg immediately jumped in to answer, and when I heard his answer I knew I would want to share it here in this book. Gregg's answer went something like this: "I know everyone says that. I have heard it my whole life. But I have a different point of view. I have never met a single person that was willing to put in the long days and do the hard work and dedicate themselves to the industry that wasn't able to find a job. I am not saying they all got rich, but they all found careers in a business they love. Every single one of them."

My number one objective for writing *Runnin' Down a Dream* was to give everyone as much permission and as much confidence as they need to pursue a career they love. I know what many smart, pragmatic, and well-intentioned people may have told you—that you should focus on good-paying jobs in classic industries where the risk is low. But just as Gregg did that day at SXSW in Austin, I hope to reprogram the classic advice that work must be work and hobbies must be hobbies and that it is best to keep those separate. It can be different. You can make a career, and even thrive, in a job you truly love.

Life is a use-it-or-lose-it proposition—how do you want to use yours?

EPILOGUE

THE VENTURE CAPITALIST (MY STORY)

A few years ago, as my venture capital career began to wind down, I started to ponder "What comes next?" I had often thought of writing a book, but I had no interest in writing a book about myself or the venture industry. I was, however, quite enthusiastic about writing *this* book.

I have always been fascinated by the elements of success. Much of my reading over the years has been directed toward the stories of people who achieved great things. It appears to me that our society overweights good fortune versus intentional hard work and methodical process. I have also observed that too often, young people's ideas for interesting careers are deemed nonstarters by parents and advisers, and perhaps that should not be the case. I wanted both to help people believe in a future they might have thought impossible or low probability and give them the tools to make that dream a reality.

When I began speaking with book agents and publishers about this idea, the vast majority were hell-bent on my writing about my own career instead, a "how-to" book for venture capital, or even worse, some type of memoir. Fortunately, I found my way to an agent and a publisher who understood my motivations and inspiration for writing *this* book.

I did not intend at the outset of this project to write about myself. But as my cowriter and I interviewed hundreds of people to learn about their own "dream job" pathways, I slowly became convinced that including my own story here at the end would add to the book and not take away from it. When asked about their careers, some successful people demur entirely with false humility (and I understand why), stating, "It was all luck" or "I am just so fortunate." But this approach is much less helpful to others, as we have no way of learning from an untold story.

So, in the spirit of Principle Six—"Always give back"—here is the story of my own journey. In it, you will find echoes of each principle you have read about in the preceding chapters.

I grew up in the town of Dickinson, Texas, which is nestled along I-45 about halfway between Houston and Galveston. My father had chased his own dream job, becoming an early employee of NASA, which had necessitated moving from Virginia to Houston. He had fallen in love with gas-powered model airplanes as a child, and he parlayed this fascination into an aeronautical engineering degree at NC State, graduating in 1958. After a short stint working in air tunnels at Langley Air Force Base, he was recruited to join the Manned Spacecraft Center (now Johnson Space Center) in Houston in 1961. Johnson Space Center was eventually moved to Clear Lake, Texas, which is right next to Dickinson. I would speculate that half the families in our neighborhood were connected to NASA. It was "in the water," as they say.

Like many before me, I became fascinated with computers at an early age. I also benefited from the fact that my lone sibling, my sister Beth, was quite skilled in math and science. While I was playing with my Commodore Vic-20 hooked up to an old black-and-white television, she was off at Rice University majoring in electrical engineering.

She would go on to be an early employee at fast-rising Compaq Computer Corporation. I have no doubt that my father's journey—being willing to take risks and move across the country—and my sister's—joining an early-stage venture-backed start-up in the PC industry—were both critical influences in my life. Both of them gave me permission to think bigger and bolder than I might have otherwise. I am deeply grateful for that.

I would eventually graduate from the University of Florida with a computer engineering degree. It was a hybrid of hardware and software engineering, giving me useful experience with both coding and electrical engineering. While at Florida I also clung to the end of the roster of the men's basketball team. Being even a small part of a top level D-1 athletics program had a big impact on me. I was exposed to a level of hard work I might not have been otherwise, juggling my classwork with three to four hours a day of practice and training. I also spent every day with people who were having a very high level of success early in their adult lives (two of our teammates would go on to have lengthy careers in the NBA). I realized that if I wanted to be successful at a similar level I would need to be in a different lane, where I could develop my own competitive advantage.

While I was at Florida, I became part of a close group of friends who were a combination of people from the basketball team and some industrial engineering friends of my teammate Joe Lawrence. After college, we began meeting once a year, starting with gambling trips to the famous Horseshoe Casino in Vegas, where we would try not to be noticed "counting cards" playing single-deck blackjack. I have always had a fascination with gambling and the analytics, strategies, and concept of "edge."

Looking back, I think this group of friends were quite inspirational to each other. We saw each other start to amass wins, and it pushed all of us to work hard. Joe and his brother Pat would go on to build very successful careers in the wealth management business. Joe would precede me to both MBA school and New York City, "lighting the path," if you will. Our friend Eric Gies would fly navy jets in the Gulf War before entering the investment world. Eric Poms, my roommate and manager of the basketball team, would go on to become CEO of the Orange Bowl, a role he has held for two decades. Rodney Rogers would start not one but two venture-backed companies. He sold the second one, Virtustream, for $1.2 billion and eventually would go on to work for Michael Dell. Not bad for a rat pack of college "drinking buddies."

AFTER COLLEGE I had a choice of joining IBM or Compaq, where my sister had helped me secure an internship the summer before graduation. When I visited the two it became a bit of a no-brainer choice. IBM was slow, calculated, and stodgy. Compaq was none of those things. I wanted to work where people wore jeans and T-shirts and had fun. They also offered me more money in a town with a lower cost of living. This was one of the easier choices I made along the way.

The name Compaq is a bit lost in time now, but back then it was the most "disruptive" tech start-up in the country. We were challenging IBM as a "clone" PC company, but rather than attacking from the low-cost flank, we were attacking on the high-performance flank. This made the journey much more exciting. I was fortunate to be placed under a gentleman named Bill Hanlon, who was without a doubt the first career "mentor" I had outside of my sister. Bill gave me bigger and bigger opportunities each and every day and would express sheer joy when I (and I am sure others) solved problems. I can still picture his smile.

After working for Bill, I would join another team at Compaq led by Wayne Flournoy. This team was known as a "firefighter" group that worked to bring new projects to market. It sat between the product engineering team that designed new products and the test team that made them fail. We were tasked with figuring out what was going wrong—a perfect match for my degree that blended knowledge of hardware and software. Because the launch of products was held up by our "debugging" efforts, my team was often at the center of attention. As a result, we would often work sixteen-hour days, living off pizza when staring down a critical bug. I loved those long days—especially the moment we were able to solve the key problem that was delaying product launch.

In that group, I met the first peer who would meaningfully influence my career: Gary Thome. At the time, no one would have considered Gary to be my peer because he was one of the hottest rising stars in the company. However, I appreciated that he would always take the time to help others learn and understand. This contrasted with some who were sharp-elbowed and territorial. Gary is top-percentile bright, has a near-photographic memory, and is genuinely kind. I am grateful to have worked with him for a short time. He would go on to spend thirty-two years at Compaq/HP.

Outside of work, I had developed a casual interest in the stock market. I had read Peter Lynch's book *One Up on Wall Street* and found it fascinating. I had also purchased the Value Line subscription, a loose-leaf binder that had one-pagers on every stock. They would occasionally send you updated pages in the mail. I would trade stocks over Prodigy, an early internet precursor to AOL, and even bought the stock of software company Borland the day of its IPO. I was in love with their products—both Quattro Pro and their programming tools like Turbo Pascal.

After two years of work at Compaq, I was also offered stock options for the first time as part of my compensation, and I noticed that managers had way more of these than the engineers. As I pored through the industry trade magazines, it was dawning on me just how big the tech world was becoming outside the walls of Compaq.

As I began work on my third project at Compaq, a restlessness came over me. This project felt a lot like the first two, and this level of repetition was less exciting than what I was learning about outside of work. I wanted to pursue something broader than engineering and felt that an MBA would give me the opportunity to explore a richer set of choices. My teammate from Florida Joe Lawrence had jumped from engineering to an MBA, and he gave me confidence that this opened up the right kind of opportunities. I began work on MBA applications, and starting in the fall of 1991, with only two years and change under my belt as an engineer, I moved to Austin and enrolled in the McCombs School of Business. This all seemed quite natural to me.

It was in business school that I really developed a thirst for reading. In grade school and college, I had a distaste for it. I do not really know why, but perhaps it links to passion. Suddenly, I found business books that I could not put down. Unlike the engineering world, the problems had no "one right answer." Also, the stakes appeared higher. The decisions were more grand and consequential. Reading about them did not feel like work—it felt effortless and fun.

While at McCombs I was heavily influenced by two faculty. The first was a man named Jim Fredrickson. Jim is the single best professor I have encountered. He had complete command of the classroom. Always dressed impeccably in suit and tie, he demanded both preparation and attention. The class, corporate strategy, embodied all the questions that would become paramount in the rest of my career. I was drawn to his office hours for extra debate. I also took an entrepreneurism class from E. Lee Walker. Lee was the former president of Dell and an active venture capitalist. He also looked me in the eye at six foot nine. Lee told stories about the early days of Dell that felt like a hero's journey. I was taking it all in—hook, line, and sinker, as they say.

I toyed with the idea of becoming a venture capitalist while at McCombs. I wish I could remember when I first heard the term *venture capitalist,* but I was interested in investing, and it struck me as the ultimate job in the field. It seemed to be at the perfect intersection of technology, investing, gambling, business, and corporate strategy. From my obsessive reading I knew the right thing to do was to land a few information interviews, so I did. I ran into more skepticism than enthusiasm, as well as the unhelpful advice of "Go work for twenty years," so I put these plans on ice for a bit. A second idea that had crept into my mind was inspired by the pages of *Fortune, Forbes,* and *The Wall Street Journal,* which I also had started reading enthusiastically. I noticed that the sell-side tech analysts (analysts who wrote reports on individual companies for Wall Street firms) at Goldman Sachs were frequently quoted as experts on their respective industries. Dan Benton, Rick Sherlund, and John Levinson were all "axes" on the stocks they covered, and everyone knew what they said mattered.

Enamored with this Goldman team, and having recently read Michael Lewis's classic finance tale *Liar's Poker,* I now set my sights on Wall Street. (It's interesting to note that Lewis intended for *Liar's Poker* to be a book about why you *shouldn't* go to Wall Street. He finds it ironic that so many people like me read it and had the opposite reaction.) Borrowing techniques from books I had read, I knew the right thing to do was to show up cold in New York City to knock on doors and ask for meetings. I was skeptical of the formal interviews offered on campuses. I scheduled a week in the big city, and, by cold-calling, I was fortunate enough to grab a meeting with Levinson and Benton. While this did not lead to an opening at Goldman, it did kindle my enthusiasm. Luckily, I also called around to other banks and booked a half-dozen other meetings, including one with Al Jackson, the head of equity research at Credit Suisse First Boston.

This meeting with Al proved fortunate for two reasons. First, Al liked taking chances on young new hires, especially those with an athletic background. He felt that working hard, practicing, and competing in athletics were transferable skills into the workplace. Second, CSFB and one other firm had a "trial by fire" strategy of letting brand-new MBA hires become full-fledged analysts on day one. You would not spend years and years as a backup hoping one day to ascend to the top spot. You had to sink or swim right away. Al Jackson gave me the big break that I needed.

During my first week in New York City, I met a mentor who would have a profound impact on my career. Charlie Wolf was a larger-than-life Columbia professor turned equity analyst. He had an amazing smile and a uniquely charming personality, and he flat-out loved to talk about stocks. When I arrived, he was an institutional investor ranked analyst covering the PC industry, the one industry that I knew from my background. Shortly after I joined, I heard a rumor that Charlie was considering moving to a mentor role in the equity research department and might give up his direct analyst coverage.

While I did not know what industry Al would assign to me, I would obviously be super excited (and advantaged) to have the chance to cover the industry I already knew. Without any directive from the firm, I spent the entire weekend locked in my walkup brownstone apartment writing a "PC Industry Analysis Report" of about twenty pages. That Monday I surprised Al and Charlie with the document, stating, "If the rumor is true, I would be honored and thrilled to pick up coverage of the PC sector." It worked. Within months, I was on a plane flying back to Houston to meet with the CFO at Compaq, the company where I formerly worked as an engineer.

I had another breakthrough early in my career that I attribute to all the business books I read during my MBA program. During the orientation we would do rotations with other groups in the business, including sales and trading. As I met with each member of the sales team, they made it quite clear that our true customers were the "buy-side" accounts—the mutual funds, hedge funds, and endowments that trade stocks each day. This gave me another idea: What if I learned how to optimize my career by talking directly to the customer? I asked each sales representative if each of them would find me one customer to whom I could naively ask questions to kick-start my career. Perhaps surprised that anyone would ask this, everyone complied, and I made a list of twenty or so questions, all on the theme "How can I help you the most?"

I learned so much during those calls, and I also believe I kick-started my relationship with each of these accounts with a clear understanding that I was there to serve them. One of the questions I asked was "Who do you like in the PC sector and why?" Two of the obvious answers were Dan Benton and Charlie Wolf (luckily I already knew both of them!), but they would all mention a third person, David Korus. David covered the PC industry for Kidder Peabody and was the third-ranked analyst alongside Dan and Charlie. Why did they like David? First, he was radically outspoken in his critique of the industry. Many analysts needed to curry favor with companies to protect banking interests. This conflict was well understood by the buy side, which differentiated David even further. Kidder wouldn't do any banking in the sector, but the buy side adored David for being fearless. David also expressed his views on the industry in an atypical weekly "fax" that he sent to clients.

Within my first year or so as an analyst, David and Dan would both move on from the sell side into more exciting investing jobs on the buy side. The top three—David, Dan, and Charlie—had all left the scene, which was fortunate for me. Also, I had built a friendship with each of them, despite being "competitors." These "peers" would each share with me their financial models and thoughts about covering the industry. Two weeks after David left the scene, I launched my own *Above the Crowd* newsletter—initially distributed via fax—an idea clearly borrowed from David. This newsletter would become a defining element of my career.

Yet another person at CSFB would have a profound impact on my life and career—Michael Mauboussin. Michael was a few years ahead of me at CSFB and interestingly covered the food sector—seemingly far removed from PCs and technology. But Michael had a deep curiosity about investing and business and was close with Charlie Wolf. Michael and I would frequently share stories, books, and ideas. Michael introduced me to new analytical frameworks (such as ROIC, return on invested capital) and some super smart clients too, like the legendary investor Bill Miller. Though we worked together for only three years, I have maintained a lifelong learning friendship with Michael. He has gone on to author numerous investing books and is considered one of the sharpest minds in the field. We also share a common interest in the Santa Fe Institute, along with Bill Miller.

Armed with Michael's new tool, I applied ROIC analysis to all the players in the PC industry. I was surprised by the results. One company—Dell Computer—stood out profoundly from the other companies in the sector. Their cash flow conversion cycle was simply way better, and you could link it back to how they built PCs to individual custom order. Because they never built to inventory, only to preorders, they had near-zero finished-goods inventory. This meant less of the company's capital was tied up in the business, which was the key contributor to the high ROIC.

Despite this, their stock was under pressure because of an option hedging strategy gone bad (if you aren't a finance person, don't worry—the details aren't important) and a notebook product that had unexpectedly caught on fire (I mean, literally, going up in flames). This left their stock depressed, trading at something like six times earnings. The bottom line: Dell was a very low price stock with an unnoticed ROIC advantage.

Armed with confidence from the ROIC analysis, and with the support of Charlie and Michael, I initiated coverage of Dell with a "strong buy" recommendation, a very rarely used sell-side technique. Fortunately for me, the analysis was spot-on—Dell did have a durable competitive advantage apparent in its financials. The stock price would go on to advance over 100X in the public markets, thanks to the leadership of Michael Dell and his amazing CFO Tom Meredith. This all left many buy-side clients like Bill Miller quite pleased, as well as the sales team. I would add both Michael and Tom to my mentor/peer connections, and I consider both friends today.

There is one more CSFB story worth mentioning. Charlie arranged for me to be invited to the famous Agenda Conference in Arizona, hosted by Stewart Alsop. This conference was the epicenter of high-tech business. Nearly all the key executives, including Michael Dell, Bill Gates, Steve Jobs, and Larry Ellison, were there. It so happened that this particular year, Palm was launching the Palm Pilot. This unconnected "PDA" was essentially a digital Rolodex. They were selling them in the lobby of the conference, and I noticed one extra perk—they came loaded with all the attendees' contact information—including fax numbers. I'm not sure what gave me the gumption to do this, but I quickly procured the device and the very next week spammed the top 350 executives in the high-tech industry with my *Above the Crowd* newsletter. Some have said that "distribution is key," and if so, I was now perfectly distributed.

I had found quick success as a PC sell-side analyst. My second year I made the II All-Star list (partially thanks to Charlie, Dan, and David leaving the scene), and though CSFB was not strong in high-tech investment banking, I was able to work on the IBM-Lotus merger, which was exciting. All that said, as I rounded year three, I knew this was not my dream job. It was thrilling, and I had access to the best minds in the industry, but I simply could not imagine doing it for twenty more years. So I started to put out feelers.

I WAS PRETTY far down the process to join the highly respected buy-side team at Capital Group in Los Angeles when I received a call out of the blue from a gentleman named Frank Quattrone. Frank was a legendary high-tech investment banker in the heart of Silicon Valley who had just shocked Wall Street by leaving Morgan Stanley and attaching himself to the much lesser-known Deutsche Morgan Grenfell. I immediately called Roger McNamee, who was a client at Integral Capital Partners on Sand Hill Road. His advice: "You must take this meeting."

Frank was eager to build an A-plus team of sell-side analysts, and he was curious to see if I would be interested in joining his team. Of course I had a problem: I had mentally decided to move on from this career. So I delicately explained this to Frank. He then asked me a profound question: "What is your dream job?" I immediately thought back to that initial spark from my days at McCombs. "I have always dreamed of being a venture capitalist," I responded.

Frank quickly replied, "Come work for me. I will move you to Silicon Valley, and I will introduce you to every VC I know." And he knew them all. With this pitch (along with a substantial salary increase), I would soon be leaving New York and headed to California.

It is important to convey that I never once had any regrets about my undergrad degree, my two years as an engineer, or my three years in New York City. Even though they did not turn out to be my "dream job," I viewed them all as exciting learning experiences and stepping-stones. I still appreciate having a technical start. Being in the center of Wall Street in New York City was an exhilarating experience that I cherish to this day. And perhaps most importantly, it was in New York City that I met my future wife, Amy. We have three wonderful children and have been together for over twenty-five years.

I would only spend thirteen months working with Frank at DMG. In this short window of time, I switched industries—I decided to cover the "internet" instead of PCs to move closer to what was new and current. We were also fortunate enough to compete for and win the lead underwriting position on the Amazon IPO, edging out Morgan Stanley and Goldman Sachs. Jeff Bezos was confident enough to bet on a somewhat brandless investment bank, but one with the most experienced banker in the land in Frank. I also now had developed yet another critical relationship in Jeff Bezos, who would become a mentor and supporter throughout my career.

People always ask if I knew what Jeff would accomplish back then. If I had known, I would have put my life savings into the stock. Also to this day, I find it a fun trivia question to ask people, "Who was lead-left on the Amazon IPO?" Very few can muster up the name DMG.

Frank overdelivered on his promise, and I quickly received an offer to join a VC firm. I said yes immediately and joined Hummer Winblad in 1997, not long after the Amazon IPO. Ann Winblad was a super famous software investor and John Hummer was interestingly a six-foot-ten former NBA player. We hit it off immediately, and I am still close friends with John today. About two weeks after the announcement of me joining Hummer Winblad, I ran into Andy Rachleff, one of the Benchmark Capital founders, at a conference. "Why didn't you call us!" he asked when our eyes first met. Frank had indeed introduced me to many VC firms, and I had done multiple meetings at Benchmark. I was so eager to enter the VC world and considered it so rare to have an offer, I had not considered there were multiple options available.

After about a year and a half, I did eventually land at Benchmark. VC was my "dream job," but it turns out Benchmark was my "dream firm." Andy, Bruce Dunlevie, Bob Kagle, and Kevin Harvey had cofounded an unusual "equal partnership" VC firm, after seeing the downside of traditional hierarchical partnerships. On day one, I was given equal economics with the hottest team on Sand Hill Road.

More importantly, one key reality of an equal partnership is the built-in incentive for everyone to take an active interest in each other's success. There were no competitive elbows—only direct and sincere advice and help. I immediately had four amazing mentor/peers in venture capital. This unstructured but highly performant model was a perfect fit for me.

I joined Benchmark at the peak of the dot-com bubble, which

means after less than twelve months of market bliss, I was enduring the dot-com crash. In many ways this made the job much harder, and it certainly led to what many would consider "grindy, difficult" years. But I think it was a better environment for learning and doing true company building. The peaky times in venture capital like the dot-com boom are quite sporadic and unsustainable.

Over the next five years I would find my footing as a venture capitalist. The companies I invested in began to experience liquidity events. First a few companies were acquired, but eventually several of the companies would file for their own IPOs. After a few handfuls of liquidity events, most competitive VCs set their sights on finding a "big one"—one of the companies that truly changes the world and becomes quite valuable on Wall Street—a "home run" type outcome. They are hard to plan for or make happen, but I would fortunately find such an opportunity with Uber.

◢

I WOULD GO on to serve for over twenty-five years in my dream job at Benchmark. We would add other partners that I also had a chance to learn from—people like Dave Bierne, Alex Balkanski, Peter Fenton, Mitch Lasky, and Eric Vishria. I loved every aspect of the work. I loved dissecting high-tech business strategy and technology disruption. I loved defending and promoting our companies to the external world. And I truly loved the investment part: putting capital to work behind your ideas, and seeing it work, all while working with some of the best people in the businesses.

Somewhere in the past few years, after working with some of the most amazing companies and amazing entrepreneurs in the business, I realized it was time for me to "declare victory" and leave the highly competitive field of venture capital. It also was a very peaceful decision. First, I had accomplished everything I aspired to in the field.

Second, I knew this business bends to youth, and it was time to move out of the way. Last, it was time for me to start giving back.

This book is a key part of that new journey.

Do something you really like, and hopefully it pays the rent. As far as I'm concerned, that's success.

—Tom Petty

ACKNOWLEDGMENTS

It is imperative that I begin by recognizing and thanking my cowriter—fellow Texan Michael Mooney. Over the past three decades, I have developed a deep passion for the art of great nonfiction writing. I constantly check the Longreads website, which is a wonderful resource. At some point years ago, I stumbled upon a 2012 article in *D Magazine* titled "The Most Amazing Bowling Story Ever." I am not going to tell you what is in the story (you should read it), but the author of that article was Michael Mooney. And it is still one of my favorite pieces of nonfiction writing. I shared it widely and still do.

Years later, around 2021, I would receive a direct message on Twitter from this very same Michael Mooney. I "followed" him after reading the bowling story. And it turns out he had just seen the YouTube video of my University of Texas presentation of *Runnin' Down a Dream.* He also attended Texas and found the content compelling. I mentioned I might turn it into a book, and before you know it we were completing each other's sentences. I felt I needed a cowriter, due to my other commitments, and I knew then and there—it had to be Michael.

From that first meeting to the book finally being published would turn out to take close to five years. Michael and I so much enjoyed researching the stories (as well as just catching up on current affairs) that we would frequently expand the scope of the project, or come up with four more people we should talk to versus actually starting to write. We were having too much fun. Luckily, we found a way to eventually land the plane.

Through the entire process, it was very clear to me that Michael understood exactly what we wanted to accomplish with the book. That alignment has been amazing. I cannot thank Michael enough.

Eventually I began the search for a literary agent. I am fortunate to have met many great writers over the years. One of them introduced me to a lawyer who recommended I speak to Elyse Cheney at the Cheney Agency. As part of this process, I spoke to probably five or six other agents. When I pitched the idea of a book about finding your dream job, every single one of them (except Elyse) tried to spin me into writing a book about myself, or venture capital, or Uber. I guess they didn't want to bet on a VC writing a self-help book. Elyse never wavered. She was 100 percent behind the idea—which I still greatly appreciate.

Next was the search for a publisher. I ended up flying to New York City and doing a "pitch-off." As a VC, I am way more accustomed to being on the other side of the table, but I obviously could see the similarity to a founder pitching an investor. But now, I was the one pitching. As with the agent search, many publishers wanted the VC industry deep dive—which is not what I was selling.

I had several great meetings and started a follow-up process with a handful, but then something unexpected happened. Paul Whitlatch, a senior editor at Crown Currency (part of Penguin Random House), sent me a letter pitching why he should be the one to edit the book and why his firm should be the one to publish it. If they would allow me, I would put Paul's letter right here in the book after the Acknowledgments. It was *so* good. He made it clear that he had a deep understanding and appreciation for the purpose and goal of the book—rooted in the fact that he had found his own dream job and that the path was not straightforward. It was a "close" that rivaled the best I had seen in investment banking or venture capital!

Alongside Paul, I've been fortunate to work with other talented members of the Crown Publishing Group, including David Drake, Gillian Blake, Tara Gilbride, Mason Eng, Coalter Palmer, and Keely Brewer.

We were on our way. I am deeply grateful that we had a team that was so aligned and willing to share the same goal, purpose, and hopeful impact on the world.

I WANT TO share another story that was crucial to this project ever seeing the light of day. A few years back, I was invited to a bespoke conference called "Powwow" that Chris Sacca held in the Montana mountains. He would invite a small group of people (fewer than fifty) from a wide variety of backgrounds. We would debate the key topics of the day, while also enjoying the great outdoors.

At that conference, Chris introduced me to Brian Koppelman, the famous producer who did the movie *Rounders* and the TV series *Billions*. After chatting for some time, Brian asked me if I had worked on anything creative. I mentioned the presentation and he said, "You have to turn that into a book!" For those who know Brian, he takes great pride in encouraging creativity in others, and he was very insistent that this was something I needed to do. I'm not sure I would have taken the idea seriously without his nudge. And now Brian is acting on *The Bear*—so he even pushes *himself* to try new things.

While the book was still in its early stages, my friend Tony Fadell released his book *Build*. He also became a catalyst for me to move forward. "It's the best thing I have ever done—you have to do it! When will it be finished?" Special thanks to Brian for sparking the idea and Tony for pushing me to finish.

I also want to thank James Clear for finding the original YouTube video and promoting it. Knowing that a legend in the field like James found the material compelling was very confidence inspiring.

Last, special thanks to Malcolm Gladwell, who gave me some structural advice early in the development of the book. Moving from a one-hour presentation to a 250-page book was nontrivial, and his advice was a huge unlock for Michael and myself.

WE SPOKE TO a number of people as part of planning and researching the book. Early on, Malcolm connected me with Joseph Fridman, a book researcher. Joseph helped me and Michael dig through an enormous number of academic papers on career happiness and success. He even connected us with several professors. We spoke with Ryan Duffy at the University of Florida and Amy Wrzesniewski, one of the top voices in the country on the "meaning of work."

These conversations led to our doing an internet survey that showed an amazingly high percentage of people with career regret. As we dug deeper on this issue, I reached out to Dan Gilbert, who introduced us to Adam Grant at the Wharton School of Business. This led to our partnering with Wharton People Analytics and eventually connecting with Angela Duckworth. During this process, Amy Wrzesniewski would join that same department from Yale. Special thanks to everyone at Wharton, especially Laura Jane Zarrow, Matthew Bidwell, and Reb Rebele, who helped drive the research that we would eventually use in the book.

AS WE WORKED on the key stories for the book, several very important and busy people took the time to share their detailed stories with us. I am forever grateful to Danny Meyer, Lorrie Bartlett, Jen Atkin, Chris Del Conte, Scott Stricklin, Greg Byrne, Jimmy Donaldson (MrBeast), Tony Fadell, Dee Gardetti, Jay Sweet, Sal Khan, Tito Beveridge, and Sam Hinkie. I have high confidence that these stories will be inspiring to others, and I cannot thank you enough for taking the time to share them. We would call back many of you not just once or twice, but perhaps even a third or fourth time. Thanks for your patience.

FOR OVER TWENTY YEARS, I've had the privilege of working with the same extraordinary personal assistant, Amie Fineberg. It's impossible to count the number of times people have said to me, "Your assistant is amazing." Amie has a remarkable ability to tackle any problem—no matter how daunting or how trivial—and always find a solution. She also has a uniquely deft touch with people, an invaluable skill in venture capital that proved equally essential in writing this book. Amie, I am incredibly grateful for your unwavering help and support over these many years. I know, without question, that my success and every accomplishment along the way have been made possible in part by you.

From a personal perspective, I owe an unlimited amount of thanks to my parents—John and Lucia Gurley. We lost my mother, Lucia, to Parkinson's in 2022. Throughout her life, she always embraced new adventures, and I know she would have been proud to see this book and new direction for me. As I wrote in the book, my father was the first person I saw up close who chased a dream job—moving from a rural farm in North Carolina all the way to Houston to be an early part of NASA. I could see what that meant to him and his peers. Also, my sister made it look easy to go from high school to college to a top engineering role at one of the hottest companies in the high-tech industry. Thanks to both of you for paving the way for me to follow.

Last, and most important, I want to thank my amazing wife, Amy. We are two native-born Texans who serendipitously met in Manhattan, spent twenty-five years raising a family in Northern California, and recently started a new empty-nest adventure in Austin, returning to our roots. Our life together has been one amazing adventure after another—so much so that it seems surreal. Thank you for being my lifelong partner and for always having my back. I love you.

Together, we have had the privilege of raising three wonderful young adults who are early in the process of identifying and chasing their own dreams. We wish them the best of luck and unlimited love and support along the way.

BILL'S BOOK LIST

The nonfiction books listed below have profoundly influenced not only the writing of *Runnin' Down a Dream* but also my broader career journey. While I've intentionally omitted fiction titles (though my shelves feature plenty of Cormac McCarthy and Larry McMurtry), please don't mistake their absence as a lack of interest. My hope is that you'll discover valuable insights and inspiration from these books, just as I have.

BOOKS ASSOCIATED WITH THIS BOOK

These books had a huge impact on me either in terms of inspiring the work (the three biographies) or in terms of helping us think about shaping and organizing the framework.

Setting the Table: The Transforming Power of Hospitality in Business, by Daniel Meyer (2006)

One of the first three books that birthed the idea for *Runnin' Down a Dream*. Danny's book shares the story of his success but also recounts a lifetime of learning about the hospitality business. Lessons for everyone.

Knight: My Story, by Bobby Knight (2002)

I originally read this book as a basketball fan, but I discovered Knight was one of the most ambitious learners you will ever discover (and one who would eventually become an ambitious teacher as well). If you want to attack a new career, do it with the fervor and gumption Knight did.

Chronicles: Volume One, by Bob Dylan (2004)

What I love about this story is how intentional Dylan was. He called himself a "musical expeditionary." One person called him a sponge. He studied, studied, studied. His 2022 book, *The Philosophy of Modern Song,* shows that he has never stopped learning and studying his industry.

Range: Why Generalists Triumph in a Specialized World, by David Epstein (2019)

This second part of *Range* does a deep dive on what I would call external learning and the breakthroughs that come from borrowing far analogies. We mention this in both Principle Two: Hone Your Craft and Principle Four: Embrace Your Peers—encouraging you to step a bit further away from center as you evolve.

Build: An Unorthodox Guide to Making Things Worth Making, by Tony Fadell (2022)

My good friend wrote an amazing book that is partly an account of his historical journey and partly a playbook for new founders. It appropriately expresses Tony's independent spirit. You never dent the world using the traditional strategy.

Blowing My Way to the Top: How to Break the Rules, Find Your Purpose, and Create the Life and Career You Deserve, by Jen Atkin (2020)

Somewhere in our cowriting journey, someone suggested to us that the book that best illustrated our original speech was this one. Jen's rise from next to nothing to the top of her field is awe inspiring.

But in her personal account of that trajectory you see so many bold and intentional steps. They all paid off.

What Color Is Your Parachute?, by Richard Bolles (1970)

This is a great book for anyone who doesn't have confidence about which direction they want to go. Time-tested and worth your time. It may not give you an exact answer, but you will definitely leave with a better perspective and multiple options to explore.

Designing Your Life: How to Build a Well-Lived, Joyful Life, by Bill Burnett and Dave Evans (2016)

Burnett and Evans take a modern approach to helping you find your direction, with less introspection than *What Color Is Your Parachute?* and more prototyping and scenario planning. Many exercises are provided. If you need help with that first step of identifying your core curiosity, I say you must read both books.

Moneyball: The Art of Winning an Unfair Game, by Michael Lewis (2003)

This extremely well-known book that went on to become a blockbuster movie had a big effect on Sam Hinkie, inspiring him to leave Bain and Australia to chase his dream job and completely changing his life.

Grit: The Power of Passion and Perseverance, by Angela Duckworth (2016)

My cowriter Michael and I had the privilege of talking to Professor Duckworth about our book. Her own bestselling book *Grit* drives home the notion that effort can easily beat talent and reinforces this with studies. When you know the path you want to take, *Grit* will give you the tools (and support) you need to give it your all.

Mindset: The New Psychology of Success, by Carol Dweck (2006)

The definitive book on self-driven external learning. Satya Nadella credits this book with changing the culture at Microsoft—which led to perhaps the biggest turnaround story in the history of business. It's impossible to continue to "hone your craft" throughout your career without a growth mindset.

The Power of Regret: How Looking Backward Moves Us Forward, by Daniel Pink (2022)

Our book starts with the finding that over half of the population eventually has career regret and would like a "do-over." Daniel Pink teaches you to put that nagging "regret" voice to work and let it power changes in your life. If you are having trouble with the boldness required to leap toward something new—read this!

Swing Your Sword: Leading the Charge in Football and Life, by Mike Leach (2011)

We mention Mike Leach only briefly in the book, but his spirit was with both of us throughout the entire writing process. We simply love his story and his "way." Mike rose to the top of his dream job by abandoning a legal career and starting over at the very, very bottom. Also, his journey was prototypical of this book: learning widely, connecting everywhere, and leaving a massive mark on the game.

A FEW BOOKS ON WRITING

My cowriter Michael and I are huge fans of modern storytelling in nonfiction writing. We first connected in a conversation where we discussed the key nuances of this writing art form. As a result we agreed that we wanted our book to have a unique structure interleafing profiles with principles. If this interests you, these books might be for you.

The New New Journalism: Conversations with America's Best Nonfiction Writers on Their Craft, by Robert S. Boynton (2005)

This book on using storytelling techniques in modern nonfiction writing is a follow-up to a previous book on the same topic called *The New Journalism,* by Tom Wolfe. The book studies the key elements used by the modern greats of nonfiction writing: Malcolm Gladwell, Michael Lewis, Jon Krakauer, and others. I have read everything those three have written—and their writing has had a major influence on me and this book.

The Storytelling Animal: How Stories Make Us Human, by Jonathan Gottschall (2012)

Gottschall argues that humans are inherently "storytelling animals." He explains the science behind why this is the case and the implications for everyday life.

On Writing: A Memoir of the Craft, by Stephen King (2000)

King's own career could have easily been one of the core stories written in our book. It has all the pieces that we describe. What's great is that he took the time to write a book about the way he writes, and why, and what's important to him. This is a literary classic, a must-read for aspiring writers, and another story that might inspire you to chase a nonobvious career.

GREAT SELF-HELP BOOKS

One thing that kept coming up during our research was that in many cases the people we were studying would go through a time where they read one, two, or maybe more classic self-help books. And in each case, something in one of those books gave them a push in the right direction. I am not saying that every word in every one of these books is perfect. That said, these are the classics and they are on the bestseller list for a reason. Many people have found them very useful in their journey, including me.

How to Win Friends and Influence People, by Dale Carnegie (1936)

Warren Buffett often says, "The most important degree I have is from Dale Carnegie. Without it, I wouldn't be where I am." This is a foundational book about interpersonal skills that is as important today as it was in 1936 when he wrote it.

Move Ahead with Possibility Thinking, by Robert H. Schuller (1967)

An active minister, Schuller believed in the transformational power of what he called "possibility thinking"—the exploration of what could go right. If you aim to shoot for the stars with a new dream job, this attitude shift will likely help.

The Seven Habits of Highly Effective People, by Stephen R. Covey (1989)

Arguably the grandaddy of the category, with over twenty-five million copies sold, *Seven Habits* gives you the tools you need to be successful and to do it in the right way. An important foundational read for anyone.

Awaken the Giant Within: How to Take Immediate Control of Your Mental, Emotional, Physical and Financial Destiny! by Tony Robbins (1991)

Robbins is one of the most successful motivational speakers in the world. He is exceptional at giving you the boost you need to kick it into gear and start doing what you inherently want to do. If you know what job you want to go chase but feel you don't have the gumption or energy to go do it, Robbins's book might be the key.

Atomic Habits: An Easy and Proven Way to Build Good Habits and Break Bad Ones, by James Clear (2018)

If you want to chase your dream job, you will need to be productive and efficient. *Atomic Habits* teaches you how small changes in how you go about your life can make that happen.

Stumbling on Happiness, by Daniel Gilbert (2006)

Some might categorize this book under behavioral psychology, but I've included it here intentionally. If you're going to commit to a long pursuit of your dream job, it's important to ensure that the destination will truly make you happy. Gilbert's book serves as an insightful checkpoint, prompting you to confirm that your goals and values align clearly with the effort you're about to undertake.

Finite and Infinite Games, by James P. Carse (1986)

It is super important to understand whether you are playing a finite game or an infinite one. Most of our perspective about competition and game strategy comes from finite games. Many of the issues you face in life, including your career, are different. And your strategy should reflect that. Always know which is which.

The Creative Act: A Way of Being, by Rick Rubin (2023)

As mentioned earlier in the book, if you intend to chase a dream job in any creative field, this book is a must-read. Rick has a proven ability to maximize the creative output of a diverse set of talented individuals. These are his life lessons that could help you as well.

FAVORITE BOOKS FOR FOUNDERS

I have often been asked what books I recommend for founders. I have settled on these six below and would probably add a seventh with Fadell's Build, except that we have already listed it above in the first section.

The Structure of Scientific Revolutions, by Thomas Kuhn (1962)

Kuhn introduced the concept of "paradigm shifts," describing how science progresses not linearly but through revolutionary shifts in thinking. Such shifts create massive start-up opportunities. A critical book to understand innovation, disruption, and the evolution of ideas.

Competitive Strategy: Techniques for Analyzing Industries and Competitors, by Michael Porter (1980)

Most founders have never taken a business class. You need some structures and frameworks for how to analyze and critique different business decisions and strategies. This is an excellent place to start. A cornerstone read.

Crossing the Chasm: Marketing and Selling High-Tech Products to Mainstream Customers, by Geoffrey Moore (1991)

Moore figured out that there is a classic go-to-market strategy for most start-ups that sell to enterprises (businesses). The key is to attack the first customers first (innovators and first adopters). The trick is to know how to do that correctly and then eventually to cross the chasm. Many start-ups die that don't follow this advice.

The Innovator's Dilemma: When New Technologies Cause Great Firms to Fail, by Clayton Christensen (1997)

Like *Crossing the Chasm,* Christensen's book identified a "truism" that holds for most technology business. The reason that a "start-up" can break in and take share from an "incumbent" is that the incumbent's product gets bloated. This "rotation" around new tech trends is pervasive, but to be successful you have to play it right.

Shoe Dog: A Memoir by the Creator of Nike, by Phil Knight (2016)

The story of Phil Knight and the birth of Nike. So well written. So many great stories. A window into just how many times the company almost didn't make it. In the end a gritty story of business success that should inspire you.

Startup: A Silicon Valley Adventure, by Jerry Kaplan (1995)

We all study successes, and there are plenty in this book—but sometimes it's even more valuable to learn from failure. Go Corp had everything: the best founder, a talented team, and top VCs—but it still didn't succeed. Kaplan tells the story in captivating detail, providing a humbling reminder of how difficult entrepreneurship can be. The silver lining? Most of the individuals involved went on to achieve great things afterward.

BOOKS ON WALL STREET AND INVESTING

I am very happy that my career veered through Wall Street before heading out to Silicon Valley. The experience was thrilling, and I learned a ton along the way. It's a special place with plenty of very smart people. But it's also a place that can rip your head off if you don't know what you are doing. If you want to lean in, being knowledgeable will pay dividends.

The Intelligent Investor, by Benjamin Graham (1949)

Warren Buffett cites this as the most important book on investing written by the man you now know was his key mentor. What else is there to say?

A Random Walk Down Wall Street, by Burton Malkiel (1973)

This is the first book everyone should read before they think about investing. It provides a clear overview of how capital markets function, along with the essential math you need to assess the probability of success between aggressive and more conservative (perhaps even boring) investment approaches.

One Up on Wall Street: How to Use What You Already Know to Make Money in the Market, by Peter Lynch (1989)

This is the book that got me hooked on investing. Super practical and approachable, it gives readers the confidence needed to enter the stock market. However, I still recommend reading *A Random Walk Down Wall Street* first!

Liar's Poker: Rising Through the Wreckage on Wall Street, by Michael Lewis (1989)

Lewis's debut book offers a compelling insider's view of Wall Street. Though Lewis intended it as a cautionary tale, many readers, myself included, were instead drawn to its depiction of the excitement and fast-paced nature of finance.

More Than You Know: Finding Financial Wisdom in Unconventional Places, by Michael Mauboussin (2006)

My good friend illustrates how psychology, philosophy, and science intersect with investing. He skillfully addresses the roles of skill, luck, and behavioral biases in financial decision-making.

The Big Short: Inside the Doomsday Machine, by Michael Lewis (2010)

Another home run by Lewis, this book deeply explores the causes of the 2008–09 financial crisis and the mortgage collapse. It provides an insightful view into how and why Wall Street can be deeply flawed.

Flash Boys: A Wall Street Revolt, by Michael Lewis (2014)

Lewis again exposes imperfections in the American trading markets, this time delving into high-frequency trading and revealing how certain market players created unfair advantages.

Billion Dollar Whale: The Man Who Fooled Wall Street, Hollywood, and the World, by Tom Wright and Bradley Hope (2018)

Simply too captivating to miss. This gripping account chronicles Jho Low's massive fraud involving the Malaysian sovereign wealth fund and the numerous accomplices and high-profile connections he made along the way. It reads even better than fiction.

FANTASTIC BUSINESS BOOKS

Here are a few gems from my collection of favorite general business reads. No matter what industry you're in, and whether you're just gaining momentum or tasting success, these books offer powerful insights and practical wisdom to elevate your game.

Swim with the Sharks Without Being Eaten Alive: Outsell, Outmanage, Outmotivate, and Outnegotiate Your Competition, by Harvey Mackay (1988)

Providing classic negotiation and networking wisdom, this book is a straightforward, highly practical, and foundational read. It can serve as your introduction to sales, negotiation, and management—all things you will need—and can easily be the first business book you read.

Customers for Life: How to Turn That One-Time Buyer into a Lifetime Customer, by Carl Sewell and Paul B. Brown (1990)

I read this in business school. A local Texas car dealership magnate offers lessons for anyone who runs a service business. Really good.

Getting Past No: Negotiating in Difficult Situations, by William Ury (1991)

An essential guide to overcoming difficult negotiations by focusing on empathy, patience, and strategic thinking. Ideal for those frequently navigating complex deals or disputes.

Good to Great: Why Some Companies Make the Leap . . . and Others Don't, by Jim Collins (2001)

A must-read for anyone aiming to understand what separates truly outstanding companies from the merely good. Timeless lessons on leadership, culture, and disciplined management. One of the classics. Valuable to have in your vault.

The Success Equation: Untangling Skill and Luck in Business, Sports, and Investing, by Michael Mauboussin (2012)

Super insightful for understanding the contribution of luck versus skill in success. Essential for decision-makers and investors aiming to sharpen analytical thinking. Great read, as the author covers many different industries.

Negotiating the Impossible: How to Break Deadlocks and Resolve Ugly Conflicts (Without Money or Muscle), by Deepak Malhotra (2016)

This is an advanced-level negotiation course offering modern, sophisticated strategies for your toughest situations. Highly recommended for experienced negotiators or executives facing high-stakes scenarios. Deepak is one of the smartest people I know.

Play Nice but Win: A CEO's Journey from Founder to Leader, by Michael Dell (2021)

As discussed previously, I met Michael in 1994. His success even then was unbelievable, but since then he has continued to grow, pivot, and extend the company. The structure of this book inspired what we did with our own book. Michael alternated chapters between the history of Dell and chapters on his fight with activists for the company. Make sure you listen to the audiobook to pick up on Michael's emotions.

BEHAVIORAL SCIENCE BOOKS

I have always been drawn to behavioral science and behavioral psychology books because they help us understand how our minds actually work, rather than how we think they should work. Armed with this knowledge, you might use totally different approaches in your business and your life. Here are some of my favorites:

Influence: How and Why People Agree to Things, by Robert Cialdini (1984)

The author brilliantly breaks down the psychology behind persuasion, revealing how seemingly insignificant details can significantly influence decisions and behavior. Essential for anyone interested in human behavior and marketing.

The Tipping Point: How Little Things Can Make a Big Difference, by Malcolm Gladwell (2000)

The first of many big hits for Malcolm Gladwell. Explores how small ideas or trends reach critical mass to become major phenomena. Essential for understanding virality, marketing strategies, and consumer behavior.

Blink: The Power of Thinking Without Thinking, by Malcolm Gladwell (2005)

Investigates the power and pitfalls of intuition and rapid decision-making, revealing how our unconscious mind can lead us toward effective—or flawed—judgments.

Predictably Irrational: The Hidden Forces That Shape Our Decisions, by Dan Ariely (2008)

Ariely reveals the surprising ways humans consistently act irrationally, challenging assumptions about rational decision-making. Highly readable, insightful, and often entertaining.

Nudge: Improving Decisions About Health, Wealth, and Happiness, by Richard Thaler and Cass Sunstein (2008)

This powerful exploration of how subtle shifts in framing and choice architecture can lead to significantly better decisions offers actionable insights for policymakers, businesses, and individuals.

Think Twice: Harnessing the Power of Counterintuition, by Michael Mauboussin (2009)

Another insightful read from Mauboussin, this book challenges readers to question intuitive decision-making, highlighting common pitfalls and providing strategies to improve outcomes.

Thinking, Fast and Slow, by Daniel Kahneman (2011)

Kahneman's groundbreaking book explores the dual systems of thought—fast, intuitive judgments versus slow, analytical reasoning—and explains why we make systematic errors in judgment and decision-making. This is now the bible. Long but worth it.

Thinking in Bets: Making Smarter Decisions When You Don't Have All the Facts, by Annie Duke (2018)

Annie Duke, a former poker champion, demonstrates how embracing uncertainty and probabilistic thinking can dramatically improve decision-making in business, investing, and daily life. Her "Always think about it like a bet" is quite provocative.

HOW THE WORLD WORKS

These are some of my favorite books that explore the big picture of how the world operates. They're profound, substantial, and arguably the most important of all the books listed here—but also are among the most challenging to digest.

The Blind Watchmaker: Why the Evidence of Evolution Reveals a Universe Without Design, by Richard Dawkins (1986)

Dawkins describes evolution by natural selection with clarity and precision, arguing persuasively that complexity and order emerge naturally without design. I concur. This is crucial reading for appreciating evolutionary thinking applied broadly across disciplines.

Complexity: The Emerging Science at the Edge of Order and Chaos, by Mitchell Waldrop (1992)

This is my favorite book. It's about the rise of the Santa Fe Institute, where I now sit on the board. No other book has affected me quite the way this one has. The institute and the book study the dynamics of complex multivariable systems. Most important systems are complex and very hard to study and understand. Yet many assume they are simple.

Thinking in Systems: A Primer, by Donella Meadows (2008)

Meadows helps managers understand that their products and services exist within complex systems. Without this understanding, unintended consequences are prevalent. Conversely, fully grasping system dynamics can help identify precise points for effective change.

The Rational Optimist: How Prosperity Evolves, by Matt Ridley (2010), and ***How Innovation Works: And Why It Flourishes in Freedom,*** by Matt Ridley (2020)

These are two of my favorite books, and I recommend you read them in order, one right after the other. Ridley gives us an ultrawide time lens to show how technology spreads and drives prosperity gains. His concept of "ideas having sex" is etched in my brain. I wish every policymaker could be forced to read both of these.

Sapiens: A Brief History of Humankind, by Yuval Noah Harari (2011)

Harari's groundbreaking narrative explores human history, examining how *Homo sapiens* became the dominant species through unique cognitive and social abilities. It also touches on the critical power of storytelling used by many to control large swaths of the population.

Enlightenment Now: The Case for Reason, Science, Humanism, and Progress, by Steven Pinker (2018)

Pinker presents compelling evidence that the Enlightenment ideals of reason, science, and humanism have significantly improved global living conditions. And I am here for it. A critical antidote to pessimism, advocating for continued commitment to rational progress.

INDEX

A

Above the Crowd (Gurley), 212
Abrams, J. J., 79
Acquired (podcast), 29–30
Alexander, Les, 189–90
Alford, Steve, 145
Angelou, Maya, 79–80
Apple, 125, 134
appreciation, expressing, 147–48, 152–55, 157
Ariely, Dan, 236
artificial intelligence (AI), xxii, 64
"the ask," 86–87
Atkin, Jen, 114–23, 198, 200, 226–27
Atkinson, Bill, 125
Atomic Habits (Clear), 28, 80, 230
Auerbach, Red, 140
Awaken the Giant Within (Robbins), 28, 230

B

Babcock, Whit, 96, 97–98
Bain Capital, 184–86
Barker, Ali, 13
Barkley, Charles, 148
Barnett, Charlie, 59–60
Bartlett, Bob, 40, 48
Bartlett, Lorrie, 40–50, 52, 59, 152–53, 198, 199
Beane, Billy, 186, 188
Beard, Chris, 145
Beck, 166
Beck, Simone "Simca," 175–76
Bee, Clair, 140
Benchmark Capital, 78, 201, 216–17
Benton, Dan, 210–12
Bertholle, Louisette, 175
Beveridge, Tito, 26, 180–82, 198, 199, 200–201
Bezos, Jeff, 33, 215–16
The Big Short (Lewis), 233
Billion Dollar Whale (Wright and Hope), 233
Bjork, Ross, 92–93, 95–98
Blaik, Earl "Red," 139
Blanco, Alma, 123

The Blind Side (Lewis), 188
The Blind Watchmaker (Dawkins), 237
Blink (Gladwell), 236
Blowing My Way to the Top (Atkin), 122, 226–27
"Blowin' in the Wind" (Dylan), 73
boldness regrets, 169–70
Bolles, Richard Nelson, 24–25, 227
boredom, 31–32
Boynton, Robert S., 228
Brown, Paul B., 234
Brown, Sam, 14
Bryant, Kobe, 58–59
Buffett, Warren, 56, 75–77, 80
Build (Fadell), 226
Burach, Todd, 34–35
Burnett, Bill, 25, 227
Byrne, Bill, 91
Byrne, Greg, 90–98
Byrne, Nick, 98

C

"career regret," xx–xxii
career(s)
  AI and, xxii
  being in epicenter of, 129–31
  burnout, 31
  college and, xv–xvi, xxi, 24
  false starts, 33
  five-year plans for, 26–27
  giving back and advancing, 150–51
  (as) infinite games, 150
  most important decision in, 23
  on-the-job experience, 5, 6, 8–9, 10–11
  pursuing with intention, xvi–xvii
Carlsen, Magnus, 21–22, 62–63
Carnegie, Dale, 28, 229
Carrey, Jim, 162–63
Carse, James P., 149–50, 230
Chappelle, Dave, 59–60
"chasing your curiosity," 23
Child, Julia, 173–77
Christensen, Clayton, 231
Chronicles: Volume One (Dylan), 226
Cialdini, Robert, 235
Cinema Speculation (Tarantino), 52
Claiborne, Craig, 176
Clancy, Liam, 69–70
Clear, James, 28, 80, 197, 230
Close, Del, 156–57
collaboration, 103–4, 112–13
college, xv–xvi, xxi, 24
Collins, Jim, 234
Columbus, Chris, 79
Compaq, 207–9
Compass Exercise, 26
Competitive Strategy (Porter), 231
Complexity (Waldrop), 237
confidence, 79, 105, 106
consistency and success, 49
Covey, Stephen R., 28, 149, 229
Cranston, Bryan, 151–52
The Creative Act (Rubin), 230
credibility and success, 49, 55
Crossing the Chasm (Moore), 231
Cunningham, Bubba, 96–98
curiosity
  as beginning of learning, 53
  fascination and, 21
  identifying key, 197
  passion and, 84
Currie, John, 92–93, 95–98, 109
Customers for Life (Sewell and Brown), 234

D

Damon, William, 23
Dangerfield, Rodney, 170
Darwin, Charles, 61
Dawkins, Richard, 237
Del Conte, Chris, -88–98, 109
Dell, Michael, 235
Dell Computer, 213–14

Del Rey, Lana, 75
Designing Your Life (Burnett and Evans), 25–27, 227
dislikes, tapping into, 31–32
Donaldson, Jimmy, 99–103, 112
Donati, Jeremiah, 98
Donati, Richard, 89
dream jobs
  Gurley's journey, xvii–xviii, 205–17
  Hinkie's journey, 186–95
  luck and, xiii
  Meyer's journey, 8–17, 52, 57, 59
  relocating for, 127–31, 133–34
Duckworth, Angela, 22–23, 30–32, 62, 337
Duke, Annie, 236
Dunlevie, Bruce, 216
Dweck, Carol, 28, 227
Dylan, Bob, 47–48, 65–74, 198–99, 226

E

87 Capital, 194
Einstein, Albert, 57
Embiid, Joel, 192
Enlightenment Now (Pinker), 238
epicenters of industry, 128–33
Epstein, David, 61–62, 226
Epstein, Theo, 185
Ericsson, Anders, 112
Evans, Dave, 25, 227
experiences, sharing, 153–54
external learning, 57

F

Fadell, Tony, 124–28, 134–35, 200, 226
far analogies, making, 61
Farrelly, Peter, 162–63
fascination
  curiosity and, 21
  finding your, 24–28, 32–33, 181
  hobbies and, 29
  passion and, 21
  perseverance and, 23
  recognition of, 30–31
  sense of purpose as element of, 36
  side hustles and, 29–30
Fedarko, Kevin, 29
Ferriss, Tim, 86
Finite and Infinite Games (Carse), 149–50, 230
Flash Boys (Lewis), 233
Flournoy, Wayne, 207–8
Fracchia, Eugene, 14
Fredrickson, Jim, 154–55, 209
Freeman, Morgan, 170
The Freewheelin' Bob Dylan, 73

G

Gandhi, Mahatma, 56
Gardetti, Dee, 126–27
Gates, Bill, 179
General Magic, 125–27, 134
generosity of time, 152
Gersh Agency, 43–45
Getting Past No (Ury), 234
Gies, Eric, 207
Gilbert, Ben, 29–30
Gilbert, Daniel, xx, 230
Gimbel, Tom, 201
giving back, 147–55, 157
  See also mentors
Gladwell, Malcolm, 112, 235–36
Glover, Tony, 67–68
Good to Great (Collins), 234
Gottesman, Greg, 29
Gottschall, Jonathan, 228–29
Gould, Stephen Jay, 62
Graham, Benjamin, 75–77, 80, 232
Grant, Adam, xx
Grateful Dead, 158–59
Grit (Duckworth), 22, 227
grit, elements of, 22–23, 37, 227

Gurley, Bill
basic facts about, 205–7
books read by, xviii
dream job journey of, xvii–xviii, 205–17
mentors of, 207, 211, 215–16
peer groups of, 206–7, 212, 214
Guthrie, Woody, 68–69, 72, 74

H

Hammer, Jon Ludvig, 63
Hammond, John, 71–72
Hanlon, Bill, 207
happiness and job satisfaction, xxii
Harari, Yuval Noah, 238
Harrison, Philip Arthur, 147–48
Harvey, Kevin, xxiv, 216
Havlicek, John, 137, 139–40
Herman, Tom, 96
Hershberger, Sally, 118
Hertzfeld, Andy, 125
Highlight Artists, 122
Highwomen, 167
Hill, Joe, 71–72
Hinkie, Sam
basic facts about, 183–86
dream jobs, journey of, 186–95
mentors of, 187–88
Holyoak, Keith, 61–62, 111
Hope, Bradley, 233
Hopkins, Anthony, 151–52
Houston Rockets, 189, 190–91
"How (and Why) Athletes Go Broke" (Torre), 35
How Innovation Works (Ridley), 237
How to Win Friends and Influence People (Carnegie), 28, 229
Huffington, Arianna, 170
humility, 149, 152
Hummer, John, 216
Hyler, Joan, 42

I

Iba, Henry, 140
ICM, 45, 48–49
imposter syndrome, 127
Influence (Cialdini), 235
information, power of, 47
The Innovator's Dilemma (Christensen), 231
The Intelligent Investor (Graham), 75–76, 232
intentionality and success, 18

J

Jackson, Al, 210–11
Jackson, Samuel L., 170
job satisfaction, xiii, xxii
Jobs, Steve, 62, 78

K

Kagle, Bob, 216
Kahneman, Daniel, 236
Kaleidoscope Films, 41
Kaplan, Jerry, 232
Kardashian, Khloé, 119
Kardashian, Kim, 119
Kardashian, Kourtney, 119
Kerr, Eric, 29
Khan, Sal, 177–80, 198
King, Stephen, 52, 57, 229
Knight: My Story (Knight), 226
Knight, Phil, 231–32
Knight, Robert Montgomery "Bobby"
basic facts about, 136–38, 145–46, 155, 200, 226
as coach, 138–39, 141–45
on finding your fascination, 33
learning by, 62, 110, 137–38, 141–42
mentors of, 138–42, 145peers and, 139, 140–41
Korus, David, 212
Kroc, Roy, 170

Krzyzewski, Mike, 139, 145
Kuhn, Thomas, 231

L

Langhorne, Bruce, 70
language of chosen field, 54
Lapchick, Joe, 138, 140
Lasseter, John, 56
lateral learning, 62
Lauder, Estée, 171–73
Lawrence, Joe, 206–7, 209
Lawrence, Pat, 206
Leach, Mike, 155–56, 228
Learning
  in areas outside field, 61–62, 141
  curiosity and, 53
  deep and continuous, 52–54, 56–59, 63, 116–20, 124, 137–138, 142, 194, 197
  foundational, 53–59
  from mistakes, 44, 78
  overlooked areas in field, 59–60
  passion and, 197
  setting goals for, 63–64
  See also mentors; peer groups
LeCompte, Andy, 118
Lee, Stan, 170
Lehrman, Gregg, 202
Levinson, John, 210
Lewis, Michael, 186, 188, 210, 227, 233
Liar's Poker (Lewis), 210, 233
Life Design Compass, 26, 36
likes, tapping into, 31–32
Livengood, Jim, 90
losses, analyzing, 50
"loud quitting," xxi–xxii
"Loves and Strengths" career exercise, 26
luck and dream jobs, xiii
Lyell, Charles, 61
Lynch, Peter, 232

M

Macdonald, Kelly, 45
Mackay, Harvey, 234
The Mailroom (Rensin), 198
Malhotra, Deepak, 235
Malkiel, Benjamin, 232
Marathe, Paraag, 187–88, 193
Marshall, George C., 156
Marshall, Tom, 160–61
Martin, William, 37–38
Mastering the Art of French Cooking (Child), 175–76
Matthews, Dave, 115
Mauboussin, Michael, 212–13, 233–34, 236
May, Scott, 143–44
McMillan, Chris, 118
Meadows, Donella, 237
mentors
  examples of, 75–80
  of Gurley, 207, 211, 215–16
  of Hinkie, 187–88
  importance of, 77–79
  of Knight, 138–40, 142, 145
  Knight as, 145–46
  of Meyer, 87
  Newell as, 137, 141, 145
  peer groups compared to, 103
  types of, 80–87
Metcalfe's Law, 111
Meyer, Daniel
  basic facts about, 198, 225–26
  characteristics, 18–19
  dream job journey of, 8–17, 52, 57, 59
  mentors and, 87
Meyer, Ray, 138
Microsoft, 58
Middle-Aged ADs, 95–98, 109
Miller, Bill, 213
Mindset (Dweck), 28, 227
mistakes, learning from, 44, 78

Mitchell, Joni, 167
Moneyball (Lewis), 186, 227
Moore, Geoffrey, 231
More Than You Know (Mauboussin), 233
Morey, Daryl, 189, 190–91
Morrison, Toni, 170
Move Ahead with Possibility Thinking (Schuller), 229
MrBeast (Jimmy Donaldson), 99–103, 112
Munger, Charlie, 63
Myers-Briggs test, 25–26

N

Nadella, Satya, 58
Naismith, James, 142
Negotiating the Impossible (Malhotra), 235
The New New Journalism (Boynton), 228
The New York Times, 70–71
Newell, Pete, 137, 141, 145
Newport Folk and Jazz Festival, 164–67
"Next Gen" (peer group), 92–94, 109
Nudge (Thaler and Sunstein), 236

O

"obsessive interest," 23
Odyssey Plan, 26–27
Olajuwon, Hakeem, 58–59
O'Neal, Shaquille, 147–48
On Writing (King), 229
One Up on Wall Street (Lynch), 232
Outliers (Gladwell), 112

P

Parcells, Bill, 141
The Parent's Tao Te Ching (Martin), 37–38
passion
  curiosity and, 84
  as element of grit, 23, 37
  fascination and, 21
  finding peers and, 107
  ignoring, for job with money, 160
  learning and, 197
  as necessary for success, 21, 197
  perseverance and, 37
  sense of purpose as element of, 50
  taking risks and, 161–63, 169, 196–97, 202–3
  See also fascination
peers/peer groups
  benefits of, 93–94, 104–6, 112–13
  as collaborators, 103–4, 112–13
  described, 103
  expanding beyond field, 110–11
  finding, 106–8
  of Gurley, 206–7, 212, 214
  Knight and, 139–41
  maintaining relationships, 108–10
  mentors compared to, 103
  "Next Gen"/"Young ADs"/Middle-Aged ADs, 92–98, 109
  on social media, 107–8, 121
  success and, 101–3
performance and job satisfaction, xxii
perseverance
  as element of grit, 23, 37, 227
  of Fadell, 125–27
  of Hinkie, 188
  as necessary for success, 198–201
  passion and, 37
Philadelphia 76ers, 191–93
Phish, 160–61
Picasso, Pablo, 51–52, 57
Pink, Daniel, 169, 228
Pinker, Steven, 238
Play Nice but Win (Dell), 235
Politico, 60
Poms, Eric, 207
Porter, Michael, 231

The Power of Regret (Pink), 169, 228
Predictably Irrational (Ariely), 236
Principles of Geology (Lyell), 61
purpose, sense of
as element of fascination, 36
as element of passion, 50
prevalence of, 23
wandering with, 31

Q

Quattrone, Frank, 214–16
"quiet quitting," xxi–xxii

R

Rachleff, Andy, 216
A Random Walk Down Wall Street (Malkiel), 232
Range (Epstein), 61–62, 226
The Rational Optimist (Ridley), 237
regrets, xx, xxi, 169–70
relocating for dream job, 127–31, 133–34
Rensin, David, 198
Rickman, Alan, 170
Ridley, Matt, 237
Riley, Lincoln, 155–56
risks, taking
passion and, 161–63, 169, 196–97, 202–3
regrets and not, 169
success and, 198, 202–3
Robbins, Tony, 28, 230
Rogan, Joe, 132
Rogers, Maggie, 166–67
Rogers, Rodney, 207
Rolling Stone, 125
Rosenthal, David, 30
Rotolo, Suze, 73
Rubin, Rick, 52–53, 230

S

Saban, Nick, 97
Sandberg, Sheryl, 82
Sanders, Colonel, 33
Sapiens (Harari), 238
Sarkisian, Steve, 97
Schembechler, Bo, 141
Schuller, Robert H., 229
Schwartz, Lorraine, 119
Seeger, Pete, 164–66
Seinfeld, Jerry, 20–21, 27–28, 31, 52
self-regulation, importance of, 31–32
Setting the Table (Meyer), 225–26
The Seven Habits of Highly Effective People (Covey), 28, 149, 229
Sewell, Carl, 234
Shake Shack, 17–18
Sheinberg, Sidney, 78–79
Shelton, Robert, 70
Sheridan, Taylor, 46
Shoe Dog (Knight), 231–32
side hustles, 29–30
Simon, Paul, 167
social media
chronicling self on, 119
education and, 177–80
peers on, 107–8, 121
Sommerfeld, Arnold, 156
Sperry, Neil, 29
Spheeris, Penelope, 47–48
Spielberg, Steven, 78–79
sports, 35, 88–89, 186, 188
stagiaires (stages), 8–11
Stanford University, 25, 146, 187–88, 193
Startup (Kaplan), 232
Stefani, Gwen, 120–21
Stoker, Bram, 170
The Storytelling Animal (Gottschall), 228–29
Strasberg, Lee, 156
Stricklin, Scott, 92–98, 109
The Structure of Scientific Revolutions (Kuhn), 231
Stumbling on Happiness (Gilbert), 230

success
 consistency and, 49
 curiosity and, 21
 hard work and, 197
 intentionality and, 18
 passion and, 21, 197
 perseverance and, 198–201
 taking risks and, 198, 202–3
 tips for, 49–50
success, later in life
 Beveridge, 180–82
 Child, 173–77
 examples of, 170
 Khan, 177–80
 Lauder, 171–73
The Success Equation (Mauboussin), 234
Sunstein, Cass, 236
Surdy, Kacper, 60
Sweet, Jay, 158–67, 200
Swim with the Sharks Without Being Eaten Alive (Mackay), 234
Swing Your Sword (Leach), 228

T

Tarantino, Quentin, 52
Taylor, Fred, 137
Taylor, James, 166–67
teaching, learning when, 154
"Ten-Thousand-Hour Rule," 112
Thaler, Richard, 236
Think Twice (Mauboussin), 236
Thinking, Fast and Slow (Kahneman), 236
Thinking in Bets (Duke), 236
Thinking in Systems (Meadows), 237
Thorne, Gary, 108
The Tipping Point (Gladwell), 235
Tito's Homemade Vodka, 182
Toffler, Alvin, 56
Torre, Pablo, 35

U

Union Square Cafe, 13–17
Ury, William, 234

V

VanDerveer, Tara, 145–46
Van Ronk, Dave, 69–71

W

Waldrop, Mitchell, 237
Walker, E. Lee, 209
Wang, Vera, 33, 170
Wein, George, 164–65
What Color Is Your Parachute? (Bolles), 24–25, 227
White, Ron, 132
Wilder, Laura Ingalls, 170
William Morris (agency), 42–43
Winblad, Ann, 216
Winfrey, Oprah, 79–80
Wisman, Jimmy, 143–44
Wolf, Charlie, 210–214
Women's Wear Daily, 122
Wooden, John, 51
Wright, Tom, 233
Wrzesniewski, Amy, xx

Y

You Have to Pay the Price (Blaik), 139
"Young ADs" (peer group), 94–95, 109
YouTube, 99–103, 177–80

Z

Zemeckis, Robert, 79
zero-sum mentality, 150
Zimmerman, Robert. *See* Dylan, Bob
Zuckerberg, Mark, 78

ABOUT THE AUTHOR

Bill Gurley is a general partner at Benchmark, a leading venture capital firm in Silicon Valley. Over his venture career, he has invested in and served on the board of such companies as Nextdoor, OpenTable, Stitch Fix, Uber, and Zillow. Born in Dickinson, Texas, Gurley earned a bachelor's degree in computer science from the University of Florida and later received an MBA from the University of Texas at Austin. In 2025, he received the Distinguished Alumnus Award from the University of Texas alumni association. For more than two decades, Gurley has written about technology and other subjects on his popular blog, *Above the Crowd,* and on his social media accounts.

ABOUT THE COWRITER

Michael J. Mooney is a *New York Times* bestselling author. He writes for *The Atlantic, GQ,* and *Texas Monthly.* His stories have appeared in multiple editions of *The Best American Sports Writing* and *The Best American Crime Reporting.* He's also the cocreator and cohost of the Audible Original podcast *Hold Fast,* about the rise and fall of the site Backpage.com and the nationwide newspaper empire it funded. He lives in Dallas with his wife, Tara.

THE RDAD FOUNDATION (RDAD.ORG)

When I set out to write *Runnin' Down a Dream*, I knew I wanted it to be more than just a book of stories and principles. Principle Six—*Always Give Back*—calls for action, not just words. The **Runnin' Down a Dream Foundation (RDAD Foundation)** is how I intend to live that principle.

The RDAD Foundation's purpose is simple: to help people who are inspired by this book chase their own dream jobs—especially those for whom financial challenges stand in the way. Too often, the only thing separating ambition from progress is a small amount of help at the right moment.

Here's how it will work:

- **Grants:** Each year, the RDAD Foundation will award grants to winners. The dollar amount of grants and the number of winners will be determined annually.
- **Milestones:** If a recipient demonstrates meaningful progress after a set period of time, they will be eligible for a second grant. The dollar amount of the second grant will be determined annually.
- **Advice & Support:** Alongside funding, the RDAD Foundation aims to provide guidance and recommendations to help recipients move forward.
- **Community:** Past recipients will be encouraged to support new ones by contributing to the RDAD Foundation financially and/or providing guidance and recommendations, thereby building a community of dream-chasers who learn from and help each other.
- **Evergreen Vision:** In the long run, those who succeed may one day give back to the RDAD Foundation, keeping the cycle alive for future dreamers.

The RDAD Foundation will launch with an initial donation from me. Also, I will include an amount that matches all the proceeds I personally receive from this book. Applications and details will be available at **rdad.org**.

The truth is, chasing your dream is hard enough. It shouldn't be limited to those with financial means. The RDAD Foundation exists to make sure that anyone with the drive and courage to run down their dream has a fair shot at starting the chase.